Lady Dicks and Lesbian Brothers

TRIANGULATIONS
Lesbian/Gay/Queer ▲ Theater/Drama/Performance

Series Editors
Jill Dolan, Princeton University
David Román, University of Southern California

Lady Dicks and Lesbian Brothers

Staging the Unimaginable at the WOW Café Theatre

KATE DAVY

The University of Michigan Press

Ann Arbor

First paperback edition 2011
Copyright © by the University of Michigan 2010
All rights reserved
Published in the United States of America by
The University of Michigan Press
Manufactured in the United States of America
♾ Printed on acid-free paper

2014   2013   2012   2011   5   4   3   2

A CIP catalog record for this book is available from the British Library.

Library of Congress Cataloging-in-Publication Data

Davy, Kate.
    Lady dicks and lesbian brothers : staging the unimaginable at the
WOW Cafe Theatre / Kate Davy.
        p.   cm. — (Triangulations: lesbian, gay, and queer theater)
    Includes index.
    ISBN 978-0-472-07122-7 (cloth : alk. paper)
    1. WOW Cafe Theatre (New York, N.Y.)   2. Music-halls (Variety-
theaters, cabarets, etc.)—New York (State)—New York—History—20th
century.   3. Lesbian theater—New York (State)—New York.   I. Title.
PN1968.U5D38   2010
792.02'2—dc22   2010007942

ISBN 13: 978-0-472-05122-9 (pbk. : alk. paper)
ISBN 10: 0-472-05122-9 (pbk. : alk. paper)

Cover illustration: Holly Hughes (*right*) and Sharon Jane Smith (*left*) in *The Lady Dick*, 1986. Photo by Dona Ann McAdams.

For Maureen
. . . and the boychik

Preface

This book captures the erotically charged, heart-thumping excitement of the WOW Café Theatre, aka WOW, since 1980, when it first arrived on the cultural scene in New York City's East Village. The book's title is taken from a play, *The Lady Dick,* and a theater company, the Five Lesbian Brothers, as examples of productive neologisms that could only be imagined at WOW, shifting old paradigms to enable alternative visions. As a whole this project is in homage to all the women of WOW who created those visions and have sustained the theater over the years. Against formidable odds, they keep it going.

The story of WOW's evolution clearly demonstrates how the conditions and dynamics of WOW are inextricably linked to the significant and influential aesthetic developed there. Since first crossing WOW's threshold in 1984, I have stood in awe of work made by such women as Jen Abrams, Maureen Angelos, Karen Campbell, Susana Cook, Karen Crumley, Babs Davy, Dominique Dibbell, the Five Lesbian Brothers, Alice Forrester, Heidi Griffiths, Peg Healey, Holly Hughes, Lisa Kron, Deb Margolin, the Millies, Cheryl Moch, Claire Olivia Moed, Madeleine Olnek, Reno, Peggy Shaw, Sharon Jane Smith, the Split Britches Company, Kate Stafford, Alina Troyano (aka Carmelita Tropicana), Lois Weaver, Susan Young, and so many others. To crib from a remark Claire Moed made on her first encounter with WOW, I, too, became a different person because of this work.

I began collecting material for this book in 1985 with the understanding that not only had WOW come into being at a turning point in the women's movement and feminist critical thought, but it is representative of this historical juncture. Although I was convinced that the theater itself was a central player in the work emerging from it, I had little understanding of the challenge writing this book would present. WOW artists tell of many a scholar arriving at the theater over the years with plans to document its history. The reason it hasn't happened until now, however, has more to do with the nature of the beast than any lack of interest. Providing a history of WOW is slippery business, even when one is simply trying to record the series of public events.

The WOW Café Theatre is a hugely amorphous entity. The absence of staff and infrastructure is a hallmark of its anarchic approach, and hence record keeping has never been part of its modus operandi. Further complicating WOW's purposeful disorganization is the fact that the majority of WOW productions were not reviewed. This is due in part to WOW's status as "community" (as opposed to "professional") theater. Extant flyers and programs list the month and days of particular events but not the year. In the early 1990s I rifled through materials that had been tossed into boxes at the Lesbian Herstory Archives, then located in archive cofounder Joan Nestle's apartment on the Upper West Side of Manhattan. Years later I revisited the archives when it had moved to a large Brooklyn brownstone and acquired even more boxes of WOW material. These boxes held whatever individual WOW participants had had the forethought to contribute to the archive.

Another collection housed at WOW, informally referred to as "the WOW archives," helped to fill in the gaps. Neither collection is complete, however. Both are made up of a hodgepodge of press releases, flyers, programs, videotapes of productions, scripts, and newspaper clippings. Over the years I have attempted to track down accurate information from the artists and producers themselves, but because of the collective's in-flux membership, it has not always been possible to locate individuals. Even when located, WOW participants did not always respond to my requests for information. This is very much in keeping with WOW's foundational ethos and, paradoxically, part of the reason why the theater has endured for three decades. The personal collections of several individuals have been immensely helpful during this project, and I'm grateful to those who made them available to me, particularly Pamela Camhe, Jimmy Camicia, Alice Forrester, Jordy Mark, Peggy Shaw, and Lois Weaver.

The appendix at the back of the book captures the breadth of work produced at WOW since its inception in 1980. The purpose of including this production history is to acknowledge as many WOW artists as possible and to spark interest in further study. One founding member of WOW has said that hundreds of shows were presented during the theater's storefront years (1982–85), at 330 E. Eleventh Street, before the collective moved to its current location at 59–61 E. Fourth Street. Much of the documentation is lost, however, and the production history does not include shows that ran for a single night. There were dozens of such instances, sometimes two different shows a night, during what one WOW member has described as "hit-and-run theater." In the late 1980s WOW artist Susan Young graciously lent her expertise to the effort of preparing an initial list of productions. I expanded that document in the 1990s, and a current member of the collective, Parker Pracjek, has fleshed it out further. In the hope of getting each production in the correct time period, shows are listed in two-year spans rather than by theater season.

At some point the WOW collective began to keep a notebook in which the house manager would record the name of the show, the show's producer, and the total of box-office receipts handed over to the producer each night. Although it cannot be assumed that this practice was followed consistently, these notebooks were saved over the years. And even though they are not organized by year, they were an invaluable source for compiling WOW's production history—sometimes the only remaining documentation of a production's existence. It is almost always the case that a show's producer was also its creator, although it is of course possible that only the producer's name was listed in the production history and that of the writer, performance artist, or choreographer is missing. In short, there are undoubtedly omissions in the production history I have compiled, and for this I apologize. As new information surfaces, it will be posted on WOW's Web site (http://www.wow cafe.org).

During most of the theater's existence, I have lived in other parts of the United States. With the exception of my discussion of WOW's inaugural festivals in 1980 and 1981, I have limited this book to productions I personally attended, including influential work that predated WOW in the 1970s by the playwright Charles Ludlam and the troupe of drag queens known as Hot Peaches. In addition to archival material, I have relied on dozens of interviews I have conducted with members of WOW's collective, past and present. I have also interviewed women who attended WOW productions in the early years, such as the poets and novelists Jewelle Gomez and Eileen Myles, who have generously shared their recollections and perspectives. Jen Abrams, a current WOW member, was enormously helpful in responding to a variety of questions such as those related to WOW's struggle to hang onto the performance space it had occupied for more than two decades. Quotations from unpublished interviews and plays are cited in the notes. Several newspaper articles and reviews were obtained in clipped and copied form, often missing publication data, particularly page numbers, which I tracked down when possible.

I am indebted to the many reviewers who wrote with passion about WOW's founding festivals for a number of publications, particularly the playwright Jane Chambers and the journalist Barbara Baracks, along with several writers who covered the first two WOW festivals for *Womanews*. Without this documentation the festivals would be mostly lost to cultural memory. In the absence of the festivals, much of what is important about the WOW Café Theatre as an enabling enterprise for women at a turning point in feminist cultural production would be misunderstood. This book is also indebted to the many writers who have repeatedly turned their attention to WOW's work over the years, C. Carr, Jill Dolan, Alisa Solomon, and Laurie Stone among them. Their thoughtful and insightful analysis has enriched this endeavor immeasurably.

Capturing the "there" that is WOW has been a process spanning twenty-five years. Many people in my personal and professional life have made this process possible. My sister Babs Davy was an active member of the WOW collective from the mid-1980s to the mid-1990s, and she provided a sense of continuity for the project that I would have otherwise missed. Babs arrived at WOW with no training in theater whatsoever and made her debut with a couple of lines in Lisa Kron's 1987 production of *Paradykes Alley*. Like so many women, Babs went on to appear in many other WOW productions and to create her own work. She is a founding member of the Five Lesbian Brothers, a troupe that emerged directly from WOW. When Babs appears onstage, it always catches me a bit off guard, and her work never fails to take my breath away.

Friends, lovers, and family members have been a source of inestimable support throughout this endeavor. I am grateful for the brainpower and solace provided during the early years of this project by Hilary Harris, Mimi McGurl, Lisa Merrill, Ruth Sternglantz, and especially Jane Fisher, the best researcher ever. I am equally grateful to friends and colleagues who agreed to read the book proposal or chapters and provided helpful feedback, including Barbara Boyce, Clare Davidson, Betsy Farrell, Gail Leondar-Wright, Sheila Moeschen, Janelle Reinelt, Marc Stern, Sara Warner, Christine R. Williams, and especially Cyrus Veeser. I will never be able to thank Peggy Shaw enough for her prompt, unfailing assistance in helping me to track down the contact information for early WOW participants. Amy Parker is a most supportive friend who served as my local editor during the years I lived in Cambridge. The knowledge and keen insights she brought to careful readings have surely made the book stronger.

Bentley University, where I served as Dean of Arts and Sciences from 2002 to 2009, is a visionary place. I was fortunate to work with a great number of stellar colleagues there, all of whom mean a lot to me and were supportive in more ways than they will ever know. Lynne Durkin, as both my friend and associate dean at Bentley, has been a rock, personifying patience and making all things possible. She is a scholar and gentlewoman whose judgment I trust absolutely and to whom I owe the deepest debt of gratitude. Two women who served as administrative assistants in the dean's office at Bentley, Martha Keating and Kathryn Nettles, also deserve many thanks. As this book goes to press, I serve the University of Michigan-Dearborn as Provost and Vice Chancellor for Academic Affairs. My wonderful assistant there, Debbie Parker, was enormously helpful during the final stages of preparing the manuscript.

My dear friend Jill Dolan discovered the WOW Café Theatre with me in 1984. For her I reserve a special note of appreciation, not only for her sage advice and skillful editing over the years, but also for her many upbeat, encouraging e-mail messages at those times during the writing process when I most needed encouragement. Jill's confidence in this project kept me going.

My son, Isaac-Davy Aronson, read various versions of different chapters over the years. As a writer in his own right and as someone who has seen all the work of the Five Lesbian Brothers, Isaac provided many insightful comments and thoughtful editing, which was particularly helpful as I struggled for months with chapter 6, "Challenging Whiteness." When he thought I had finally nailed it, dancing in the streets commenced. Isaac probably doesn't remember a time when I wasn't working on this book. His unflagging interest, patience, and encouragement constantly amaze me, and his love is a source of energy and inspiration. In my life, he is joy.

Because the work that produced this volume has spanned almost three decades, I regret that I have surely forgotten some of those who helpfully participated in this process. In recompense, and in the ever generous spirit of WOW, I hereby dub as honorary "WOW girls" all who contributed to making this book happen. It is my hope that this marks only the start of reexamining an organization and multiple bodies of work that are well worth further consideration. As indicated by the extensive production history detailed in the appendix, there is so much more to be explored. In addition to making a contribution to extant knowledge of WOW and its cultural production, I hope this book will inspire another generation of scholars to dig in. It is a project with larger implications that speak to the historical and continuing relevance of the WOW Café Theatre.

Contents

Lady Dicks and Lesbian Brothers

Chapter 1

Introducing WOW: "A Miracle on E. 4th Street"

When confronted with the big questions and surprising obstacles of what it means to be women in the theater, we did what we had to do. We took off our hats and danced.

—LOIS WEAVER, 1998

"The most daring offering of the Broadway season! A smart, graceful, 100-minute revelation!" (*Newsday*), "One of the most thought-provoking comedies in Broadway history!" (*NY1*), "Uproarious, touching and joyously alive!" (Associated Press).[1] These publicity blurbs were culled from a rash of unqualified rave reviews for a Tony-nominated play called *Well* by Lisa Kron. *Well* premiered off-Broadway in 2004 at the Public Theater in downtown Manhattan, where it also garnered raves, and then moved uptown to Broadway in early 2006. The show's rise to the pinnacle of commercial success is extraordinary because, as one reviewer put it, "It's not everyday—or every year, for that matter—that an avant-garde theater piece opens on Broadway. [I]t certainly isn't conventional or commercial."[2] *Well* is premised on a paradox—"a solo piece with other people in it," according to Kron.[3] Because the play's characters rebel against the author, several reviewers found themselves reaching back a century to Italian playwright Luigi Pirandello as the source of the play's conceit and Kron's aesthetic. However apt this nod to Pirandellian influence might be, Kron's sensibility is the product of a more recent, more local, and less canonical source.

Kron is a veteran of the WOW Café Theatre, an entity that has rarely, if ever, appeared in the official annals of either "legitimate theater" or avant-garde performance. WOW is a small, hand-to-mouth women's theater collective housed today in what was once a factory in Manhattan's East Village. The organization was born of two ambitious international theater festivals called Women's One World (WOW), which were produced in the fall of 1980 and again in 1981. Although *Well* was not developed at WOW, Lisa Kron

was, and her play reflects that. Her apprenticeship at WOW is important because it so closely resembles that of numerous others. Through Kron's experience—from her first encounter with the WOW Café in 1984 to the premier
of *Well* in 2004—we can neatly track WOW's history and aesthetic trajectory.

Kron may be the first WOW artist to have made it all the way to Broadway, but she is among many playwrights, performance artists, and theater
troupes that produced work at WOW and crossed over into professional, if
not commercial, venues. A sampling of others includes Holly Hughes, Deb
Margolin, Cheryl Moch, Madeleine Olnek, Reno, Peggy Shaw, Alina
Troyano (aka Carmelita Tropicana), Lois Weaver, the Five Lesbian Brothers,
and the Split Britches Company. Kron herself is adamant that her work
would not exist today were it not for the WOW Café Theatre, and she is not
alone in this sentiment. WOW provided a space for theater artists like Kron
to produce work at a time when women were overwhelmingly absent from
the creative domains of playwriting, directing, and designing in New York's
mainstream theater venues.

WOW's influence on Kron and so many others who began their careers
there involves aesthetic and political sensibilities in combination with the dynamics of WOW as an organization. Like the punk rock music scene that
permeated WOW's neighborhood at the time of its founding in the early
1980s, WOW was unapologetically amateur in its approach and chaotic in its
organization. With no staff and no artistic director, WOW's participants focused on getting themselves and their material onstage, eschewing such dis-
tractions as bookkeeping, grant writing, and finely-honed performance skills.
WOW's driving force—and much of the reason audiences attended its productions—was a passionate enthusiasm for women's cultural production and
social agency. Opening nights were charged with heightened expectations
that had little to do with consummate production values. Haphazardly
thrown-together sets and costumes, missed entrances, and actors fishing for
their lines served to expand rather than diminish the experience. As the novelist and literary critic Walter Kirn observed, reminiscing about a performance by the poet Allen Ginsberg in the 1980s, "Oracular spontaneity is rare
these days, and heartfelt, inspired sloppiness underrated."[4]

The "sloppiness" factor of the heartfelt performances at WOW was the
by-product of an ecstatic moment in which a group of women came together
in a rush to make theater and to unleash desires that had been too long reined
in: the desire for voice, imagination, and sex free from censure and the stric-

tures of gender and race. Over the years WOW's inspired messiness has evolved into a distinguishing characteristic of the collective. Ironically, a chaotic, anarchic approach to organization became a productive operating principle, ensuring WOW's longevity; and an abiding sense of tumult combined with desires released from constraint have informed many aesthetic choices. As the theater scholar and critic Alisa Solomon so aptly put it in 1985: "The WOW Café is a force more than a place."[5]

Regarding WOW's enduring status as a *women's* theater, the collective takes the position today that, like the neighborhood's self-identified punks of the 1970s and 1980s, identifying with the category "women" is a matter of self-selection and self-identification. The same is true of WOW's membership. According to the collective's mission statement in 2005, "WOW welcomes the full participation of all women and transpeople in solidarity with women. WOW especially welcomes women and transpeople of color, and women and transpeople who identify as lesbians, bisexual and queer."[6] Expansive notions of identity have underpinned WOW's milieu since its inception. Predictably, however, issues of identity, philosophy, and politics have continued to arise at WOW, often leading to heated, sometimes prolonged, and unresolved debates. This constitutes yet another distinctive feature of WOW: the collective has been arguing about the same issues for three decades. A concern is raised, debated, dies down, sometimes for years, and lives on to resurface another day. For example, men are welcome in WOW's audience and on its stage, but the *extent* to which they can participate in a production has been a matter of ongoing debate, not because of any prejudice against men but simply because there are many more opportunities for men as playwrights, directors, and designers in New York theater worlds.

Theater scholar David Savran made this point in a provocative essay on theater as "the queerest art." He identified the emergence of "the new American queer theater" in such contexts as Broadway and beyond: "The new queer theater has done little to redress the long history of the exclusion of women as playwrights, protagonists, directors, and designers in prestigious, commercial venues." He continues, "Almost invariably, gay men have achieved levels of visibility and power in theater that are routinely denied to women, whether straight or lesbian. . . . And this denigration of women tends to be echoed by the relative exclusion of both lesbians and gay men of color from major administrative and artistic positions in prestigious theaters."[7] Savran cites the impresario Joseph Papp's off-Broadway theater complex—the

Public Theater—as an exception to this rule. Exclusionary practices prevail, however, making venues like the WOW Café Theatre a continuing necessity.

Since its founding, WOW has operated out of an unarticulated and fluid notion of feminist space inhabited by participants who do not necessarily agree on what constitutes "feminism." Members of the collective have lived and worked out of dozens of differing and changing perspectives. My conversations with some of WOW's many participants over the years bear this out; it is sometimes difficult to believe they are referring to the same organization. Although most of the collective's members agree that WOW was a positive, productive, and in many instances life- and career-altering experience, others experienced the organization as being rife with conflict and tension. Some participants recall the acute pain produced by instances of betrayal, an inevitable by-product of WOW's operational dynamics as collaborative alliances and allegiances shifted and reformed over time.

In its three decades, WOW has trudged through the minefields of psychological, social, and cultural differences with the occasional disastrous, if not fatal, misstep. The collective's most salient accomplishment has been the ability to sidestep any single party line, successfully keeping its sights set on accommodating multiple perspectives while achieving both individual and common goals. In this light, WOW serves as a model for building coalitions. If achieving social change requires sustained collective action among culturally marginalized groups with varied political affinities, then the ways in which WOW has managed to negotiate the disparate worldviews, aesthetic sensibilities, and political perspectives endemic to a heterogeneous category like "women's theater" shed light on some crucial aspects of successful coalition building beyond theater. In ways alternately obvious and nuanced, WOW was and continues to be a place of cultural activism as well as a player in the extraordinary theater made possible by its existence.

This chapter highlights some of WOW's most intriguing aesthetic and organizational dimensions and sketches an overview of the theater's early history. Lisa Kron's experience is an appealing place to start not only because her sojourn at WOW typifies that of many others but because it helps to explain what made WOW so exciting when it first burst on the scene of women's theater internationally and "downtown performance" locally; why it continues to be relevant for feminist, lesbian, and queer performance today; and the enduring significance of its contributions to theater history and avant-garde cultural production.

Discovering a Place Called Women's One World

At WOW . . . shows were put up in a month, or sometimes a few days, with sets and costumes made literally out of trash from the streets. They were full of magic.

—LISA KRON, 2006

When Kron arrived in New York in 1984 to pursue a career in theater, she did what actors do: she ordered photographs of herself known as "head shots," she blanketed the city with mailings to potential agents, she worked temp jobs during the day to pay the rent, and she faced the grind of cattle-call auditions. Claire Moed, an acquaintance of Kron's at the time, told her about WOW and encouraged her to present something at one of WOW's weekly "Variety Nights." Kron hired a pianist, rented rehearsal space, and put together a few minutes of material for her debut. "When I arrived," she recalled, "I realized I didn't have to be quite so prepared."[8] In WOW's tiny storefront space, Kron encountered an energetic, rowdy assembly of women informally presenting a hodgepodge of performances for each other.

Kron took the stage, told a story, ended with a song, and exited through the back of the building, where she stood until it dawned on her that the audience was still applauding. One of WOW's designers at the time, Susan Young, approached Kron and said, "Go back in there and do something else." But she didn't have anything else prepared. This rarely stopped anyone from going onstage at WOW. An impromptu approach was widely and appreciatively accepted and could be quite inspiring. For instance, the notorious persona "Carmelita Tropicana" emerged during just such a Variety Night. It was an evening emceed by performance artist Alina Troyano, who was then a fledgling actress. Because the night's offerings were scant, one of WOW's founding members, Peggy Shaw, convinced Troyano to "go out there and do *something*." Reaching back to her country of birth as a source for inspiration, Troyano addressed the audience in a Cuban accent, recited some poetry, and sang the Cuban national anthem. The audience loved it, and Carmelita Tropicana was born.

Kron did not return to the stage that first night, but she did attend the collective's next meeting. She recalls feeling shy and awkward because, as she says partly in jest, "no one in the room demonstrated any social skills, with the possible exception of Alice Forrester," a stage manager and one of WOW's all-around techies at the time. The playwright and performance artist Holly Hughes would later echo Kron's description of WOW's general ambience: "We were a bunch of oddballs and malcontents with sharp elbows. We were not 'make nice' girls."[9] Irreverence, the freedom to be "bad girls," and an implicit feminism were the impulses underlying WOW's milieu. The theater was also characterized by a "why not" attitude of "anyone is capable of doing anything and everything in the theater." Kron learned this when Forrester turned to her at the meeting and said, "Hey, you were good the other night. You want a time slot next month to do a show?" Stunned, Kron agreed: "When someone opened a door, I had to walk through it." In doing so, she entered a theatrical world antithetical to the one she had anticipated. Rather than waiting to be cast in someone else's play, Kron was about to create a performance piece of her own. "It was nothing I could imagine," she recalled, "and everything I wanted."

Throughout WOW's history the enterprise has steadfastly maintained an antiauthoritarian stance. As Hughes has written of the organization: "There are few rules, but breaking them is not only tolerated, it's almost encouraged."[10] WOW operates as a collective based on labor or "sweat equity," which means, simply, "if you work on my show, I'll work on yours." It has survived in part because its members keep to a minimum those things on which they are required to reach consensus. The collective sets policy on as little as possible, and all policies are strictly operational. There are no official leaders; all decisions are made at meetings held every Tuesday night. Depending on who shows up, a decision made at one meeting might contradict one made the week before. This structure leaves abundant room for confusion and conflict, but members stick to the principle of anarchy, agreeing to disagree, and muddle through whatever issues arise. Another founding member, Lois Weaver, has described WOW as "a bureaucracy waiting to happen."[11]

Dozens of women's theaters existed in the 1970s and 1980s only to collapse under the demands, pressures, and pitfalls of collective organization. WOW beat the odds by surviving its own working methods—not because its participants are more committed or because it is better organized but because of a continuous recommitment to remain as amorphous as possible. WOW's contradictions are so legion that categorizing it is slippery business. More of an endeavor than an entity, WOW eludes facile definition by exceeding and at times skewering attributes that typically attend words such as *theater, community,* and *subculture.* At any one time there are thirty to thirty-five active members, while lapsed or "associate members" number in the hundreds. Because membership in the collective is a matter of self-selection, Hughes provides but one example of a WOW participant who arrived with no experience in theater of any kind. Showing up at a Tuesday night meeting is still the only requirement for membership. When Kron showed up for that first meeting in 1984, she was in.

Shortly after her debut at WOW, Kron attended a performance that changed everything she thought she knew about theater. She saw a revival production of a play called *Split Britches* (written in 1980–81) performed by a three-woman troupe of the same name.[12] "*Split Britches* blew me away," Kron recalled. "I had no idea such a thing was possible."[13] The piece constitutes a revelatory moment common to many women from WOW's early years. The writer and filmmaker Claire Moed had a similar experience: "Everyone talks about that; they see *Split Britches* for the first time and their lives change. My life changed. I became a different person in that hour and a half."[14] As the Split Britches Company, Deb Margolin, Peggy Shaw, and Lois Weaver created original work together for many years. In the beginning, Split Britches was WOW's unofficial resident company because the troupe's origins and WOW's coincide in place and time. As two of WOW's founders, Shaw and Weaver guided the organization in unofficial leadership roles during its formative years. Weaver's influence was pervasive from WOW's inception as a consequence of the acting workshops she taught, which she has described as "encouraging the independent artist rather than teaching an actor."[15] Through their work individually and together as Split Britches, Margolin, Shaw, and Weaver influenced a large number of WOW artists in a great many ways.

Kron's trajectory as a theater artist began with a series of short and then longer solo pieces, trying them out at WOW's weekly Variety Night while simultaneously working on and appearing in productions by other members of the collective. Like many WOW artists who followed this developmental path, Kron then segued into creating her own plays, *Paradykes Alley* in 1987 and *Paradykes Lost* in 1988. Mirroring other WOW productions at the time, these plays were driven by parody—parodies of classical narratives, genres, historical figures, popular icons, and cultural norms, sometimes all in the same show. *Paradykes Alley* takes place in an out of the way bowling alley, where a group of women have been meeting once a week for years. The production was billed as "a funny play with music about a bunch of women with their own balls." *Paradykes Lost* is a zany comedy that parodies the screwball and mystery film genres of the 1930s and 1940s. The press release described it as "a madcap mystery farce that depicts sinister deals, mistaken identities, and Sapphic romance with double-edged dialogue and expeditious pacing."[16] Both plays were conceived and directed by Kron and written in collaboration with the cast using improvisational techniques to generate material.

Kron's *Paradykes* productions had all the hallmarks of WOW's aesthetic. They assumed and playfully addressed a lesbian audience, irrespective of who might actually be in the audience, and male characters in *Paradykes Lost* were played *by* and *as* women in drag. For example, theater director Kate Stafford was cast as the show's classic film noir detective dressed in a Humphrey Bogart–like hat and suit. She played the role as the strong, silent-type male character all such detectives indubitably were, but she also played it as a butch lesbian. The detective was referred to as "she" and "her" by the other characters in the play. Desires abound in this single character—to play a man, to play a detective, to play Humphrey Bogart, Cary Grant, or a butch lesbian playing a detective, to seduce the heroine, to get the girl—thus offering several points of identification for audience members. In his review of the play, the *Village Voice* editor and critic Robert Massa quipped, "As a gay man, I feel less left out at WOW than at straight burlesque. Kate Stafford as the detective manages to suggest Cary Grant without caricature. Even I swooned."[17] Stafford's performance opened a space where Massa could project his desire and act on it. At the same time the production's aesthetic devices positioned women as the event's prime movers, claiming and acting on their *own* desires. Strategies that posit women as subjects who devise, drive, and enact their own representation made feminism intrinsic to the production rather than subject matter for the narrative. Similarly, lesbianism was assumed onstage and in the audience. At WOW lesbianism is a *given* rather than an issue to be addressed—a given *not* in the sense of being mandatory but as something unremarked upon, a syllable not stressed.

Heidi Griffiths, another early participant, has described how WOW encouraged imaginative transformations both offstage and on. "You could reinvent yourself, become your fantasy," she recalled. "If you didn't find the little slot you fitted into, you'd just make it or invent something else. The categories were slippery and ever changing."[18] In contrast to the normalizing dictates of heterosexuality in the culture at large, at the WOW Café Theatre "lesbian" is not a prescribed identity. Instead, it is one of many possible identities, and lesbianism is one of a wide range of sexual practices. For example, unlike Shaw and Weaver, Margolin—the third member of the Split Britches troupe—identifies as heterosexual, and her work has reflected this identity. In

discussing the play *Split Britches,* she has pointed to the "political importance of Shaw and Weaver's commentary on sexuality as embedded in the
text of the play. They filled the gap between fact and fiction with their own
passions (an inherently political methodology when you let it show)."[19] Margolin stresses the embedded nature of such commentary, the choice to
"show" rather than "tell." Fluid approaches to identity and sexuality at
WOW have informed the ways in which women imagine and reimagine
themselves and their work.

Following on the heels of Kron's *Paradykes* plays, a new troupe was
formed in 1989—the Five Lesbian Brothers. This company represents a cul-
minating point in the trend of early WOW work, launching its next generation. Kron herself is a member of the Brothers, as they call themselves, and
three of the group's other members appeared in her *Paradykes* plays (Maureen Angelos, Babs Davy, and Peg Healey). The fifth member is Dominique
Dibbell. Each Brother arrived on the scene separately with varying degrees of
theater experience—from lots to none at all. Each participated in many
WOW productions before finding the others and coming together artistically.
As a company, the Five Lesbian Brothers presented their first show in 1990,
developed subsequent work, and crossed over into other downtown Manhattan venues, making it as far as off-Broadway with four of their plays.
Their aesthetic strategies and method of creating performance material mark
them as descendants of the Split Britches troupe. But like the activist group
Queer Nation, founded in New York in the same year, the Brothers adopted
the in-your-face attitude and approach exemplified in Queer Nation's brash,
unapologetic slogan: "We're here. We're queer. Get used to it."[20] The tagline
"Commercially Viable Yet Enchantingly Homosexual" appears on the Brothers's letterhead. In the early 1990s this was a particularly startling declaration
for a theater company to make.

WOW productions throughout the 1980s tended to sidestep directly addressing issues that surround heterosexuality as a cultural institution lest they
reinscribe and reinforce its dominance. For instance, coming-out scenes were
not enacted on WOW's stage. By its very nature a "coming-out play" requires heterosexual normalcy to take center stage as that which the character
emerging from the closet of homosexuality is up against. The Five Lesbian
Brothers faced institutionalized heterosexuality head-on, staring it down,
wittily of course, and with an audacity that echoes the rhetorical strategies of
Queer Nation. For example, in the Brothers's first play, *Voyage to Lesbos,* a
character remarks in passing, "Then after lunch I killed a man. He called me

'sweetheart.'. . . I really surprised myself. I never thought of myself as a 'can-do' kind of person."[21] In the edgy outrageousness of their work, the Brothers are both a product of feminism and a precursor of "queer."[22] Indeed, *Voyage to Lesbos* is an instance of the "new American queer theater." Proponents of queer politics maintained that focusing on identify categories such as "women" or "gays and lesbians" as the centerpiece of liberation politics tended to define and solidify those identities as forever marginal. Like a good feminist, the character in *Voyage to Lesbos* is a "can-do" woman. But in casually deploying that agency villainously, she explodes the characteristics that typically append the identity category "woman."

If the Brothers' work represents a second phase in WOW's history, Kron's later work signals a third phase. Two decades after she discovered WOW, the influence of WOW in general, and of Split Britches in particular, is abundantly apparent in *Well*. The production not only captures the concerns and dynamics of WOW but its aesthetic and operational history as well. Kron's conflation of a one-woman show with a multicharacter play—a solo piece with other people in it—is but one in a profusion of contradictions and oppositions that pervade the play. *Well* is a calculated and unabashed mess—a signature feature of the WOW Café Theatre.

Considering Well and Split Britches

Audience and performers, as cocreators of meaning in performance, might strive together to imagine the potential for radically altered social communities in the momentary suspension of disbelief that constitutes theater.

—JILL DOLAN, 2008

Well's incongruities are signaled from the start in the production's design. As spectators file into the theater, they encounter a divided stage. One side is open, flexible space capable of representing any number of different locations where the play's several vignettes will be enacted with energy and enthusiasm. The other side is heavily cluttered domestic space, a slice-of-life portion of a living room rendered in realistic detail. Its centerpiece is a La-Z-Boy recliner where one of the characters is snoozing, oblivious to the audience. Kron enters and stands under a spotlight that carves out a space she will return to whenever she feels the need to talk "privately" with the audience. She introduces herself and tells the audience that the woman in the recliner is her mother. Kron plays herself, Lisa, while the role of her mother, Ann Kron, is played by the actress Jayne Houdyshell. Lisa stands trim and fit, wearing an attractive suit with lapels that sparkle in the light. Ann lounges in a faded, loose-fitting housedress, a long, droopy cardigan, and open-toe slippers. Words used by reviewers to describe Ann physically include "dumpy," "frumpy," "squat," "disheveled," and "slovenly." One reviewer summarized these attributes succinctly when he described Ann as the "embodiment of a figure that tony Manhattan has been conditioned to dismiss."[23] Lisa suggests that her mother is a "housewife savant."[24]

The contrasts Kron sets up extend beyond the visual to questions of identity and authorial voice. Speaking directly to the audience at the top of the show, she makes a number of assertions, establishing her vision as the play's author. She tells the audience that the play is emphatically *not* about her and her mother. Instead, *Well* is "a multicharacter theatrical exploration of issues of health and illness both in the individual and in a community." Apropos of this theme, she describes her mother as "a fantastically energetic person trapped in an utterly exhausted body." Ann's character suffers from allergies that have incapacitated her for her entire life. Lisa's character also once suffered from debilitating allergies but got better. Intertwining stories juxtapose a time when Lisa was so sick she signed herself into an allergy clinic for an extended stay with a time when her otherwise impaired mother led the neighbors in a successful effort to racially integrate their declining neighborhood in Lansing, Michigan.

As the narrative unfolds, Lisa's dramatic vision is alternately developed and repeatedly undermined. The play's action is driven by a dynamic tension between focused, artistic intent and disruptive chaos engendered by characters who fail to play by the rules. Flying in the face of Lisa's plan, Ann, too, addresses the audience directly. She engages them warmly as guests and then proceeds to interrupt Lisa periodically, asking questions, adding details, and gently correcting her daughter's version of things. Four actors, two white and two black, play multiple roles in the allergy clinic and neighborhood scenes. As Ann talks to the audience over one of these scenes, the action halts, and she seizes the moment to meet the actors. Frustrated, Lisa begrudgingly introduces them as actors to Ann, who remains in character. As the interruptions continue, Lisa increasingly loses control, and the production runs amok. Scenery falls apart. Actors drop character to debate how a scene should be played and steal moments to interact with Ann on her side of the stage. The character of Ann is so unpretentious, warm, and funny that the actors fall in love with her. Lisa admonishes the audience, "Don't bring your mother onstage with you. It's a very bad idea." And, "Wow! This avant-garde meta-theatrical thing will just bite you in your ass!" When the play careens toward the implication that Ann should be able to heal herself since she was able to heal an entire neighborhood—suggesting her illness is willfully psychosomatic—the actors perceive this as a daughter's betrayal and, offended, they walk off the stage and out of the play.

Of *Well*'s seeming disintegration, one critic wrote, "By the play's end it all collapses, leaving Lisa and her grand ideas in the proverbial dust."[25] But like so much of the work created at WOW, calculated failure prevails to decidedly fruitful ends. Kron's grand ideas are played out and made even grander by the richly complex ways she renders them. The triangulated roles of playwright, daughter, and actor all reside in the character of Lisa. When her authorial voice is subverted, it jettisons the playwright's control, throwing her authorial identity into relief and its reliability into doubt. All identities are portrayed as unstable. Describing what it was like to be the only Jewish family in the neighborhood, Lisa's character says, "The assumption [is] that although you might be a Jew, you're also still a Christian. Judaism, you know, is viewed in the Midwest as a kind of an accessory that you wear on top of your Christianity."

Ann's character is drawn as an inveterate invalid, a frumpy housewife easily dismissed. But this maternal object—"exhibit A" in Lisa's narrative—hijacks the play and steals the show, ultimately demonstrating as much presence and more agency than the author herself. Simultaneously, Ann represents the voiceless, objectified woman of early feminist musing and the dynamic, feminist "eccentric subject" that critical theorist Teresa de Lauretis has posited as a hopeful alternative.[26] About her mother, Lisa finally admits to the audience, "she doesn't make any sense at all as a character." Kron explodes stable identity categories, the idea that people are unified, recognizable, securely fixed subjects. She reveals instead the untidiness of multiple, shifting identities and perspectives that reside within single characters.

This is only one example of the complexities pervading *Well*, a play that spins together enormously funny contradictions, deeply challenging ideas, and emotionally touching moments in a truncated, ostensibly haphazard way. In this scheme particularly the influence of the Split Britches Company is apparent. The ways in which the troupe created material for production sheds light on *Well* not only as a play chaotic in structure but also as one that portrays identities as messy, social constructions rather than indelibly etched traits of the human condition. The company's process for developing material produced characters of a different stripe. Margolin, Shaw, and Weaver worked collectively and collaboratively to create the textual, visual, and aural dimensions of each Split Britches production. They believed strongly that desire is the starting point and through-line of their artistic process. They asked themselves what they wanted to play, to say, to wear. The initial source for each character might have been a specific person or type, a character from classical drama or popular culture, or it could have been a particular image. Instead of developing characters designed to convey universal themes that speak across the ages to the collective experience of all women, the troupe engaged a process in which they imagined in detail all the little moments their characters might have experienced alone and in relationships. At the same time they brought their own personal desires and fantasies to bear on each character. Margolin has described this process as "mining my own business."[27]

The troupe devoted rehearsals to discussion and improvisational work to, as Weaver put it, "try to bring up images and impulses that come out of an associative side of the self rather than what you know." She has called this "multiple-choice acting," explaining that "you have lots of choices. One of them could be an intention, an 'I want to' or an action, but it could also be a physical impulse or an image that doesn't necessarily relate to that moment. You can use that and work from that to create moment-to-moment acting."[28] The company kept notes on all that emerged from this process—images, themes, dialogue—which was then scripted by Margolin with additional text written by Shaw and Weaver. The material was "edited" as the group worked it into a piece during the later stages of rehearsal.

The actors themselves were typically quite different from the characters they portrayed in any given production. In the piece *Split Britches,* for example, Margolin, Shaw, and Weaver played three of Weaver's ancestors—sisters who lived an impoverished, isolated, rural life together in a dilapidated farmhouse in the Blue Ridge Mountains. As part of their creative process, each actor freely played out her heart's desires in a variety of roles she herself might have played in life as well as those conceivably played by the character. Company members captured the resulting flights of imagination and incorporated diverse aspects of these into their final performances. This expansive process ensured that each production was built around characters that operated out of multiple senses of identity, and it produced pieces that were nonlinear, highly theatrical, richly imagistic, and sometimes fantastical. Of the fantasy their process encourages, Weaver has pointed out that "fantasy often takes us outside the realm of roles the way they are designed for us by the outside world."[29] In performing the roles prescribed for women by society while simultaneously playing out alternative visions, characters in the work of Split Britches, along with those of Lisa and Ann in *Well,* offered a multitude of possibilities for alternative ways of being in the world.

The process in which the Split Britches Company engaged inevitably produced what they refer to as the "breakdown moment." This occurred in the course of generating material for a show, representing an instance of conflict the company could not get past. The breakdown moment brought the creative process to a halt and prompted heated debate about any number of issues, often including their personal feelings about the dynamics of working together. The issues and emotions leading to this moment were knotty, complicated, and largely irresoluble. The strategy for moving forward in the absence of resolution was to work creatively *on,* rather than *through,* the breakdown moment. The conflict was transformed into what Margolin, Shaw, and Weaver have called the "Split Britches Breakdown Scene," which was then incorporated into the final production of a piece.[30]

Because all the moments in a Split Britches production are a consequence of this way of working, from a spectator's point of view it is impossible to determine just where "the breakdown scene" might occur. Likely places to look are those moments in the production when the participants interrogate their own performance practice.[31] For instance, in their third play, *Upwardly Mobile Home* (written in 1984), the characters prepare to rehearse the final scene of a play within their play while they complain and argue about nearly every aspect of it. One character says she wants to do a different play because this one is "racist and sexist," while another counters that "it's not racist and sexist. It has a very high consciousness."[32] A third character wants to sing a song and is told by the character playing the scene's "director" that she can indeed sing but not right now because this final scene is the one in which she is strangled. When the characters finally get into the rehearsal, the staged moment of strangling goes on and on until the director calls "cut" and enters the scene within a scene to demonstrate how strangling is done. Whatever its source, this scene is a hilarious rendering of performers who work closely together momentarily at each other's throats. In the case of *Well,* with its rebellious characters and recalcitrant actors, it is as if Kron took a Split Britches breakdown scene—with all the fraught issues and emotionally charged dynamics of close relationships—and made of it a whole play.

Underpinning these and other aesthetic devices typical in WOW productions is a deep-seated commitment to an autonomous sexuality for women—that is, women as sexual subjects or agents, whether heterosexual or lesbian. In *Well,* for example, the character Ann believes her daughter's allergies were cured during her time in the clinic. But Lisa contends it happened when she moved to New York, began to make theater, found a girlfriend, and chose to be healthy. "It's sex," she proclaims. "I've got this girlfriend who's cured me with sex." The notion of art and sex as transformative is inconceivable to the character of Lisa from Kron's allergy clinic days but not to the ethos of WOW where Kron discovered this transformative power. Lisa refers to her girlfriend this one time only in the play; her sexuality is not spotlighted again. This demonstrates one of the ways performance work can be "lesbian" and "feminist" without being about either lesbianism or feminism.

In keeping with WOW's historical arc, *Well*'s driving conceit grew out of Kron's fascination with the idea of putting characters onstage who do not know the rules—characters who are not "theater people" and thus, unintended, break into the action. For example, during one neighborhood scene a black girl named Lori bursts into a memory from Lisa's childhood, taunting and bullying her. In the throes of their fight, Lisa tells the audience that the scene is meant to depict the experience of integration in a positive light: "Lori is not helping to establish that. Seeing her is just going to play into any stereotypes you might already be holding." As Lori knocks Lisa down and drags her offstage, Lisa wails, "I can't believe I'm getting beat up in my own play!" *Well* repeatedly gestures toward the complexities of race and foregrounds the prerogatives and fantasies of white liberalism by putting a character onstage who ostensibly does not know the rules.[33]

Analogously, many women stepped onto WOW's stage who had no training in the skills and conventions of theater art and were subsequently encouraged to make their own theater pieces. Innovation was often the result of such risk taking, and uneven acting abilities have always been a part of WOW's aesthetic charm. The theater may be conceptually, organizationally, and aesthetically messy, but it is undeniably productive. When the *Village Voice* awarded WOW the Obie for "Best Performance Space" in 1991, the *New York Press* wrote: "Run entirely by volunteers, supported mostly by the box office, and managed by consensus, the Women's One World Café is a miracle on E. 4th Street. . . . Wide, wild variety and enthusiasm give WOW its staying power."[34] To deem WOW a miracle is not entirely hyperbole; its longevity alone is remarkable. The theater received Obie recognition because it produced some of the most significant performance work of the time. That it managed to accomplish this given the conditions under which it operates is the miraculous part: with no paid staff, no overarching artistic vision, no funding, and—until recent years—no phone. Even today the theater's annual operating budget is a mere seventeen thousand dollars, yet its production history is largely uninterrupted. The mess that is WOW constitutes both its challenge and its promise.

Mapping WOW

There is no WOW. . . . WOW is whoever you talk to.
—PEGGY SHAW, 2001

Alisa Solomon's inspired concept of WOW as a *force* rather than a *place* is the impulse underpinning this book. Extrapolating from her premise, I posit that WOW is a force to be reckoned with. Over the years scholars and theater critics have written much about WOW artists and their work, yet the connection with WOW itself as a significant contributing factor has largely been missing from these accounts. Critics covering *Well,* for example, repeatedly locate Kron as a product of New York's "downtown arts scene." This is true, but it falls short. WOW is unlike other downtown performance venues in unique and compelling ways, producing its own ripple effect in the larger performance community. As a production space and an organization, WOW is vitally linked to the aesthetic and political importance of the work it enabled and foreshadowed. Its productions at the dawn of the 1980s, for instance, anticipated the emergence a decade later of an important theoretical, political, and aesthetic phenomenon encompassed by the rehabilitated term *queer.* This book articulates the impulses, influences, and conditions that conspired to establish WOW in the first place. But what exactly has made WOW and the work it launched so important?

The notion of WOW as a force is entirely in keeping with its inaugural moment—two hugely ambitious international women's theater festivals presented at venues across the East Village in 1980 and again in 1981. The poet and novelist Eileen Myles has said of the first festival, "It was a momentary convergence of power and a sense of possibility—an urban Woodstock."[35] Although such festivals were common at the time, WOW's festivals were perceived as startlingly new. Those who attended have described the experience as transformative and share a deeply felt conviction that these events were without precedent. The evidence to support such singularity, however, tends to elude collective memory, perhaps because cultural memory, as the theater historian and critical theorist Joseph Roach has reminded us, "is a process that depends crucially on forgetting."[36] The festivals embraced features antithetical to the preponderant feminist sensibility coming out of the 1970s—cross-dressed and sexually explicit performances, festival-goers who showed up dressed to kill (nary a Birkenstock sandal or flannel shirt among them), and the erotically charged atmosphere that permeated nearly every dimension of the festivals. What distinguished these festivals cannot be recalled because today there exists the belief that "feminists didn't do that kind of thing back then." But they *did* and in ways so utterly out of sync with prevailing feminist sensibilities at the time that were this book a work of fiction it would run the risk of being dismissed as naive and unbelievable.

Chapter 2 considers the reasons why the festivals were so anomalous in part by tracing the origins of WOW to a confluence of disparate sensibilities and influences outside the dominant screeds of feminism. WOW's four founding members were Pamela Camhe, Jordy Mark, Peggy Shaw, and Lois Weaver. Three of them (Camhe, Mark, and Shaw) came from backgrounds in visual art, not theater. Weaver, however, had been a founding member of arguably the most important women's theater company of the 1970s: Spiderwoman. While Camhe and Mark had been deeply involved in the women's movement of the 1970s, Weaver had skirted its edges. And Shaw, as a butch lesbian, spent most of the decade appraising feminists with a jaundiced eye, returning feminism's disapproving gaze on butch/femme roles. All four had participated at one time or another in a short-lived, little-known lesbian theater called Medusa's Revenge, which was located off the Bowery in the East Village. Like Spiderwoman, Medusa's Revenge was founded and operated by women of color. Shaw's work with a troupe of drag queens, Hot Peaches, would also influence WOW's aesthetic production. It was this troupe's artistic director, Jimmy Camicia, who introduced Shaw to a feminism she could relate to. In order to understand the sources of WOW's iconoclasm, then, I turn to visual art and performance in the 1970s as well to artists of color and drag queens.

While the specifics of WOW's festivals may be lost to collective memory, there remains a vivid sense that they were an antidote to the grim mood that had emerged from the women's movement of the 1970s. The opening line of a review of the first festival noted, "Women are laughing again," which is the title of chapter 2.[37] What was so troubling about 1970s feminism that women had all but forgotten how to laugh? The discussion is framed by a moment in time when WOW and the feminist movement intersected quite literally. On April 24, 1982, Lois Weaver happened to walk by Barnard College in time for the closing session of the Scholar and the Feminist IX conference, "Towards a Politics of Sexuality," where some of the most targeted shots had been fired across the bow of the women's movement, fueling the infamous "sex wars." Outside the conference hall antipornography feminists, who were also passionately against butch/femme gender roles and sadomasochistic sexual practices, leafleted passersby, while inside the hall anticensorship feminists articulated a counterdiscourse, outlining the theoretical framework for what would become known as "sex-positive" feminism. Like the work of those few sex-positive activists and theorists at the time, some performances in WOW's festivals anticipated this turning point in feminist critical thought.

Chapter 3, "Sex, Drag, and Rock 'n' Roles," recuperates the elusive festival performances and rediscovers feminism's lost genealogy. Bobbing in a sea of some eighty different performance pieces was a smattering of work representing submerged strains of 1970s feminism. Specifically, I examine Jordy Mark's seductive evening of cabaret, with its leather-dyke aesthetic (the chapter takes its title from this event); Pamela Camhe's moody, erotic "lesbian *Vogue*" photographs of sexy femmes and cross-dressed women with mustaches; the work of the irreverent, over-the-top Radical Lesbian Feminist Terrorist Comedy Group; various pieces by the Flamboyant Ladies, a black lesbian theater company so provocative that one of their productions led to the banishment of WOW from its festival space; the original production of *Split Britches*, a visionary piece considered a turning point in feminist theater; and three strippers from a working-class bar in New Jersey who talked about their lives in the business while stripping for an audience of women. These diverse examples help to explain why so many participants remember the festivals as exciting and radically different—they represent kinds of performance supposedly not in evidence until more than a decade later.

Nothing emerges from a vacuum, however. WOW was a departure from the aesthetics of a majority of feminist art and performance, but it was also very much a product of the 1970s. Although the festivals' productions manifested multiple feminist impulses in play at the time, they privileged feminism's suppressed undercurrents. This engendered an ethos particular to WOW that also resonated with what would emerge in the 1990s under the compelling and productive rubric "queer," which is not to suggest that WOW derived its significance from this development. WOW as lesbian cultural production manifested most of the attributes of queer years before the

word made the transition from an adjective—queer politics, queer theory—
to a noun. Queer evolved in part as a reaction against the identity politics and
leanings toward assimilation that characterized post–Stonewall era gay and
lesbian rights movements. Like most of the work produced at WOW, queer
does not operate out of a "we're just like everybody else" philosophy. Like
WOW, queer takes an oppositional stance toward heterosexuality not as a
practice but rather as a prescriptive social contract, a powerfully normalizing
cultural institution, and an imperative way of life. Queer is also a reaction
against particular kinds of feminism.

As queer became an ever more important site for progressive art and
thought in the 1990s, feminism came to be viewed in a peculiarly totalizing
way. All feminists tended to be lumped together and branded as dour prudes
and antipornography partisans or "good girls" by queer theorists and third-
generation feminists alike. Stereotypes do not arise out of nowhere, of
course, and early feminism admittedly produced its share of staid, upright,
humorless feminists. But it was also feminists who produced WOW's festivals, which included smart, wildly funny, erotically charged performances.
The chapter resurrects those instances of cultural production that worked to
reverse a sleight of hand that metamorphosed *all* feminists into "*the* feminists." Much exciting and important contemporary work is miscast as oppositional to an aesthetic history that profoundly informed it and, the chapter
argues, largely produced it. The theme of official cultural memory—and how
it depends on forgetting—runs throughout the chapter. Eclipsing salient features of lesbian cultural production, like that of WOW, was the necessary
condition of a process that valorized queer as an entirely new phenomenon—
a phenomenon ostensibly antithetical to feminism.

Chapter 4, "Feminist Space and a System of Anarchy," considers the roles
played by space, location, and operational dynamics in an endeavor that began more as a social club, the WOW Café, and evolved into the WOW Café
Theatre. Within four months after the second festival, WOW established its
first permanent home in an East Village storefront at 330 E. Eleventh Street.
The first contentious debate among participants was whether to build a stage
or put in a pool table—the space was too small to accommodate both. Mea-
suring approximately twenty feet from the front door to a tiny stage at the
other end, the space was some ten feet wide and crammed with about twenty-
five folding chairs. Heidi Griffiths, who went on to become the Public Theater's casting director, said it was "like watching theater on an airplane—four
people sitting in a row going back and back until they were standing in the

window bays."[38] An expanded understanding of space itself as an active player is one way to capture WOW as an aggregate that exceeds the sum of its parts. Even in the most passive sense of space as a "container" of objects and activities, it is the foundation on which WOW's sustained existence is built. Over the years little has been required to secure WOW's operation financially.[39] This made it possible for the collective to focus on developing work while taking chances that risked the very real possibility of failure. Variety Night provided opportunities for performers to take a reading of their material in front of a live audience. Pieces presented as part of WOW's regularly scheduled season were also frequently considered works in progress. The creative license to make work that is not commercially driven and can be reassessed along the way allows for the greatest possible degree of risk taking, with significant ramifications for the creative process.

By the end of the storefront years (1982–85), WOW's participants had organized themselves into a collective based on shared labor, the rules for which fit on a single sheet of paper. The source of WOW's organizational principles, its "system of anarchy," can be traced to the vibrant punk rock music scene in its East Village neighborhood. The chapter maps how this new collective structure evolved and pays special attention to how the group managed to finally ameliorate the "tyranny of structurelessness" that had characterized its early years, leaving some members feeling deeply and legitimately emotionally abused and betrayed.[40] The discussion acknowledges WOW's failures along with the collective's ability to move forward without agreement on fundamental issues of policy, politics, and aesthetics. Over one hundred women's theaters were in existence across the United States when WOW was founded. The vast majority of them closed; and WOW is the only theater of its kind still operating in New York. In the face of evidence that suggests feminist collectives are destined to implode, WOW stubbornly moves forward, refusing to be swept into the dustbin of history.

During WOW's storefront years, the collective began to attract wider attention as a key player in what became known as the East Village club scene. This short-lived phenomenon evolved in the early 1980s when a number of bars featuring performances opened on Avenues A, B, C, and D—the far east side of the East Village known colloquially as Alphabet City. In an attempt to capture a moment in history, chapter 5, "Staging the Unimaginable," describes a particular night on the club scene—my own first encounter with WOW. Affiliation with the East Village club scene put WOW on the map of "downtown performance," a label applied to noncommercial venues located south of Fourteenth Street and characterized as bohemian, experimental, and avant-garde in nature. But association with the clubs garnered greater visibility for WOW while simultaneously subsuming its singular aesthetic contributions into a larger, predominantly apolitical context. In many respects the collective's work was similar to that presented in the other clubs, but important differences were eclipsed. I use the work of the innovative theater artist Charles Ludlam to highlight these contrasts because Ludlam's sensibility had a major influence on the work of artists presenting in the clubs, and WOW productions have been repeatedly compared to his in reviews and other published accounts. I focus on Ludlam's production of *Camille* to illustrate the ways in which WOW's work carved out an alternative representational space for women as social, sexual subjects on their own terms, resisting the tendency to recuperate them into someone else's narrative.

The WOW Café Theatre staged on a microlevel that which remained unimaginable on a macro one. In so doing, the collective fulfilled a promise axiomatic to the project of avant-garde art and performance: to alter consciousness, to shift the paradigm under which consciousness operates. WOW artists made work with the capacity to productively alter ingrained patterns of perception, thought, and emotion without sacrificing women as subjects to an avant-garde representational economy that unconsciously and repeatedly objectified them. Confounded by marginalized social and symbolic identity categories of gender, sexuality, class, and race, WOW artists and their fellow travelers were compelled to open up spaces in symbolic systems to represent—on their own terms—the vagaries of their existence. Moreover, they faced the challenge of somehow inculcating mainstream culture with the means to interpret the products of their imaginations. Cofounder Shaw put it this way: "I have heard white straight theater critics at a performance created by women or people of color say, 'I don't know what everyone was laughing at.' . . . They didn't get the jokes because they don't recognize us."[41] Chapter 5 maps the nature of this dilemma for WOW artists.

C. Carr, a major chronicler of East Village performance, has marked the end of the club scene as occurring "when the clubs closed and WOW became a regular theater."[42] She is referring to WOW's move in the fall of 1985 from the storefront to an abandoned doll factory, four flights up in a city-owned building—the space it occupies today. Chapter 6, "Challenging Whiteness," details the early history of the new space and the accompanying shift in priorities to, among other changes, addressing the dynamics of oppression beyond gender. Although WOW never became a "regular theater," Carr's point is well taken since the collective's move into the walk-up altered the ambience the storefront had made possible. The collective had a choice of either the first or fourth floor in a building at 59–61 E. Fourth Street, the same block where the La Mama Experimental Theatre Club has resided since the early 1960s. Occupying the first floor would have preserved WOW's walk-in, social club environment and was tempting for this reason, but the fourth floor offered more unobstructed space for productions. After three years of mounting shows in what one critic had called a "size 6 shoe-box Café," the fourth-floor space won out.[43] Thus began the walk-up years. During the hours before the doors opened to admit audiences, the space was accessible only by shouting up from the street until someone threw a key out the window. At 1,250 square feet the space was still small, but it was possible to squeeze in as many as sixty spectators on the floor and a few risers at one end, with a small dressing room at the other end. The stage was about 21 feet square in between. As many as 30 lighting instruments could be hung from the 10-foot ceiling. By WOW standards it was Radio City.

Members of the collective continued to present at weekly Variety Nights and during WOW's annual festival of new work, but many felt the need for longer runs to further develop full-length pieces. Hundreds of shows had been mounted during the storefront years, but that had been possible only because two shows were presented each night, many for only one or two nights. The earliest version of a play written by Alina Troyano and Uzi Parnes titled *Memorias de la Revolución/Memories of the Revolution* was presented on a single night, June 7, 1985. Billed as "Carmelita Tropicana's Ciao WOW," it was one of the last performances in the storefront. Troyano and Parnes's piece was further developed during a three-week run in the new space in the fall of 1986. It opened to excellent reviews and a four-week run at P.S. 122 in the fall of 1987. Troyano and other artists who eventually moved on from WOW—touring and crossing over to other venues—often returned to showcase new work.

The Split Britches troupe had been the exception to the storefront's general practice of what the lighting designer Joni Wong has described as "hit-and-run theater."[44] By March 1984 the company had developed enough of a repertoire to place an ad in the *Village Voice* announcing upcoming productions of three plays with the following tongue-in-cheek headline:

the GREATEST GIRL GROUP . . .
SPLIT BRITCHES
their GREATEST HITS!

Split Britches had the ability not only to sustain longer runs but to tour Europe for extended periods and present work at multiple venues in addition to WOW. The company enjoyed periodic two- to three-week runs in the storefront, but these were weekend slots with other shows going up all around their productions. The comic and performance artist Reno, for example, curated a full program of stand-up comedy in the second time slot on Friday nights. In the new space each show would run from two to four weeks, and collective members began to build repertoires of their own.

The first season in the E. Fourth Street location was auspicious, establishing the character of WOW's new space in general. Although the move presaged closer attention to theater, the collective hauled its social club spirit up the four flights and continued to present a wide range of programming. Theme parties and poetry readings continued, as did some stand-up comedy and occasional appearances by performers on tour from abroad. Echoing the general ethos of WOW, a one-night "minifestival" of video and film, curated by the independent filmmakers Harriet Hirshorn and Mary Patierno in 1988, grew into an annual three-week event featuring more than sixty films and videos all made and produced by women. This was an important development in the larger women's community, and for many filmgoers it was their first encounter with WOW. Although time to produce theater had become precious, the film festival was seen as an opportunity to build audiences for WOW and demonstrate the collective's commitment to support women's cultural production more broadly.

Highlights from WOW's inaugural season included the playwright Cheryl Moch's wonderfully funny *Cinderella: The Real True Story,* in which a beautiful, plus-size Cinderella is sent off to the ball cross-dressed to win the hand of the *princess,* with instructions from her fairy godmother to "just move like you're not only entitled to your own space, but like you're thinking of taking everyone else's."[45] *The Lady Dick,* by performance artist Holly Hughes, also debuted; this dark comedy had wickedly pointed songs like a lethal rendition of "You Make Me Feel Like a Natural Woman," sung by a performer wielding a butcher's cleaver over her head. The techie-turned-writer and performer Alice Forrester's outrageous *Fear of Laughing in the*

Lower East Side played on the sexism inherent in television sitcoms through parodies of *The Honeymooners, Leave It to Beaver,* and the *Andy Griffith Show,* all presented within the frame of a televised Jackie Gleason variety hour. One of the most memorable moments in Forrester's exceedingly low-tech production was when the (shower) curtain opened on the entire cast—women of wildly different heights, shapes, colors, and sizes—hoofing together uniformly in line, in circles, and on their backs in a send-up of the precision choreography and identical body types of the ever-smiling, always synchronized June Taylor Dancers.

These inaugural performances engaged issues chapter 6 addresses. Some shortsighted feminist critical theories had posited a category of "woman" so middle-class, so white, and so straight that few women actually inhabited this narrow social realm. In small but significant ways these WOW performances gestured toward a wider view: *Cinderella* brings her princess around to an understanding of class privilege; in *Lady Dick* class functions as a structuring principle in the back-alley world of lesbian bar culture, where the play is set; and the lumbering chorus girls in Forrester's production, with their decidedly unacceptable body types, critique the pristine blonde, blue-eyed, svelte paragon of mainstream media's idealized construction of white womanhood.

WOW's first season in the E. Fourth Street space closed with an event that traversed a wide terrain of difference—a monthlong festival of original work subtitled "From the Political to the Perverse." To note just five examples from a slate of more than thirty separate bookings, the festival included the Asian Lesbians of the East Coast, who presented a slide show; Spiderwoman Theater; the band Useless Femmes; the performers Katherine Ekau Amoy Hall, Bina Sharif, and Sheila Hallet, who showcased a multimedia piece billed as "Healers—Original Whirling Lesbians/Women of Colors"; and WOW collective member Diane Jeep Ries, who performed *SEXTRAVA-GANZA,* an explicit exploration of S/M sexuality.

Another example of WOW's attention to diversity was the three to four weeks dedicated annually to a festival of work by women of color. Members of the collective provided staff for these shows in the form of technical, promotional, and house-management support, but, even as they did, the collective considered this approach a ghettoizing one and struggled with the dilemma of why more women of color—particularly black women—did not join WOW. Black women had been very much a part of WOW's founding festivals, and their participation continued for a time in the storefront. Once the collective was formed and moved to the new space, however, its membership was made up predominantly of working- and middle-class white lesbians, some heterosexual white women, and a smattering of lesbians of color. Given the diversity of its founding moment, the absence of significant numbers of women of color in subsequent years was troubling. Chapter 6 addresses this conundrum and considers race beyond the composition of the collective, analyzing the meanings generated in performance at the intersection of whiteness with gender, class, and sexuality.

Whiteness is challenging insofar as it is an unmarked category that derives its power from its invisibility. At the same time, however, whiteness *can* be challenged. Troyano's *Memorias de la Revolución* is an example of a production that takes up this challenge. Her hilariously witty, wildly imaginative rendering of Carmelita Tropicana's Cuban revolution opened WOW's second season in the fourth-floor walk-up and represents a groundbreaking work. The discussion explores the many rich levels on which the production played, including the ingenious way *Memorias* locates whiteness as a racial category in the construction of white womanhood. The piece locates the symbols of U.S. ethnocentrism and imperialism as residing in and deployed through that construction.

Significantly, the task of exposing whiteness is not relegated to WOW's few women of color. Troyano's *Memorias* foregrounds whiteness and makes it visible in performance, but it does so by playing it out on the bodies of white women in the cast, not on racial "others." Foregrounding the role white womanhood plays in the care and maintenance of white supremacy is arguably the work of white women. As the author and activist bell hooks has explained, "White avant-garde artists must be willing to openly interrogate work which they or critics cast as liberatory or oppositional. That means they must consider the role whiteness plays in the construction of their identity and aesthetic visions, as well as the way it determines reception of their work."[46] In response to hooks, chapter 6 looks closely at whiteness as a structuring principle of the work itself.

The chapter ends with an analysis of the wonderfully eccentric work of the Five Lesbian Brothers as seen through the lens of the nineteenth-century notion of "true womanhood"—an enduring concept of womanhood that is decidedly white, heterosexual, and middle class. In performing the dynamics of gender with a vengeance, the Brothers drag the historical apparatus of white womanhood along with them onto the stage. For example, the Brothers' play *The Secretaries* could be considered their answer to the 1991 film *Thelma & Louise*, starring Susan Sarandon and Geena Davis. The Brothers play straight white women who behave diabolically but escape juridical punishment, suicide, homicide, and all other variations on the theme of bad girls driving off the edge of a cliff. The Brothers' secretaries adhere so fanatically to the dictates of proper white womanhood that even serial murder cannot tip them over into "fallen woman" status. This is what makes the Brothers' work so anxiety producing—straight white womanhood runs amok, unmoored from middle-class propriety. The Brothers' work is decidedly funny, but words like "deeply unsettling," "creepy," and "terrifying" have also been used to describe it. In performance, the Brothers valorize white womanhood and simultaneously eviscerate it. The depth of their subversiveness can be measured by each performer's ability to hold antithetical constructions of white womanhood together in a single performance.

In sum, the following chapters are about cultural production, cultural memory, and the WOW Café Theatre. The context from which WOW work emerged and the ways in which it emerged are equally intriguing and inseparable from the importance of the work itself. In response to my suggestion that early WOW work was ahead of—and pushed ahead—feminist critical theory in performance, Hughes countered, "A lot of the time we just threw something up there." This comment confirms WOW's foundational impulsiveness, but Hughes is not trivializing the effort. Rather, she makes clear that WOW artists did not necessarily work from theoretical premises in premeditated ways.[47]

Whatever the "quick and dirty" strategies, much of what WOW produced throughout the 1980s and 1990s marked a distinctive shift in feminist performance, charting new political and aesthetic territory that informed feminist critical production in important ways for years to come. What WOW "threw up there" was innovative, subversive, funny, and the consequence of a rich and complicated social and aesthetic environment. WOW does not participate in the Western tradition of the artist as inspired genius. Instead, the conditions at WOW encourage, unleash, and nurture the imagination, wit, and creative energies of its participants. Multifaceted and nuanced, these conditions underpin the cultural phenomenon that is WOW and have everything to do with the notion of feminist space, however vaguely conceptualized and *as* vaguely conceptualized. A great deal has been written about WOW artists and their work over the years, and several of the plays themselves have been published. Still, the WOW Café Theatre remains largely unacknowledged. When a phenomenon like WOW goes missing, something significant is lost not only to theater history but to cultural studies in general, and when lesbian cultural production goes missing, something is lost to queer.

Chapter 2

Women Are Laughing Again: Allied Farces

It was 1979. . . . I left Michigan with visions of all the sisterly, nonhierarchical art we were going to make. We were gonna topple the patriarchy by scattering huge sculptures of vaginas around public spaces and by renaming ourselves after our mothers' favorite condiments or obscure appliances found in the attics of famous women of the past.

—HOLLY HUGHES, 1996

In 1979, the year televangelist Jerry Falwell founded an organization called the Moral Majority, four lesbians from New York City met at a women's festival in Amsterdam and began a conversation that would lead to the founding of Women's One World. They were Pamela Camhe, Jordy Mark, Peggy Shaw, and Lois Weaver—all members of a supposedly immoral minority against which Falwell rallied his forces. Mark had just left a European tour as a singer and actor with the drag queen troupe known as Hot Peaches to join Camhe at the festival, where Mark was presenting an orchestrated slide show of Camhe's photography. Shaw and Weaver were scheduled to perform in Amsterdam as part of a tour of European festivals with the women's theater company Spiderwoman.

Impressed by Europe's festivals in general and high on their experience in Amsterdam, the four women began to daydream and brainstorm about mounting a similar festival in New York. Realizing the impossibility of replicating a European-style festival in the absence of public funding, they dropped the idea and went their separate ways upon returning to the city. They had no idea then that women from a number of European countries would be in touch over the following months with eager inquiries about their phantom stateside festival. They told those who contacted them that unlike in Europe, where festivals are generously funded, there would be no such funding in New York. No one seemed to care; these artists wanted the opportunity to perform in New York, and they agreed to pay their own travel expenses if free housing could be located.

In response to this prodding, Camhe, Mark, Shaw, and Weaver came together in the spring of 1980 at the Dojo restaurant on St. Mark's Place in the
East Village to discuss the possibility of mounting an international women's
theater festival. It seemed an insurmountable task. In addition to an utter
lack of funds, the four would-be festival organizers recognized that there was
no suitable, affordable performance space in the city. At this juncture in the
conversation, Mark remembers Shaw looking intently out the window:
"Peggy pointed to the All Craft Center across the street and said, 'We could
do it there.'"[1] The All Craft Foundation rented the building from the city and
ran a women's training center in the electrical, plumbing, and carpentry
trades. The building had formerly housed the Electric Circus, a hip disco with
a large main ballroom and a separate bar. By the end of the meeting, the four
women had agreed that if they could secure the space they would produce an
international festival that fall. The project was so ambitious and seemingly
implausible that they dubbed their nascent enterprise "the Allied Farces." As
it turned out, however, the festival was so successful that the Allied Farces
went on to produce a second, even larger international festival the next year.
From these festivals would emerge a women's community space called the
WOW Café, which in turn would evolve into the WOW Café Theatre.

A review of WOW's first festival written by the poet and playwright Jane
Chambers appeared in the *Advocate,* a glossy, nationally distributed gay
magazine. Chambers opens her review with three telling lines that capture
the historical moment: "Women are laughing again. Women are smiling and
singing and telling jokes. Out of the decade-long depression of the Women's
Movement a culture has emerged." She continued, "Nowhere has the blossoming of this women's culture been more startlingly evident than in the
Women's One World Festivals held in Manhattan."[2] The festival heralded a
kind of Freudian "return of the repressed," arriving on the scene at a time of
transition. As Chambers intimates, the women's movement had been so
fraught that women found little reason to laugh. She welcomed the festival as
relief from this dreary state of affairs.

In her review Chambers positioned WOW as a response to, as well as a
product of, 1970s feminism, locating the festival's performances alongside
other cultural phenomena of strength and humor. An emergent women's culture is evident, she noted, in "the throngs of women who storm Chris
Williamson's foot-tapping concerts, the sold-out houses that greet Pat Bond's
appearances, the fans who swarm comic Robin Tyler for autographs, [and]
the standing-room-only audiences who made my play *Last Summer at*

Bluefish Cove a commercial success."[3] Where WOW diverges from these examples, however, and what marks it as a turning point in feminist cultural production, is linked to a unique combination of disparate influences its four founders brought to the endeavor. The poet and novelist Eileen Myles differentiated the first WOW festival as destined to be a break from other feminist cultural production when she recalled, "The festival dropped a bomb in the middle of the scene, rewriting the look of lesbians ready to get over the seventies."[4]

The varied experiences, talents, and perspectives of the festival's founders converged in political and aesthetic sensibilities that were both foundational and enduring. WOW might have developed along very different lines had the producers all hailed from similar locations. Politically, Camhe and Mark had been active in New York City's feminist community throughout the 1970s, while Weaver had spent the decade on the margins of the women's movement, sympathetic but on the outside looking in. Shaw, however, considered feminists no less than the enemy, having met with disapproval from feminists who thought butch lesbians like her represented little more than a pathetic attempt at male impersonation. Artistically, Mark was a visual artist, singer, and actor, Camhe a photographer. They had met in 1974 in a clown workshop at the city's second Women's Liberation Center and shortly thereafter they became a couple. Weaver was an actor and director trained in traditional and experimental forms of theater, while Shaw was a visual artist who had stumbled on the world of drag queen street theater and received her performance training as a member of Hot Peaches. Upon moving to New York, Weaver had joined three women of color as founding members of Spiderwoman, a descendant of the 1960s experimental theater movement. Weaver and Shaw became a couple in the late 1970s after Shaw joined Spiderwoman. Mark and Shaw had worked separately with Hot Peaches, and together they wrote a cabaret theater piece they performed at Medusa's Revenge, an explicitly lesbian theater in the East Village established and operated by women of color.

Collectively, then, the four women were informed by the aesthetics and sensibilities of work produced by three important, sometimes overlapping groups: women of color, feminists, and drag queens. Women of color making work in the 1970s, for example, could be straight or lesbian, feminist or not, and it was the artistic director of a male drag troupe who introduced Shaw to a kind of feminism with which she could connect and productively engage. WOW's inaugural moment thus signaled a new era, bringing together multiple aesthetic impulses at a time of transition in the women's movement and contemporary feminist thought.

Hot Peaches: All Have Voices, All Can Sing

Some members of the Hot Peaches company cannot sing, dance or act, in spite of the fact that they do so; others are quite talented. . . . [R]ather than apologizing for their frequent lapses into an unprofessional status, they proudly boast about it as the very quality that distinguishes them.

—KEVIN VANCE, 1974

A significant portion of WOW work over the years has been compared by reviewers to that of the playwright and actor Charles Ludlam, a founder and exemplar of Theatre of the Ridiculous. But it was another gay male troupe, Hot Peaches, that had the greatest impact on WOW's development. Certainly Hot Peaches had much in common with Ludlam's work. Like Ludlam's theater, Hot Peaches thrived on camp and shtick. One reviewer wrote in 1978, "The look of the Peaches is strictly haute couture. There's nothing straight about their act or their clothes. They love razzle and adore dazzle."[5] In the 1970s "The Peaches" and "The Ridiculous" were often mentioned in the same breath, but the importance of Hot Peaches to WOW's development lies in the differences between these two troupes.

In a 1974 interview Ludlam himself maintained that Hot Peaches was more about fashion than theater and therefore fundamentally different from his work.[6] In this regard, he was right. Early Hot Peaches work was often written around individuals who wanted to perform a particular "look." Jimmy Camicia, the troupe's artistic director, did not come from a background in theater and had never written a play when in 1972 he encountered the group of street queens who would become the Peaches. "One of them said, 'I want to sing this song,'" he recalled, "and another said, 'I want to wear this dress,' and I said, 'Okay, I'll write a play.'"[7] The *Village Voice* said of the 1973 Hot Peaches production *The Watergate Scandals of '73* that it "seemed to provide an excuse for the company to appear in drag."[8] The same year Camicia told another reporter, "We're not actors, we're entertainers. Rather than becoming the script, the script becomes us."[9]

In Ludlam's theater characters were sometimes played in drag, while Hot Peaches shows revolved *entirely* around female impersonation. *The Watergate Scandals of '73* included a wicked portrayal of Martha Mitchell, then wife of the country's attorney general, frantically making her infamous late-night telephone calls while sitting on the toilet. Ludlam himself would have played the character as realistically as possible, not to fool the audience into thinking he was a woman but to play on the conceit in multiple ways. The Peach who portrayed Mitchell, however, unabashedly approached the character as a drag queen playing Martha Mitchell and conversely as Martha Mitchell playing a drag queen. The work of Ludlam and Hot Peaches was equally flamboyant and fabulous but in different ways. While Ludlam mounted highly theatrical productions of what were first and foremost *plays,* Hot Peaches mounted plays that were first and foremost *productions.*

Ludlam may have been right about fashion as the impulse behind the founding of Hot Peaches, but he was entirely off the mark in his assessment of the troupe as "the Stepin Fetchit of gay theater," a historical reference to Lincoln Perry, a black actor whose stage name was Stepin Fetchit. Perry is infamously credited with inventing the stereotypical "shuffling Negro" role he played in dozens of films in the 1930s. Although Perry has since been recuperated as an accomplished actor who was able to succeed in a white-controlled industry, at the time Ludlam made this remark Stepin Fetchit was considered an example of demeaning negative stereotypes.[10] Hot Peaches could only be considered the Stepin Fetchit of gay theater if its performances were addressed primarily to straight audiences in ways analogous to those in which Perry's work supposedly played to white audiences. Instead, and unlike Ludlam's theater, the work of Hot Peaches was addressed specifically to the gay community.

In his 1978 book *Queer Theatre,* the poet and theater historian Stefan Brecht indirectly acknowledges Ludlam's Stepin Fetchit analogy but suggests that Hot Peaches represents a break from what he referred to as "coon-status." Of Hot Peaches he wrote, "Gay theater, entertaining parade of female impersonators liberated from their coon-status in burlesque shows for straight salesmen, stages the party-parade by which drag-queens realize their phantasies [*sic*]."[11] And of Hot Peaches's audience, Brecht added, "Being catered to and being told it is catered to, it will more readily forgive qualitative lapses of the performance. None of this excludes satire, didacticism or tragic pathos, though it does exclude offensive satire (agreement on issues is presumed)."[12] Camicia put it this way: "Gay theatre that talks to everybody is not gay; it's straight. . . . Charles was headed for Broadway, and gay was poison."[13] Which is not to suggest that Ludlam's theater pandered to straight audiences, but by invoking Stepin Fetchit he suggests that this is something he might have feared. Ludlam remained adamant that his work was not "gay theater."[14]

Theater itself was secondary to Hot Peaches. Of the troupe's earliest incarnation, recalled Camicia, it represented "a place where Lower East Side street queens were welcome and felt comfortable." Hot Peaches continued to be a place where gender outcasts could proclaim, "This is who I am. Ain't it hot?" The troupe was primarily about creating a supportive environment where people could perform who they were and who they wanted to be—a sensibility that would characterize WOW's evolution. As the playwright, director, and critic Michael Feingold wrote in the *Village Voice*, "The Peaches of course don't *act,* but each Peach has constructed a star-type personality." Camicia further explained, "Theater was so tedious compared to TV and Hollywood. Hot Peaches was broad-based as opposed to theater-based." Weaver offered this insight: "Hot Peaches was a lot like WOW in the sense that *anybody* could be a Peach. It was an unspoken thing; if you ever did a show, took tickets, swept the floor, or made a costume, you were a Peach." Shaw added, "That's a lot of Peaches."[15]

Writing for the *Advocate* in 1978, the cultural historian Steven Watson noted, "Although Hot Peaches originally grew out of [troupe founders] Jimmy and Ian [McKay]'s relationship, the group now has built a huge pool of gay talent that it uses regularly: street queens, musicians, off-off-Broadway actors, poets, divas and punks. And much of the fun and electricity of the Hot Peaches shows still works, no matter who the Peaches are."[16] Theater was merely the medium available to this grassroots group. "We knew exactly what we were doing," Camicia recalled. "We had no theatrical aspirations." People were his primary focus: "Everyone has talent. The question is will you let them find it? All have voices, all can sing."[17]

Peggy Shaw is a case in point. Her experience with Hot Peaches mirrors the experience many women would later have at WOW. The role she subsequently assumed for other WOW women echoes the role Camicia played for her during her years with Hot Peaches. Of the first time she saw the troupe, Shaw recalled, "I'd never thought about theatre until that moment. Before long, I was making sets for their group."[18] She was with Hot Peaches for two years before she went onstage. By way of explanation, Camicia said, "Dykes came in as crew and did not want to go onstage." This is an interesting observation given that a few heterosexual women performed regularly with Hot Peaches over the years. By the time the Peaches toured Europe in 1975 and 1976, Camicia had discovered feminism, in part because Mallory Jones, sister of the influential feminist writer Kate Millett, had become a member of the troupe. Of feminism, Camicia recalled, "I found it intellectually fabulous."

He realized that "Hot Peaches and other gay shows had a tradition of putting women and dykes down." Encouraging Shaw to perform was Camicia's first step in turning this around. "Feminists were the enemy for me during the 1970s," Shaw reflected. "Jimmy introduced me to feminism."[19]

Camicia wrote the following monologue for Shaw and encouraged her to perform it.

> HISTORY!!! You mean HIS-STORY
> His story in which every great
> If they're to rate
> Must first turn male then white then straight
> From adam down to jesus christ
> They very neatly sliced away
> The dark
> The feminine
> The gay
> Until today
> When they've mystified the story
> And debased our former glory
> Mythified the truth of matriarchy
> Sacrificing virgins upon burning faggots for the glory
> For the glory of their gory hoary patriarchy
> Do you wonder at my fury?
> Do you wonder why
> You don't get high
> Upon the lie
> His-Story?
> Well, get real Mary.[20]

Shaw performed this monologue and thereafter considered Camicia her teacher. She "learned how to write because Jimmy said, 'We don't have any lesbian material. Go in there and write something, Peggy, and come back in fifteen minutes.'" Shaw returned with a monologue called "Dyke."[21] Before she began performing, she was strong but silent. "Peggy hardly ever spoke," recalled Camicia, but when she began to speak onstage, what came across the footlights was anger. Shaw was the only lesbian among the troupe's women, and Camicia thought, "maybe this is how dykes present themselves. Peggy was very angry and suppressed."[22]

Shaw described her experience this way: "The rage wasn't exactly con-ducive to comedy. I learned that from the drag queens. The whole style of drag queens is competitive. You have to be taller, use more glitter, be funnier. The life is combative, in-your-face theater. The drag queens in the company had high consciousness. They didn't wear tits. They were boys in dresses, but their look created instant humor, an instant clown persona. When I worked with Lois [Weaver], I learned about subtlety and seduction."[23] With both Weaver and Spiderwoman, Shaw would learn an alternative way of working as well as new ways to address a different kind of audience.

As critic Laurie Stone pointed out in her review of a 1988 Hot Peaches "greatest hits" event, the troupe addressed the gay male community in par-ticular. "Although there are three women in the cast," wrote Stone, "the show represents male experience. The women do feminist shtick, but they sing about gay male sexuality, not their own."[24] Shaw later told Stone about an epiphany she had in the 1970s: "I remember the moment I realized I hated women. It was in Berlin, and a woman came into a meeting, and I realized I knew nothing about this woman, and yet I hated her, thinking I hated her the way a man would. I saw I thought I *was* a guy, that I had taken on all that stuff [over a lifetime]. I had to tear it all down and build it back up."[25] From the Peaches, Shaw had learned the empowering dimension of addressing a specific audience as well as the value of an "everyone has talent" approach to performance. Now her challenge was to make work emerging from a differ-ent kind of specificity.

Spiderwoman Theater: Challenging One Size Fits All

By exploding the constraints of the realist form, as well as those of a hegemonic notion of feminism or "postfeminism," groups like Spiderwoman have the po-tential to transform feminist theater once again into a site of radical political ac-tion for the 1990s, by working at the intersections of race, ethnicity, and gender.

—JILL DOLAN, 1993

Of the many women's theaters in existence during the 1970s, the work of Spi-derwoman Theater had the greatest impact on WOW's developing aesthetic. Weaver had a six-year affiliation with the group and Shaw a shorter tenure. In college Weaver had studied a new phenomenon known as experimental theater. When she arrived in New York in 1974, she headed straight for a venue that had been recognized for this kind of innovation, the Theater for the New City. There she met theater artist Muriel Miguel, who had worked with the Open Theater, one of the most important experimental groups of the 1960s and early 1970s. Weaver became a founding member of the Spider-woman Theater in 1975 along with Miguel and Miguel's sisters, Lisa Mayo and Gloria Miguel.[26] Spiderwoman's influence on WOW stems not only from the ways in which it was like other feminist theaters operating during the 1970s but also from the important ways in which it was different.

Feminist theater had evolved from two newly developed practices in the 1960s—consciousness-raising and experimental theater. In New York, for example, the It's Alright to Be Woman Theater—one of the very first women's theaters—emerged in 1969 directly out of consciousness-raising, a feminist practice grounded in the premise that "the personal is political." In consciousness-raising groups, women who shared their experiences with other women quickly realized that not only were these experiences quite common but this commonality was peculiar to their social status as women rather than a consequence of nature or their actions as individuals. These groups then considered their common experiences in light of larger political implications. Theater historian Charlotte Canning has commented on this phenomenon: "The majority of feminist theater artists working in groups consistently strived to create connections with the audience that emphasized commonalities and similarities."[27] According to WOW cofounder Jordy Mark, the It's Alright to Be Woman Theater was an inspiration for other feminist theaters and a site for community building. "It was such an important part of the women's community in the city then," she recalled. "It served as a magnet for feminist women, empowering them. A lot of women came out of the closet in the context of that theater."[28]

The other important catalyst for feminist theater was the experimental theater movement, particularly the Open Theater. Members of this company broke with traditional approaches to making theater, eschewing the authority of the playwright and generating original material through innovative improvisatory techniques developed in workshop settings. Actors were the central creative force underpinning this endeavor. In collaboration with directors and playwrights, actors explored their own creative impulses and generated new work centered on their bodies as the primary expressive dimension of theater, resulting in plays that were often nonlinear in structure and dependent on the performance of visual images as much as on spoken text. By privileging the actor's presence over the play's text, experimental theater sought to achieve a more direct and visceral connection with the audience.

A number of important feminist theaters would be founded by women who worked with the Open Theater—Spiderwoman's Muriel Miguel among them. Like many others, Miguel became increasingly disillusioned by her experience with the Open Theater Company, however. She eventually left because of the theater's steadfast male point of view and unwillingness to address women's issues as political rather than merely personal. Among other women who departed the Open Theater were the director Roberta Sklar, who went on to cofound the Women's Experimental Theatre in 1977 with Sondra Segal, and the playwright Megan Terry, who cofounded the Omaha Magic Theatre in 1968 with Jo Ann Schmidman.

A genealogical line can be drawn from the It's Alright to Be Woman Theater directly to WOW's festivals by way of groups like the Women's Experimental Theater, with an important difference: most feminist theater pieces were about serious matters presented seriously. Spiderwoman's work also addressed serious topics, but it did so mostly with humor. A signature feature was the company's exaggerated, no-holds-barred performance style. This approach was engaged not to trivialize the issues but to explore them more expansively. In its early years critics described the troupe's humor as "women's locker room," "extreme," "ribald," and "zany." The British reviewers Carole Spedding and Jill Nicholls each wrote about Spiderwoman's very first production, *Women in Violence,* when the troupe performed it in London in 1975. Echoing familiar themes of women's theater at the time, the piece was about violence against women, violence among women, and the violence a woman commits against herself. "When Spiderwoman arrived and burst on stage confronting us with their lives in the most *garish carnival style,*" Spedding wrote, "we were stunned."[29] Nicholls observed, "The show works as a montage—the women clown, joke, repeat themselves hypnotically, talk over one another, jostle for position with the audience. Their clothes dazzle with tricks and colour, their faces bend like rubber, their timing is perfect."[30] As these descriptions suggest, the piece lacked the solemn tone of much women's theater production. Spedding's review went on, "It was the first time that I had ever laughed at pies-in-the-face and the fact that it had me in fits [of laughter] within a play entitled *Women in Violence* seemed an almost impossible achievement." Nicholls added, "It makes English plays and players look so staid and prim. Ideas run riot, lines feed on one another, the women work from their own experience, let their bodies be fully themselves, and so spin off beyond stage realism or true confessions." Performance scholar Rebecca Schneider has described Spiderwoman as performing both a "slapstick style and hysterical behavior around extremely serious topics."[31] Spiderwoman

Theater was flamboyant in ways different from Hot Peaches but flamboyant nonetheless.

Reviews of Spiderwoman productions over the years have made note of the performances of large women among the group. What has often struck the reviewers is that these women have performed extravagantly, as if size does not matter. In other words, performers with bodies out of sync with mainstream ideals did *not* limit the material they could perform; these women did not present themselves as asexual, move in restricted ways, or position themselves in the background. Rather, Spiderwoman's large women were sexual and sexy; they assumed all the attributes and behaviors that ostensibly belong to svelte women alone, performing them forcefully and with confidence. By mainstream standards, then, performances by Spiderwoman's large women were excessive, but by the company's standards they were absolutely in keeping with the overall intent of the work. Presaging the stance the Split Britches troupe would take with regard to lesbians, the Spiderwoman company presumed women's differing sizes as a given rather than as something on which to comment.

For Spiderwoman, women's experiences were common up to a point. As Canning has pointed out, "Rather than stress commonalities, as was prevalent at the time, Spiderwoman explored differences. The . . . experiences they wanted to express did not exist in other theaters. For much of their history they have been a coalitional theater, committed to working across the differences of race, sexual preference, and class."[32] This dimension of Spiderwoman grew organically out of the company's particular way of working in combination with the group's diverse composition. The Miguel sisters are Native Americans of Cuna and Rappahannock descent, and Spiderwoman takes its name from the Hopi goddess of creation, who taught her people how to create designs and how to weave. The Open Theater's improvisatory approach to creating work in combination with this Hopi tradition inspired Spiderwoman to develop a working technique called "storyweaving." With this method, designs or patterns are created and stories emerge from a process of weaving words with movement.

Long after Weaver and Shaw had moved on from Spiderwoman, members of the company described this process: "Challenging the 'one size fits all' view of feminism, [we] . . . use our diverse experiences . . . to defy such generalizations as 'blondes have more fun' and 'all women's theatre is the same.' Our stories can be told or thought of at any time—on the street, over meals, in the tub. Then we rehearse, improvise and brainstorm to investigate various aspects of our stories, dreams and images. We usually begin with a theme, someone tells a story, another repeats it, and we work together to transform it into movement or reduce it to its essence."[33] Weaver helped to develop this approach and then took it with her to the company she would cofound with Shaw and Margolin in 1981, Split Britches. Weaver expanded on this notion of storyweaving, disseminating it throughout WOW's membership by means of the workshops she conducted, the classes she taught, and the productions she directed.

Initially Spiderwoman was feminist theater less by design than as a consequence of using the personal experiences of women in the group as fodder for storyweaving. Although the company had an enthusiastic following, feminists did not always welcome their performances. Of the troupe's experience during the 1970s, cofounder Muriel Miguel told a reporter, "We were performing, spilling our guts on the floor and these middle-class women were telling us they weren't sure we were politically correct." Gloria Miguel elaborated, "I've suffered more in my life as an Indian than as a woman."[34] Performing the dynamics of class and race, as well as gender, age, and body image, became defining features of Spiderwoman's work. Because the company's approach allowed for the representation of multiple differences, the work was decidedly not exclusionary. Maintaining gaps and fissures in their storyweaving as openings for the representation of difference was characteristic of Spiderwoman and would later become crucial to WOW both aesthetically and operationally.

Spiderwoman's over-the-top performance style combined with the diversity of its performative address meant that the group would be considered what Canning has described as "confrontational" by default if not intention. "Muriel Miguel understands very keenly that it is Spiderwoman's marginalized and contradictory status that makes them so controversial," she wrote. "When presenting to the Native American community, their feminism is problematic; when presenting to the feminist community, their commitment to exposing and confronting racism is often unwelcome; and when presenting to the theater community, their non-traditional style as a deliberate choice and commentary on theater is confusing."[35]

When Shaw joined Spiderwoman in 1978, sexuality became yet another constitutive difference in Spiderwoman's work. Muriel Miguel invited Shaw to join the group because Spiderwoman wanted to create a cabaret piece. Shaw had experience mounting cabaret theater with Hot Peaches, and she played the saxophone. She was a member of Spiderwoman for two and a half years before she and Weaver split off from the group to produce their own work. By the mid-1980s Spiderwoman was the only feminist theater from the previous decade still operating in New York City. If the It's Alright to Be Woman Theater was the mother of feminist theater in New York during the 1970s, then Spiderwoman gave birth to the city's feminist theater of the 1980s. In keeping with this sentiment and in acknowledgment of this lineage, Spiderwoman performed the opening act for WOW's twentieth anniversary event in 2000.

Medusa's Revenge: A Homo-esthetic Sensibility

Medusa's Revenge is a young, exciting company that could very well be at the vanguard of the "second wave" of theater for women.
—BARBARA SCHWARTZ AND MARA SHELBY, 1978

Lesbian content was primarily on stage at Medusa's Revenge . . . the first theater in the world willing to produce our work. [It] has never made it into any of the official histories of feminist or lesbian theater.
—SARAH SCHULMAN, 1998

Little has been written about Medusa's Revenge, a short-lived but important lesbian theater founded in 1976 at 10 Bleecker Street, off the Bowery in the East Village. In many respects this theater was the prototype for WOW. Medusa's Revenge cofounder Ana Maria Simo recalls that the lighting instruments and dimmer packs in WOW's first permanent space were gifts from Medusa's Revenge when it closed in 1981.[36] For many years this was the only lighting equipment WOW had. Medusa's Revenge was run by two Cuban exiles, Simo and cofounder Magaly Alabau. Their initial impulse sprang from a desire to create a lesbian community space. "I had a girlfriend at the time," said Simo of Alabau, "who was an actress in the Spanish theater in New York and she also worked at LaMama. . . . She was very dissatisfied with the roles she was getting, as a woman. She suggested the idea of the lesbian space and a theater where she could express herself."[37]

Although Alabau had experience in professional theater, she and Simo recruited performers for their theater by leafleting local lesbian bars. An early press release stated, "Medusa's Revenge is an experimental theatre of women dedicated to the creation of original plays . . . exploring a homo-esthetic sensibility. It operates from its own performing space: a white, vast, air-conditioned basement theatre. The theatre also conducts an ongoing acting workshop, geared toward the creation of a permanent ensemble."[38] Composed mostly of women with no previous theater background, this ensemble developed a new piece each year. Like Hot Peaches and WOW, Medusa's Revenge was purposefully a community-based enterprise. Unlike Hot Peaches and WOW, however, the theater focused primarily on developing new plays and solicited scripts from women outside its membership, producing them around the ensemble's annual major production. Medusa's Revenge also instituted a yearly playwriting award for work reflecting a lesbian sensibility.

Like WOW in its early days, Medusa's Revenge presented outside artists and companies, which included work by artists of color like the Flamboyant Ladies and Edwina Lee Tyler's troupe, A Piece of the World. During a month-long engagement at the theater in the fall of 1978, the Spiderwoman troupe performed *Women in Violence, The Lysistrata Numbah!* as well as three shorter pieces in repertory. Medusa's Revenge had a women-only policy, with mixed audiences restricted to specific nights. A flyer from 1978 explained, "Medusa's Revenge—both the theater space and the resident company under the same name—continues to be fully committed to the exploration of lesbian culture and the development of a women-only audience." Like the WOW Café, some performances were followed by women-only dances, and over the years a number of imaginative theme parties were held in the space as fund-raisers. Shaw has described Medusa's Revenge as a "very welcoming place" as well as a kind of "secret." "It was a word-of-mouth affair," she recalled. "You almost had to live in the 'hood to hear about it."[39]

Simo's experience with Medusa's Revenge would be echoed later by that of some women at WOW. Because her background was in political activism rather than theater, she assumed the role of manager or executive director, which meant she provided much of the operation's labor—organizing, cleaning, and fighting with the landlord. Simo reflected that "one day, the actors were doing improvisations and they felt that they weren't getting anywhere. I was cleaning the bathroom and I was asked if they gave me all their voluminous transcripts, if I could possibly write a play."[40] She did. The resulting play, *Going Slow,* became the ensemble's first production. Simo then wrote a play called *Bayou* for the ensemble to perform, which she described as "very, very different from the feminist women's theater that was happening at the time . . . a certain amount of women in the audience were walking out in a huff."[41] Shaw remembers the depiction of lesbians in *Bayou* as having nothing to do with presenting positive images of "the life"; this politically incorrect sensibility was true in general of plays developed at Medusa's Revenge.

A publicity flyer for the play announced, "*Bayou* is about a wild and mythical lesbian bar where anything can and does happen: dreams and tap dancing, nightmares and memories, torch songs, fiery sensuality, death, divas, and divine apparitions." The production's program lists eight performers playing some twenty-nine different roles. In a review for the *Gay Community News,* the visual artist Fran Winant wrote: "A great predatory feast takes place, dramatized toward the end of the play as a kind of religious communion: the bar-owner devours the lives and dreams of her customers, and is herself devoured by gangsters seeking protection-money, while the women in the bar burn out their energies dancing the night away and competing for sex. The individual woman who attempts to draw sustenance from this world goes insane and her mind is devoured by doctors who administer shock treatments." This sounds hopelessly grim, but it was not. Winant continues, "Lighting, costumes, dancing, numerous abrupt changes of scene, and a sense of sexual fascination between women combine to hold the audience's attention. A couple of high points . . . a top-hat and cane routine straight out of a '40s' Fred Astaire movie . . . and some of the particularly sexual dances are done with sticks, representing phallic pool cues. The women moved these forward and back, around and across each other's bodies." On the production's overall ambience, Winant observed: "The background music rarely stops, and at intermission you can get up and dance, join the bar scene yourself."[42]

Writing for *Majority Report,* the editor and peace activist Judith Pasternak commented on the acting in *Bayou,* "There are some very good performances, especially Georgine Gorra's quintessential butch and Keitheley Wilkinson's brief but touching appearance as a drunk baby butch."[43] A butch/femme dynamic operates in this play and prefigures an expanded vision for playing on gender roles that would be developed at WOW. *Bayou* is an early instance of incorporating butch/femme iconography into a theater production, which is perhaps part of the reason some women "walked out in a huff." In the 1970s a great many feminists considered representation of butch/femme lesbians to be the epitome of derogatory stereotypes. This sentiment carried over into the 1980s and was challenged by work presented at both Medusa's Revenge and the WOW Café.[44]

In 1979, Mark and Shaw, along with an African American woman named Honey, mounted a cabaret at Medusa's Revenge called "Acting Up and Out." Honey went on to play the black radio announcer in *Born in Flames,* Lizzie Borden's 1983 documentary-style feminist film. Shaw wrote the following ditty and performed it as part of her act:

If there's nowhere to go to when you raise your mind
And an evening's entertainment is so hard to find
Just catch the F train on the Independent Line
On the DOWNTOWN side
It's so easy to find
MEDUSA'S
They got Dykes for days
MEDUSA'S
The finest women in town
MEDUSA'S
It's on the Lower East Side
The gayest place in town
Where you can lose your mind
Have a cruise
You can't lose
Be a star
That's who you are
At Medusa's Revenge![45]

This short piece not only captures the general aura of Medusa's Revenge as a community and cultural space, but it forecasts the WOW Café's milieu as well. Cruising women and becoming a star characterize the sensibilities of both enterprises.

Unlike the WOW Café Theatre, however, Medusa's Revenge referred to itself as a *lesbian* space rather than a *women's* space. Like WOW, Medusa's Revenge produced what the British critical theorist Alan Sinfield has called "boldly sexual work" in the single sentence he devotes to Medusa's Revenge in his 1999 book *Out on Stage: Lesbian and Gay Theatre in the Twentieth Century*.[46] On the theater's continuing obscurity, Simo believes that "one of the reasons [it] is not known is precisely because neither of us [cofounders Simo and Alabau] nor the women who came to work with us were in the network of feminist theatre or lesbian feminist activities. We were totally out of the loop in terms of our social class."[47] Medusa's Revenge was as far afield of the period's white middle-class feminism as a lesbian theater space could get.

Similarly, WOW created its own cultural space, knitting together multiple activities and performances into a whole that was greater than the sum of its many parts. Its first international festival was a place where women with disparate backgrounds and resonant sensibilities could—for a brief time—

become a community; where performers from across the city, across the country, and around the Western world could interact and see each other's work; and where audiences could interact with performers and each other. Shortly after Medusa's Revenge closed, WOW made the transition from a festival to a community space, establishing itself as the WOW Café in its first permanent home. "At the time, I remember I felt relieved," Simo has said, "because I felt the mission was in good hands. It was continuing."[48] Simo went on to write a number of plays after Medusa's Revenge closed; one of them—*Pickaxe*—was produced at WOW in 1986.

Feminist Art at Decade's End: A Transitional Moment

Anything smacking of power difference or potential inequality was decisively expurgated from the feminist revolutionary canon. Good lesbian-feminists no longer did these things. Such practices were, it was said, the products of a lesbianism vitiated and contained by heterosexuality.

—CLARE WHATLING, 1992

Don't panic . . . I was born this way. I didn't learn it at theatre school. I was born butch. I'm so queer I don't even have to talk about it. It speaks for itself.

—PEGGY SHAW, in the role of "Stanley, a butch lesbian," *Belle Reprieve*, 1991

As appealing as it is to imagine WOW's youthful beginnings as a girl in a white hat riding in to save the day with twelve hundred pounds of steed galloping between her legs, in 1980 that girl would have been a nude white "womyn" riding sidesaddle—attributes that speak to the dominant strain of feminist politics and aesthetics by the end of 1970s. The printed program for the Women's One World Festivals depicted a massive naked woman on its cover, rising from Manhattan and holding the world in her hands. This visual rendering of the festival's title, graphically demonstrates how it was a product of feminism in the decade preceding it. A juxtaposition of these two images—the hard-riding, sexually potent cowgirl prepared to hogtie anyone who gets in her way and the larger-than-life woman charged with the care and nurturing of the entire world, her nakedness symbolizing her status as "everywoman"—mirrors the central debate at a transitional moment in feminist thought. Performances at this festival embodied these two distinct impulses, reflecting what came before and foreshadowing what was to come.

In terms of the many theories circulating within feminism, and the diverse works of feminist art produced across mediums throughout the 1970s, the broad brushstrokes are most important regarding WOW. Feminist debates filtered down through the women's movement and academia only sporadically to those responsible for creating the WOW Café Theatre. A woman's cultural location—her education, class, race, sexuality, her position in or outside an urban area, in or outside academia—played a role in what she would know about the movement and its theoretical underpinnings. In many cases that which would become generally known was whatever had received widespread media attention or acquired infamy within the larger feminist movement itself. Lois Weaver's experience is a case in point. She first became aware of feminism when she read about the radical feminist group Redstockings in a mainstream magazine. Although deeply interested in Redstockings' ideas, Weaver felt out of place when feminists gathered in New York coffeehouses and bookstores to discuss the movement's ideology. She was unfamiliar with the language of the New Left and uncomfortable with the stridency she perceived in much of the rhetoric. Weaver's working-class, rural Virginia roots marginalized her and ultimately positioned her outside of many feminist conversations and debates during the 1970s.

A woman's knowledge of feminism and feminist art could also be a consequence of serendipity. Feminists worked actively in video and film, theater, and visual art; however, these forms traditionally tended to exist in separate spheres or art worlds. It was possible for feminist artists working in one medium to be largely unaware of feminists working in another unless the work became famous. This was the case with such landmark pieces as Judy Chicago's sculpture installation *The Dinner Party* on the West Coast and the successful, widely covered production of Ntozake Shange's *for colored girls who have considered suicide/when the rainbow is enuf* on Broadway. Playwright and performance artist Holly Hughes was a visual artist before finding the WOW Café shortly after it opened. She has recalled being so broke at the time that she seldom saw film or performance of any kind that required admission.[49] Although the Women's Experimental Theatre was active in New York in the late 1970s, Hughes never saw a single production, and Weaver attended the theater for the first time to ask the company's members—Roberta Sklar, Sondra Segal, and Clair Coss—to participate in WOW's first festival.

In terms of feminism's influence on the development of WOW's project, what in subsequent years would be identified and analyzed as disparate strains of feminism seemed less discrete during the 1970s. In part, this was because a good deal of ideological repositioning was under way as many women theorists, artists, and activists struggled to think through what feminism might mean and what it might accomplish. Women aligned with what became known as liberal feminism, for example, tended to focus on issues like equal pay for equal work; through struggle and political action, these women sought equity and parity within existing cultural and economic structures. Material or socialist feminists were influenced by Marxist theories and embraced the premise that the dynamics of inequality and oppression are endemic to, and produced by, mainstream cultural, political, and economic institutions. They sought to expose and reform the ideologies underpinning these institutions in an effort to bring about systemic, structural change. Paradoxically, what had been known as radical feminism in the early years of the movement became incongruously conflated with its antithesis, a phenomenon called cultural feminism. This development helps to explain what Jane Chambers found "startling" about the first WOW festival. Radical feminism was "the repressed" that had returned, making a notable reappearance at the festival.

Although feminists had produced critical theory during the 1970s from a number of social, cultural, and ideological positions, the worldview of cultural feminism, which was but one strain of feminism, came to dominate the movement's politics and aesthetic production by the decade's end. In her important historical account *Daring to Be Bad: Radical Feminism in America, 1967–1975*, historian Alice Echols maps the trajectory of early feminist thinking that led to this emergent feminist ideology. She shows how the same radical feminist thought, which had sowed the seeds for a feminism that espoused political activism firmly grounded in the notion of gender as a social construction as opposed to a fact of nature, simultaneously contributed to the eventual ascendancy of cultural feminism. She describes this feminism in terms of an essentialist female counterculture. In response to a culture dominated by men—and thus imbued with the tenets of "maleness"—cultural feminists envisioned an alternative culture aligned with traditional notions of all that is ostensibly natural, positive, and nurturing about "femaleness." Echols argued that theoretical limitations in the same thinking that productively informed an agenda for social change through political action ultimately led to the demise of radical activism in favor of a localized, lived countercultural politics. Cultural feminism was manifest in individual lifestyle choices premised on characteristics supposedly common to all women in a universal sisterhood.[50]

Although other strains of feminism had been superseded by 1980, they continued their subterranean existence. Women made music, art, video, film, performance art, and theater reflecting every disparate worldview and political impulse circulating throughout the women's movement and across contemporary feminist thought. A monolithic, seamless feminist aesthetic did not exist. Filmmakers such as Barbara Hammer and Su Friedrich made important films that were both feminist *and* lesbian.[51] A play by Megan Terry was produced for the stage and adapted for video in which four women have sex with each other as a tribute to the novelist Willa Cather.[52] Lydia Lunch, a punk icon and pubescent leader of the group Teenage Jesus and the Jerks, wailed her sexual rage.[53] And the performance artist Jill Kroesen sang songs with such titles as "I Think I'm Good If Someone Wants to Fuck Me Blues" in pieces with titles like *Excuse Me I Feel Like Multiplying*.[54] This, of course, was not the kind of work that received mainstream media attention.

As an essentialist ideology came to dominate feminism's landscape, however, a predominant aesthetic emerged and found its expression in important works of art and theater, some of which became widely known. Possibly the most famous work of feminist art to come out of the 1970s, *The Dinner Party* by Judy Chicago, was significant for WOW for several reasons. Festival cofounders Camhe, Mark, and Shaw, as well as Holly Hughes, had all come to performance from the visual arts, and *The Dinner Party*'s themes and aesthetic resonated with much women's theater and performance art during the same period. This work is undoubtedly what inspired a young artist like Hughes, coming from Kalamazoo, Michigan, to believe the patriarchy could be toppled "by scattering huge sculptures of vaginas around public spaces."[55] *The Dinner Party* incorporated ideas then circulating about the nature of women's contributions to history and culture, while also bringing to the fore a newfound appreciation for the traditional materials of women's art making, such as ceramics, hand-painted china, weaving, and needlework. Each of the table's thirty-nine place settings honors a particular woman by incorporating images that are specific to her story as well as symbols cultural feminists deemed empowering and common to women in general. In response to a culture saturated with phallic references and images, much of *The Dinner Party*'s design represents variations on a single theme—the explicit rendering of a vulva and clitoris. The table itself evokes vulval iconography with its three sides configured in the shape of a triangle.

As Chicago described it, "The incorporation of vulval iconography was certainly intended to challenge the pervasive definitions of . . . female sexuality as passive. But, more significant . . . it implies that the various women represented—though separated by culture, time, geography, experience, and individual choices . . . are unified primarily by their gender."[56] The work celebrates a female lineage along gender lines, positing a stable, ahistorical, female nature that privileges women's experience and reifies the commonalities therein. A similar conceptual framework could also be found in most women's theater collectives of the period. The goal was to promote social change by creating an alternative representational space for women through productions firmly grounded in women's experiences. Common themes and issues included motherhood, daughterhood, food and the body, domestic labor, rape, and battering.[57]

Ntozake Shange's groundbreaking play *for colored girls who have considered suicide/when the rainbow is enuf* represents a similar aesthetic from a black woman's perspective, acknowledging and mining the lived dynamics of race and racial oppression. It is arguably the most famous feminist theater piece of the 1970s. First produced at the Bacchanal, a women's bar outside of Berkeley, California, the play enjoyed a run off-Broadway in 1976 and opened on Broadway later that same year, where it ran until 1978. It was produced across the country and on television. Of her drama Shange has said, "In the summer of 1974 I had begun a series of seven poems, modeled on Judy Grahn's *The Common Woman,* which were to explore the realities of seven different kinds of women. They were numbered pieces: the women were to be nameless & assume hegemony as dictated by the fullness of their lives."[58] The piece is made up entirely of a series of poems that flow together, integrating poetry with movement and music to create what Shange has called "a choreopoem." Like Chicago, Shange wanted to propagate symbols that express the specificity of women's experience, but for Shange that did not mean ignoring or transcending the specificity of black women's experience. A line representative of the play's style also captures the paradoxical nature of black womanhood: "& it waz all i had but bein alive & bein a woman & bein colored is a metaphysical dilemma / i havent conquered yet."[59] Shange explored the possibility of an alternative language to express a different kind of experience, marking differences while emphasizing commonalities.

Unlike most feminist theater and art at the time, *for colored girls* and *The Dinner Party* reached a large audience, but they were considered through a "separatist" lens, relegating them to a separate critical space.[60] By 1980 it was clear to many feminists that if women were to ever find their way out of this critical isolation and political morass, they would have to critique and subvert symbolic systems in a different way. Rather than developing a set of symbols designed to balance, if not supplant, those of patriarchy, women began to understand that they would have to actively engage the very patriarchal representational codes they had been attempting to both sidestep and reformulate. The path leading in this direction had already been mapped within the discourses of feminism itself, as Echols has argued, and an alternative aesthetic direction was evident in the work of some visual artists. When the play *Split Britches* burst on the scene in 1980 as something entirely different from its contemporaries in theater, including the work of Spiderwoman, the difference lay in part in the legacy of feminist visual art, an aesthetic manifest early and compellingly in the work of women of color.

In a largely white, middle-class, single-issue women's movement, women of color brought multiple social, political, and cultural perspectives to their work, foregrounding the constructed nature of all identities. In her 1972 piece entitled *The Liberation of Aunt Jemima,* for example, the artist Betye Saar placed a doll wearing a stereotypical mammy outfit in a vertical rectangular box. With skin rendered the blackest of black, and a face dominated by a large white smile and wide-open white eyes, the figure stands with a rifle in one hand and a revolver and a broom in the other. Propped under the doll's breast is a two-dimensional image of a similar mammy figure, also smiling. Her hand rests sassily on one hip, while on the other hip she holds a bawling white baby. The back wall of the box, against which both mammy figures stand, is papered with repeated head shots of the widely circulated commercial portrait of Aunt Jemima. The compliant, content, iconic mammy is clearly a construction of white culture. Contained literally *in a box,* the mammy image operates in a world of someone else's making. Saar's box is a display case for resistance at the intersection of gender, race, and servitude.[61]

In the spirit of black and feminist activism, another important artist, the painter Faith Ringgold, challenged the art world establishment in the early 1970s by not only making work that exposed racism and sexism but by organizing protests against particular exhibitions in which few or no women and black artists were represented.[62] In California the artist Judy Baca created enormous public murals, making visible Latino and Latina experience at the intersection of multiple social categories in the context of historical events.[63] When the work of female artists of color received critical attention at all from the mainstream press, it was typically relegated to categories of "black art" and "Hispanic art." White artists occupied the category of "women's art"— invoking once again, it would seem, Sojourner Truth's question, "Ain't I a woman?"

As if in response to this reality, black women artists like Lorraine O'Grady set about the process of reclaiming the female body with an understanding, as she has put it, of the black female body as "outside what can be conceived of as woman."[64] In a performance piece entitled *Mlle. Bourgeoisie Noire,* created in 1980, O'Grady began making unsolicited appearances at New York art openings dressed in a long, debutante-style dress made entirely out of 180 used white gloves. In so doing she manipulated and exposed the dynamics and context of representation itself. O'Grady appropriated the white gloves that signal privileged white womanhood, literally "covering over" her black female body as that which is unrepresentable as "woman," then walked her work of art into opening-night events.

In addition to its critique of mainstream art worlds and the privileged status of white women, *Mlle. Bourgeoisie Noire* was a response to a strategy that had been employed by many white feminist performance artists—the practice of performing nude. In women's performance art throughout the 1970s, nude performance could be understood as an attempt to reclaim the female body from its objectified, to-be-looked-at status by literally stripping it down to its essence.[65] By incorporating her naked body into her own work of art, the performer stepped out of the frame of Western art's tradition of the female nude as silent object, recasting the female body as a speaking subject and situating the performer within the revered position of "the artist." Visual artist Carolee Schneeman's 1975 performance piece, *Interior Scroll,* is one of the most powerful and graphic examples of nude performance as a critique of "the artist" and an art world that colludes in protecting and reserving that category for men. Standing alone and nude, her legs spread, Schneeman slowly extracts a text from her vagina, reading from it the transcription of a conversation in which a male filmmaker condescendingly critiques Schneeman's work on the basis of her gender.[66]

The practice of performing nude emerged, in part, from a belief in the naked female body as a kind of tabula rasa. Any representation of the body is already enmeshed in existing networks of meaning; but the nude female body in performance seemed available for rewriting in the symbolic order because that body was white, representing a state of unblemished purity that imbues conceptions of white womanhood historically. Given the historical fact of slavery and its enduring legacies, a black woman's body can hardly represent a tabula rasa for writing the female body in general out of its status as object. *Mlle. Bourgeoisie Noire* made visible a body largely missing from Western high-art culture, and in O'Grady's hands it was packed with multiple ironic meanings.

Although there is no evidence that WOW's founders were familiar with these particular pieces, a number of feminist visual artists in the 1970s tackled the dynamic, meaning-making apparatus of representation itself and three of WOW's four founders were familiar with that world. Like Saar and O'Grady, WOW theater artists would contribute to the project of challenging the dictates of representation. When a piece of theater was not *about* women's issues, it was often summarily dismissed with a critique posed in the form of a question: "Where is the politics?" The answer to this question— "The *aesthetic* is the politics"—was often eschewed, but it was nevertheless an important move going forward.

By the end of the decade most feminist art was exhibited, performed, or screened around such ghettoizing themes as "women's art" and "black art" in marginalized venues. The work that managed to attract wider art world attention was aligned with the prevailing feminist worldview, in which difference was elided in deference to an ostensibly universal, shared female nature. Many feminists challenged this essentialist aesthetic from its inception, but it emerged to dominate the landscape of feminist representation because it received attention and media coverage. It attracted this attention precisely because its worldview ultimately tended to support rather than challenge the status quo. After all, what is it about a belief in women as innately nurturing, fecund, peaceful, and nonhierarchical that the institutions of mainstream culture would not welcome and support?

In fairness, the essentialist dimension of a work was often just that—one dimension of it. That this dimension was seized upon to the exclusion of other interpretations demonstrates the extent to which mainstream culture recognizes and embraces all that seemingly reflects it. The speed with which feminist thought, political strides, and aesthetics could be co-opted was breathtaking and led to an understandable antiessentialist backlash by feminist critical theorists. In the process, however, much that was important and productive for women in works of feminist art was overlooked. Limited readings might bring attention to a work of art for the wrong reasons, but they do not cancel out the importance of the work's alternative meanings. Pieces like Chicago's *Dinner Party* and Shange's *for colored girls* were (and continue to be) of deep and abiding importance and political significance for countless women.

Sex Panic

We hope that the "predatory butch," modeling her actions on those of the male, will be helped to a new consciousness of sisterhood and become aware of her own male chauvinism.

—DEL MARTIN AND PHYLLIS LYON, 1972

What made somebody a lesbian, I was told, wasn't wanting to have sex with women . . . [for] if you admitted you wanted to have sex with women, you would be accused of being just like a man. . . . Apparently, sex was something lesbians used to do before they got politics and opened food co-ops.

—HOLLY HUGHES, 1996

As a woman-centered ideology played out in alternative lifestyles and cultural productions that celebrated seemingly inherent qualities of "femaleness," it also targeted for censure, if not eradication, those social and sexual practices deemed inherently patriarchal. Essentialist feminists had a jaundiced view of butch/femme social and erotic practices and took a moralistic stand against both heterosexual and homosexual S/M (sadomasochism) communities. Women who engaged in any practice considered "male identified" became the movement's pariahs. Lois Weaver recalled an incident backstage after a performance by Spiderwoman at a New England college. She was removing her stage makeup when a group of feminists arrived in the dressing room to lavish praise on the performance. The mood in the room changed completely, however, when she began to apply her *street* makeup. She could feel the visitors' disapproval of an act considered male identified. Weaver remembered, "For the first time I understood that feminists thought I was one of those misguided women who needed to be saved."[67] Pamela Camhe also traversed the 1970s in high-femme fashion, despite feminism's disapproving eye, and with an edge—Camhe added a mustache made up of little black stars to her femme couture. It was the surveillance and policing this disapproving eye required, and the implications for its targets, that made 1970s feminism so fraught for many women.

As if foreordained, on April 24, 1982, Weaver happened to walk by Barnard College on the city's Upper West Side on the closing day of an event that would mark a turning point in the women's movement, the famous Barnard conference "Towards a Politics of Sexuality." The conference was the site of a pivotal skirmish in what would become known as the "sex wars," the result of escalating tensions over opposing views of an appropriate feminist stance on sex. On her way to teach a performance workshop for children at Riverside Church, Weaver passed the college and was handed an antipornography flyer by a woman wearing a T-shirt that read "For a Feminist Sexuality" on the front and "Against S/M" on the back. After teaching her class, Weaver returned to the conference and slipped into a seat in the back, just in time for the closing session. It was author and activist Amber Hollibaugh's pioneering pro-sex, anticensorship talk in response to the antipornography and anti-S/M proponents.[68] Hollibaugh mapped the conceptual skeleton of something Weaver knew WOW had already begun to flesh out. Hollibaugh was espousing an expansive view of sexuality, and WOW was performing it.

Some of the women who performed in WOW's festivals, for example, brought what Weaver has described as "a real S/M quality." "There were women whose work was geared toward black leather and a strong sense of eroticized power play," she recalled. "Although Jordy Mark wasn't S/M identified, her style had an S/M sensibility. And all the bartenders were S/M dykes." Early WOW participant Diane Jeep Ries appeared on the festival's stage as a blushing bride in a traditional white wedding dress and veil, but when she stripped off her dress "she changed from a bride into a complete leather dyke."[69]

Throughout the first half of the 1980s WOW offered butch and femme workshops designed to familiarize performers with "the tricks of the trade." Butch workshops included instruction on the art of tying a tie and "cooking lessons" that taught participants how to order Chinese takeout. But like the erotically charged sense of power play that infused S/M performances at WOW, "butch" was not solely about style; it also celebrated the sexually potent dimension of the ostensibly "predatory butch." Peggy Shaw recalled WOW's first butch workshop, when a woman who was supposed to help her with the presentation rode into WOW's storefront space on a motorcycle in the middle of the proceedings. Shaw asked, "Where have you been?" She responded, "I've been cruising women outside the Duchess [a women's bar]." Shaw said, "That bar closed last week!" "Yeah," came the reply, "but they don't know that."[70]

At the Barnard conference issues of sexual pleasure were pitted against issues of danger and safety, making clear the debates underpinning the sex wars that were splitting the movement apart. When Hollibaugh said, "[W]e cannot afford to build a political movement that engraves the sexual reactions of nineteenth-century bourgeois women onto a twentieth-century struggle," she was not denying the egregious and pervasive nature of violence against women.[71] Instead, she was talking about the critical need for women to be able to explore all kinds of sexual desires and representations and to engage in all kinds of sexual practices free from both violence and censure. This shift in the conversation from gender to the realm of the erotic was a troubled one and more disruptive than anyone could have predicted. In their focus on gender during the 1970s, feminists had failed to take into account the culturally determined, volatile nature of sex. They were unprepared for the relative ease with which panic about sex could be stirred up and spread among members of their own ranks. But what exactly was the route feminist thought took leading up to the sex wars? The answer is important because the women who shaped WOW grappled with and reacted against a particular kind of thinking.

Within the women's movement during the 1970s the constraints visited upon the desires, bodies, and psyches of women by grossly unequal social systems and institutions had fostered a kind of breathless desire for remedies. But the *effects* of these constraints left few women prepared to confront the complexities and subtleties of the unprecedented position in which they found themselves. With newfound access to less expensive, more effective birth control methods and legalized abortion, it was possible for the first time to effectively separate the practice of intercourse among heterosexuals from the inevitability and imperative of procreation. Moreover, the article "The Myth of the Vaginal Orgasm," published in 1968, argued that sexual intercourse is not the primary source of a woman's sexual pleasure.[72] The realization of a long-held fear that men might possibly become superfluous seemed imminent. Evidence of the feverish pitch this anxiety reached can be found in such hyperbolic statements as that made by Pat Robertson, an emerging leader of the New Right: "[The] feminist agenda is not about equal rights for women. It is about a socialist, anti-family political movement that encourages women to leave their husbands, kill their children, practice witchcraft, destroy capitalism and become lesbians."[73]

Few women were in a position to fully explore and address all the knotty dimensions and far-reaching implications of such astonishing change. As a consequence of the United States' puritanical heritage, accurate information about sex had been suppressed. Sex itself had been treated as simultaneously important and trivial, beautiful and dirty, desirable and repugnant, and, for women, not infrequently frightening and dangerous. Despite the much touted "sexual revolution" of the 1960s, religious and social institutions had managed to sustain the status quo through the naturalizing discourses of heterosexual reproduction within an equally naturalized and sanctified notion of the nuclear family. Once it was possible to imagine sexual desire and practices separate from reproduction, it became equally important to analyze desire and sex separate from the gender imperatives of heterosexuality to fully comprehend the workings of gender oppression. With rare exceptions, feminism's analysis of gender inequality tended either to ignore sex as a trivial concern or to conflate it with gender.

Compounding this was the inability of many women to comprehend what desire and sex might mean for them separate from the coercion they experienced as a consequence of unequal, rigidly enforced gender positionings. For many women the idea of their *own* desire simply did not compute. All they had been able to imagine was the "desire to be desired," from a passive position within the sphere of he who—by dint of gender privilege—had the power to own and *act* on his desire.[74] The resulting confusion is evident in the feminist writer Ti-Grace Atkinson's 1975 piece "Why I'm against S/M Liberation." "Feminists are on the fence, at the moment, on the issue of sex," she wrote. "But I do not know any feminist worthy of that name who, if forced to choose between freedom and sex, would choose sex."[75] Curiously—and ironically in a piece railing against sadomasochism—Atkinson posed a hypothetical instance in which a woman might be *forced* to choose between putting an end to gender oppression and gaining sexual agency and pleasure. Freedom in this instance is not only freedom from gender inequality but freedom from sex.

The imbalance of power that permeated traditional gender roles was rightly understood as a root cause of sexism and, by extension, the seed of physical and emotional violence against women. However, somewhere in the attempt to end sexism the terms *imbalanced* and *unequal,* which had attended the word *power,* faded into the background. Power *in and of itself*—separate from how it is ascribed and enforced along gender lines—became demonized. Any exchange of power in the practice of sex, whether consensual or not, thus became synonymous with abusive, sexist, even violent sex. Even in those quarters where gender was understood as a social construction, sex was largely considered a force of nature, the operative word being *force,* its nature "male." Power was perceived as inhering in one gender, and that gender became the exclusive term of all destructive, negative sexual associations. In some feminist circles the sexual act of penetration itself was believed to be an act of aggression and therefore of oppression. In walking a sexual tightrope between pleasure and danger—an ongoing negotiation—feminists tended to fall into a consideration of danger to the exclusion of pleasure.

Given this conceptual framework it is hardly surprising that the image of the lesbian butch of the historical and contemporary butch/femme couple came to be seen as a manifestation of the damaging consequences of internalized patriarchy. She was considered male identified as evident in the male attributes she appeared to value, assume, and enact. Together, the femme and the butch embodied gender oppression by virtue of their ostensibly unhealthy, demeaning sexual role-playing. Within heterosexuality's dominant/submissive gender paradigm, the "butch" was perceived as imitating the power-mongering term of the binary in a misguided attempt at sexual agency. The "femme" was understood as imitating the victimized term. The femme was also considered male identified, as evident in the traditional female attributes she appeared to champion. Racial and class biases informed conceptions of butch/femme couples as less sophisticated, less informed, less enlightened, and in need of redemption. In the 1970s, butch/femme coupling was perceived not only as perpetuating sexism but as its very emblem. Few feminists had access to concrete images of these supposedly visible, emblematic outcasts. For many feminists, "butch" circulated solely as an idea—the "mannish woman"—separate from both iconic and lived reality. The historical, lived reality of butch/femme made access to its representations rare. Quite understandably, few butch/femme couples were willing to travel the hostile terrain of feminist venues.[76]

In contrast to the scarcity of butch/femme images, however, depictions of women in pornography were readily available. Instead of analyzing the sexism in much pornography, though, some feminists seized upon the abject violence depicted in a small percentage of pornography and used it to support the argument that *all* pornography constituted violence against women and furthermore was a *cause* of violence against women. The line between fantasy and practice was blurred. This conflation was articulated by legal scholar Catharine MacKinnon in 1993 when she wrote, "Pornography is masturbation material. It is used as sex. It therefore is sex. . . . With pornography, men masturbate to women being exposed, humiliated, violated, degraded, mutilated, dismembered, bound, gagged, tortured, and killed. . . . What is real here is not that the materials are pictures, but that they are part of a sex act."[77] Not only is pornography bad in this scenario, but masturbation is bad, sex is bad, and men are bad. To be "male identified," when the phrase was first coined, meant to lack political consciousness. By the end of the 1970s this political meaning was lost as "male identification" became synonymous over time with all things masculine.

Not much of a leap is needed to understand how S/M would be perceived as the epitome of bad sexual practice. As the cultural anthropologist and theorist Gayle Rubin wrote in 1981, "Given prevailing ideas of appropriate feminist sexual behavior, S/M appears to be the mirror opposite. It is dark and polarized, extreme and ritualized, and above all, it celebrates difference and power."[78] Aside from the mise-en-scène of S/M, the exchange of power that defines its erotic practices alone was enough to constitute violence in the eyes of some feminists. As public policy scholar Carole Vance put it in 1984, "Pornography, S/M, and butch/femme [became] the anti-pornographer's counterpart to the New Right's unholy trinity of sex, drugs, and rock 'n' roll."[79] The notion of "consenting adults" in S/M sexual practices was considered beside the point, for to engage in an exchange of power—or to assume a butch or femme presentation of self in any context—was deemed evidence of false consciousness or of an alienated male-identified self. Even women who merely fantasized about "taking" a partner in a sex act or "being taken" in the erotic scenarios of daydreams were thought to suffer from a false consciousness imposed by sexist, patriarchal psychological and social structures. Many women worried that their forbidden fantasies were indicative of something terribly wrong and strove to exorcise them. Sex had become something that feminists needed to clean up, rein in, and police.

Valorizing Lesbianism

It remained for a stunningly efficacious coup of feminist redefinition to transform lesbianism, in a predominant view, from a matter of female virilization to one of woman-identification.

—EVE KOSOFSKY SEDGWICK, 1990

The move to valorize lesbianism—not necessarily lesbians—as the ideal and model of nonsexist relationships is perhaps the best and paradoxically one of the most perverse examples of the consequences of an understanding of gender and sexuality in which (1) one gender alone is perceived as imbued with power, (2) power itself is conflated with oppression and violence, and (3) power *as* oppression and violence is attributed to certain sexual practices among consenting participants. Known as lesbian feminism, women-to-women relationships became a model of egalitarian, nonsexist bonding for many feminists in the 1970s women's movement.

In lesbian feminism, "lesbianism" was primarily about gender rather than sex and perceived as existing in a kind of vacuum outside the domain of the culture's gender dynamics. The imbalance of power that is naturalized, normalized, and enforced along sexist male-dominant/female-submissive gender lines was perceived as remedied in woman-to-woman love by virtue of sameness in gender. The fact that women rarely owned and wielded social power was construed as their not wanting to own and exercise power by virtue of their very nature. Two people without the need or will to exercise power—two women—can live a life blissfully exempt from the seemingly inherent abuses of male power since it is impossible for women to exchange what they do not have and by nature do not even desire. If the butch/femme dyad symbolized traditional sex—that is to say, heterosexually inflected, erotically charged, male-identified sex—then lesbian feminism symbolized an androgynous, gender-neutral, largely desexualized, woman-identified sex.

At the same time that lesbianism was symbolically center stage, the complex material struggles of lesbians living on the margins of heterosexual culture tended to be obscured. For some women the period characterized by woman-identified feminism *felt* a bit like "lesbians, lesbians everywhere, but nary a one in sight." As the early lesbian activists Del Martin and Phyllis Lyon pointed out in 1972, "Many Lesbians have made no attempt whatever to relate to women's liberation . . . some because they are still struggling with an uncomfortable Lesbian identity and have not yet reached the status of Woman."[80] Lesbians who because of their erotic gender identities and sexual practices had not reached the "status of Woman" were positioned by lesbian feminism as not only outside of the women's movement but outside of respectable lesbianism as well.

In what sense, then, could lesbianism be considered "respectable"? The apparent ease with which it was possible for feminism to valorize lesbianism is the consequence of a larger heterosexist view, the one that cannot imagine lesbians having sex in the first place. After all, what is it that lesbians *do*? In the absence of a penis, and therefore the supposed absence of penetration, sex is ostensibly removed from sex—a comfortable position for sex-panicked feminists. In an exceedingly ironic move, the category of "lesbian"—previously defined *by* and *as* the sexual—became a desexualized icon of nonsexist feminist imaginings. To sustain this gender-neutral, power-neutral, desexualized imaginary space required policing its boundaries for evidence of deviance. Women—both heterosexual and lesbian—who refused to relinquish their forbidden sexual fantasies, refused to surrender their unacceptable public erotic presentations of self, and refused to conform to sexual practices that denied a consensual exchange of power were considered, as Weaver has described it, "misguided women who needed to be saved."[81]

Happily, by the end of the decade, somewhere on the margins of the women's movement, there were renegade feminists already dancing to the tune of a song not yet written or recorded—Cyndi Lauper's "Girls Just Wanna Have Fun." Some of these women, hailing from disparate sectors of both the women's movement and feminist performance, gathered together in 1980 under the umbrella of a women's theater festival in New York City called Women's One World. This would mark WOW's inaugural moment.

Chapter 3

Sex, Drag, and Rock 'n' Roles: The Festivals

We're pioneers born of other pioneers—those being Spiderwoman and Hot Peaches. They were the first real explorers. And then we came and settled the territory.

—LOIS WEAVER, 1999

The Festival celebrates the diversity of women and represents many different interests, ethnic groups and lifestyles. Whatever women are is what the Festival will be.

—WOMEN'S ONE WORLD FESTIVAL PRESS RELEASE, 1980

In her review of WOW's twentieth anniversary event, *Village Voice* critic Alisa Solomon described WOW historically as a place where "now well-known artists honed their craft, giving birth to a feminist-and-tinsel-tinged queer aesthetic."[1] This lineage can be traced directly to the two international Women's One World Festivals mounted in 1980 and 1981, where the seeds of a queer ethos were already beginning to sprout. In 2001, however, when Solomon asserted that WOW had given birth to a queer aesthetic *as feminist,* "queer" as a sensibility and political phenomenon was largely understood as a reaction against certain tenets of both feminism and the gay and lesbian liberation movement. Twenty years after the festivals, I conducted interviews with a number of the women who originally attended them in an attempt to recuperate the festivals' historical significance. Through these interviews it was surprising to discover the extent to which individual remembrances were in sharp contrast to a plethora of reviews of festival performances. Such divergence reveals an important lesson about cultural memory and the painful erasures that can occur within it.

By 2000 a significant dimension of feminist history had been lost to collective memory, the consequence of a process of omission that later served to support claims of originality for certain sex-positive cultural developments in the 1990s. WOW's festivals belie this elision, however, providing evidence of a funny, parodic, eroticized, gender-bending aesthetic with roots firmly grounded in feminism. Ironically, some of the most powerful cultural production of the 1990s emerged as a reaction against a feminist aesthetic history that not only powerfully informed it but, as Solomon suggested, brought it into the world. Although accounts of the festivals vary among participants, one sentiment recurred: the festivals exceeded by far anything these women had previously experienced. A typical remark was, "I'd never seen anything like it before; there had never *been* anything like it before." In support of these claims most participants cited the same three characteristics: the festivals' international dimension, the opportunity to see women's theater, and the visibility of some identifiably lesbian work. But in these respects the festivals were not particularly unique. There were ample opportunities to see women's theater, with some 112 extant feminist theaters in the United States at the time, more than 20 of them located in New York City.[2]

Women's theater festivals were not uncommon on the East Coast, and festivals that brought together women's theater troupes from around the Western world were held annually in the United Kingdom and across Europe. Opportunities to see work acknowledging lesbian existence were infrequent, but the explicitly lesbian theater Medusa's Revenge was operating at this time in the East Village. The city was also home to the First Gay American Arts Festival, held just a few months before WOW's first festival. Organized by the playwright John Glines, this festival had spanned six weeks, included some lesbian work, and—like WOW's festivals—presented mostly theater, but it also included dance, film, music, art exhibitions, poetry readings, and stand-up comedy.[3] The notion that the WOW festivals were unique might be attributable to a kind of provincialism: although they were presented in Manhattan, the New York borough nearly synonymous with theater production, the festivals were essentially neighborhood events. Many women who worked on and attended the festivals were from the East Village neighborhood where the festivals were mounted and had not previously attended theater of any kind. Participants Sherry Rosso and Ruth Barone, for example—who would go on to throw elaborate fund-raising parties for WOW—got involved in the festivals merely as a consequence of living in the same building as two of the producers. Still, there was a felt *something* that made WOW's festivals special.

East Village resident C. Carr would eventually become one of the best-known and respected writers to chronicle East Village performance. She was a member of the Heresies collective, which was made up primarily of visual artists involved in radical feminist thinking and debates. By 1980, Carr had attended some feminist theater and performance art and followed the punk rock music scene avidly. If anyone was positioned to consider WOW's festivals as part of the larger sociopolitical and aesthetic landscape, it was Carr. In a 2001 interview, however, she, too, had difficulty pinpointing exactly why the festival felt so extraordinary. "It seemed so fresh," she recalled, "so different, so exciting. There was a sense of energy to it that most feminist events just didn't have."[4] In the absence of specifics, the *feeling* that produced this deeply held conviction clearly persists in collective memory.

The reasons WOW's festivals were genuinely groundbreaking cannot be recalled because the performances that made this so were decidedly out of sync with today's conceptions of what feminists did in 1980. Participants themselves cannot remember certain characteristics of the festivals—women in drag, erotically charged performances, and audiences sporting a variety of "looks" far from that of the stereotypical asexual, androgynous, lesbian feminist—because they are counterintuitive; after all, "feminists simply didn't do that kind of thing back then." Today there is a widely held belief in both mainstream and queer culture, as well as among a new generation of feminists, that in the 1970s and 1980s feminists were generally humorless and did not think playfully about gender or positively about sex until the 1990s.

Twenty-seven years after the first WOW festival, after reading a description of what actually took place there, Carr wrote, "Sometimes when you're changing the world, you don't know it at the time. We'd been through 'liberation' in the seventies, but how much had it really changed our lives? Then suddenly, at the festivals, we saw it acted out onstage. I remember Jordy Mark walking down some kind of runway in these big boots. Couldn't tell you what she said, but her swagger said it all. That was just one little moment in a night of such moments. I had never seen lesbians be so daring and glam and full of themselves before. I loved it."[5] This chapter returns to a moment in time when what was lost to collective memory can be found.

Magnitude, Money, and Men

I told Jordy Mark I'd like to meet the rest of her cohorts, and almost before I could hang up, she materialized at the Voice *along with Lois Weaver, Pamela Camhe, and Peggy Shaw, all of [the] Allied Farces. Each was so gung-ho, I thought they'd festival right there in my office.*

—HOWARD SMITH, 1980

Attend *is too passive a word for what I saw. . . . Women descended on the place in cabs, in cars, on bikes, on roller-skates, in Adidas, bounding into that lobby with the kind of boisterous enthusiasm that . . . women are supposed to reserve for sale day at Macy's.*

—JANE CHAMBERS, 1981

The exhilaration Carr and others have recalled as a distinguishing feature of WOW's early festivals was in part a consequence of the events' sheer magnitude. Together, the festivals presented eighty different performance pieces, representing ten Western countries, Japan, and twelve U.S. cities. Over the eighteen days of the first festival, participants could take an afternoon workshop, see three different shows daily at the All Craft Center on St. Mark's Place (at 3:00, 7:30, or 9:30), then catch an 11:00 p.m. show at Theater for the New City on Second Avenue. During the eleven-day second festival, there were an assortment of daytime workshops on offer. One could see a 6:00 p.m. show while enjoying a plate of pasta at University of the Streets on Avenue A, then attend two different shows (at 8:00 and 10:00, with a variety of entr'actes between them) in the Grand Ballroom of the Ukrainian National Home on Second Avenue, followed by a fourth show at Theater for the New City. On weekend nights a midnight cabaret was held at the Centre Pub on St. Mark's. Festival-goers could hang out, interact with each other, and network at a festival café during the day and a festival bar in the evenings. Each day concluded with a free, women-only dance for all festival participants. Although it is impossible to gauge the overall size of the audience, two local newspapers put the total number of participants at the second festival at three thousand.[6]

As mentioned earlier, Women's One World was modeled on European festivals, particularly Amsterdam's Melkweg Internationale Vrouwenfestival, where Camhe, Mark, Shaw, and Weaver had first discussed the possibility of mounting a festival in New York. The idea was to re-create the aura surrounding these festivals with their diverse sites, cultural events, and social activities. Significant participation by women of color came to be another distinguishing characteristic of WOW's two festivals, which in turn influenced the Amsterdam festival in later years. Melkweg overwhelmingly featured the work of white women until its producer attended WOW's second festival and began to book women of color from the United States. What Women's One World was unable to re-create, however, was the financial support festivals abroad received from government and corporate sources. Neither WOW festival received any public or private funding.

As a consequence, mounting the festivals was a massively labor-intensive effort. The producers begged and borrowed nearly everything—lighting and sound equipment, chairs for the audience, pasta and tomato sauce for their "Pasta and Performance" series, and garbage bags filled with ice for the festival's bar, which they schlepped across the Village every day from Bonnie & Clyde's, a women's bar south of Washington Square Park. WOW's performers were paid from box-office receipts and covered their own expenses, including travel. Out-of-town groups received three hundred dollars and local artists one hundred dollars per performance. The producers were not paid, nor was any other form of labor remunerated. Scholarships were available for women willing to work in exchange for admission.

A reasonable budget for each festival at the time, given their scope, would have been around fifty thousand dollars.[7] The producers went into the first festival with approximately a thousand dollars from a series of fund-raising events—evenings of music, cabaret, and comedy called "Summer Nights." By the second festival they had "amassed" three thousand dollars. With these limited funds, plus box-office receipts, the festivals presented a program jam-packed with multiple examples of women's theater, performance art, and one-woman shows; film and video screenings; dance concerts and cabaret; poetry readings and stand-up comedy; and concerts of women's music like that associated with the Michigan Womyn's Music Festival, along with a number of all-girl bands representing rock 'n' roll, soul, big band/swing, punk, and jazz/funk fusion.

Also featured were an African dance and percussion concert; a children's street theater show; a bilingual puppet show and bilingual theater piece (Spanish and English); performances of mime, clowning, and fire-eating; a Latin American classical guitar concert; and the music of Haydn and Mozart played by a twenty-five-piece women's chamber music orchestra. Women of color were responsible for roughly 20 percent of the performances, 5 percent of which overlapped with the roughly 20 percent of identifiably lesbian work.[8] Afternoon workshops were offered at a wide range of ticket prices (from eight to forty-five dollars) on an equally wide range of themes—from self-defense to video production, mask making, dance, clowning, lesbian playwriting, singing, feminist acting, and ritual and cross-cultural performance. Among these workshops, Lois Weaver conducted one called "Celebrating the Diva in All of Us," described in the program as "simple acting techniques used to explore real, exaggerated, or fantastical self-images . . . in a simple theater format."

The first festival presented two well-known performers from outside women's theater, "stars" whose drawing power promised to expand the festival's audience base. The West Coast stand-up comic Robin Tyler was already familiar to many in the women's music scene and comedy circuit. Billed as "feminist, lesbian, and Jewish," she had recently released an album entitled *Always the Bridesmaid Never the Groom* and was a big enough attraction to pack the house for her single Monday night performance. The black choreographer and performance artist Blondell Cummings was well known in the New York world of dance and avant-garde performance. She presented *My Redheaded Aunt from Redbank* at the festival, described as "a multi-media dance poetry reading." The piece was scheduled prominently in a weekend evening slot and concluded with excerpts from another Cummings piece, *The Ladies and Me.*[9] The second festival presented another stand-up comic, Kate Clinton, whose star was rapidly rising on the women's music and comedy circuit. She was featured in one of the festival's midnight cabarets. Local groups like the Women's Experimental Theatre also had their own followings.[10]

In addition to booking artists guaranteed to fill houses, the producers employed other strategies to attract audiences and add to their paltry coffers. A woman with a pickup truck, Judy Rosen, filled the back of it with hay and sold "hayrides" around the East Village, while others square-danced to a string band and caller. Festival performers and crew members marched in colorful parades across Greenwich Village, leafleting along the route. During the first festival a group called the Schlockettes opened every performance with a couple of hilarious musical numbers that set the tone.[11] Aping the Rockettes of Radio City Music Hall fame, they parodied the sparkling, synchronized chorus line with a motley troupe of seven white women and one black woman, all of varying heights, body types, and sizes. They danced in black tights, sneakers, and men's boxer shorts, wearing oversized, untucked pink shirts and men's ties. Perhaps because the Schlockettes included the festival's four producers, their final number was "Money"—the song's refrain, "give me money," an obvious pitch for contributions from the audience above and beyond the price of admission. A number of other calls for help were made in the local press and through other venues around the Village. This plea appeared in *Womanews:* "WOW needs volunteers for technical work and child care, vendors and concessionaires (food, crafts, printed material), and housing space (that's a big one—women from all over the world will be coming to participate. They need your extra bed, couch, floor space!). Do you have a crane for an aero-dancer? A spare piano? A van or truck you would drive for pick-ups and deliveries?"[12]

Two controversial topics stirred around the first festival before it opened. The admission price of $5.oo a day for three shows at the first festival (and $6.oo a day for two shows at the second festival) was considered "totally out of the range of many women's budgets," according to *Womanews*. It was not the only publication to mention the festival's cost as an issue of concern, but its complaint is representative. One reviewer, Susan Thames, wrote, "I know most movies are $4.50, but many women don't spend that either—and most movies are not produced by women for women."[13] Two women from Burlington, Vermont, circulated a flyer in English and Spanish decrying the expense and accusing the producers of being insensitive to the conditions of low-income women.

But the producers felt it was important to recognize and validate the performers by paying them for their work, precisely *because* the event was produced by and for women. During the second festival Weaver told a reporter from *Other Stages,* "It's important to get in the habit of paying for women's work. We believe that women performers should not work for free any more than housewives."[14] These were the days of the "sliding scale" in the women's community, and paying "more if you can, less if you can't" was a generally accepted rule. Shaw was impatient with this practice, however, especially because admission had been waived for anyone willing to contribute her labor to the event. She recalled, "When I worked the box office and people said they couldn't afford the ticket price, I said 'Empty your pockets.'"[15] Camhe and Mark tended to let people in, though. "We wanted the audience," Mark recalled.[16]

Another policy that ruffled feathers was a modified women-only rule. Men were welcome to attend festival events only when accompanied by a woman. On this subject critic and editor Erika Munk wrote a brief, scathing attack in the *Village Voice* threatening to attend the festival "in impenetrable drag, or send a flying squad of male critics."[17] In response to Munk, the feminist journalist Audrey Roth wrote in *Womanews,* "W.O.W. was conceived as a festival in which women could experience the diversity of women artists— a place where women could come together and make contacts, where performers and audiences could interact. It was *not* conceived as an anti-male, hard-line political statement to the world."[18] Camhe had explained to a *Vil-*

lage Voice reporter weeks earlier that the policy focused more on getting women *in* than on keeping men *out*. "This way," she said, "maybe more women will come."[19]

In her single-paragraph rant headlined "Outrage Department," Munk wrote, "When I called to find out why they had such a policy, the answer was, 'We want to define this as a women's space, because that way there's the right energy, sharing, and intimacy.'"[20] But the impulse behind this policy, the organizers emphasized, also had to do with protecting the performers from walk-ins. Given the generally down and dirty conditions of St. Mark's Place at the time and the fact that some women were performing in varying states of undress, it was not inconceivable that men would walk in off the street to see the "girly show." (As an example, peep shows and strip clubs were quite common in Times Square.) In any case WOW's producers ultimately dropped the women-only policy for the second festival. From then on, men would be welcome at WOW; the extent to which they were welcome to participate in *productions,* however, would be an ongoing, unresolved subject of debate for the next three decades (chapter 4 looks at this and other struggles).

Glamorous Femmes and Girls in Mustaches

Maybe you have to be a lesbian artist to understand how startling, how exciting, how overwhelming this is.
—JANE CHAMBERS, 1981

Multiple published sources over the years have credited Peggy Shaw and Lois Weaver with founding WOW, overlooking the fact that Pamela Camhe and Jordy Mark also contributed in equal measure. Together, these four women produced the festivals and founded the WOW Café. Although Shaw and Weaver's legacy is crucially important, an appreciation of Camhe and Mark's work is also necessary to understand WOW's development artistically. They produced work that made a significant intervention in prevailing feminist aesthetics and brought years of accumulated artistic acumen to WOW's festivals. They left the enterprise a year after WOW settled into its first permanent space, the storefront at 330 E. Eleventh Street, and their participation faded from collective memory even as their contributions lived on.

An oft-told anecdote illustrates what goes missing from feminist history when Camhe and Mark's contributions to WOW are eclipsed. Weaver was touring Europe with Spiderwoman in the mid-1970s when the troupe's costumes failed to arrive with them in Berlin. Luckily, Hot Peaches also happened to be in town and sent over a trunk full of costumes. When Spiderwoman opened this Pandora's box full of sequined gowns, platform shoes, and feather boas, the women realized what they had denied themselves for feminism. "Hot Peaches gave us permission to be glamorous," recalled Weaver. A gay male sensibility is thus credited with bringing a lesbian aesthetic out of feminism's dowdy closet. That the boys had to show the girls how to be glamorous is not all of the story, however.

Camhe, a photographer by training, also had a trunk full of costumes, which included both contemporary and antique women's and men's clothing—alluring dresses, spike heels, boas, trousers, suspenders, ties, and bowler and Bogart-style hats. Beginning in 1974, she opened up her trunk for women to play and photographed them in glamorous "female drag" and "lesbian *Vogue*"—both terms she used to describe her work.[21] She also photographed women in full male drag. Camhe's images from the 1970s are of women alone and together, looking self-possessed as nudes, hot butches, glamorous femmes, and men. Her contributions to the festivals were beautifully orchestrated slide shows, which she described as "naked and sexual and new."[22] Of her piece at the first festival one critic wrote, "[It is] the first truly erotic piece of slide/film work I've ever seen."[23] "Camhe's slides created a movie effect through dissolves and perfect syncing of music," observed a revewier of Camhe's work at the second festival. "The fluid motion . . . seemed to capture not only her visions but the energy created by WOW. Women everywhere, dykes for days, surging forward and folding back upon themselves."[24] Another critic wrote that Camhe "faced the fact that there's a lot of pleasure in the modelings of *Vogue Magazine* and *Gentleman's Quarterly*."[25] This pro-sex posturing, with its recuperation of femininity, precedes and resonates with queer sensibilities that came a generation later and also with third-wave feminism and girl culture.[26]

Described by a reviewer as "a cacophony of sound, sleaze and sexuality that had the audience surging to its feet," Jordy Mark's evening of cabaret titled *Sex and Drag and Rock 'n' Roles* was also precedent setting. The review goes on, "Mark slinks up and down the runway jutting out into the audience. Clad in a black dress that hugs her razor-thin body, she plays with a white boa draped around her neck. She flashes back to the stage and proceeds to pull trousers, tuxedo shirt, jacket and bow tie over her dress as her five-piece band jams on. Tipping a fedora over her eyes, Mark then seduces the audience by singing, 'Honey, honey, can I put on your clothes.'"[27] Another critic described Mark's cabaret as "feminist punk" and its choreography as "putting on and taking off everything from a nightclub slither to crotch-tight leather." Of the audience, this reviewer wrote that it "surprised me, because I've never seen a feminist audience enjoy a performance about drag. This audience understood that drag is . . . as universal (and pleasant) as sex."[28] During one performance when the soundtrack temporarily broke down, Mark invited the audience to join her onstage. They paraded up onto the runway for an impromptu fashion show for which they had come well prepared. A note in the festival's program read, "You are encouraged to attend as your drag fantasy."

Sung to a tune from the 1972 Broadway musical *Grease,* another of Mark's melodies also celebrated the pleasures of drag: "There are worse things I could do / than put on a suit or two / I don't want my sex to change / just my clothes I'll rearrange / You can say it's my bag / going out sometimes in drag." A photograph of this moment shows Mark at the mike in a double-breasted men's suit and tie wearing a mustache. Camhe is walking onstage wearing dozens of black balloons over a corset, a motorcycle cap, and a mustache. She is about to perform a droll version of "Falling in Love Again," which she sings à la Dietrich as "*Failing* in Love Again," seductively playing with and to the audience as she petulantly pops a balloon now and then with her cigarette. Feminists in drag? Feminists in mustaches? Audiences loving it? In 1980? In the work of Camhe and Mark, it is evident that a radical feminist impulse, however suppressed, not only continued to exist but prefigured a queer aesthetic.

Just as Weaver articulated being granted a kind of permission from Hot Peaches to go against the grain of cultural feminist mores, Camhe and Mark needed a way to be "good" feminists and still make the kinds of work that inspired and sustained them. "Feminism was and continues to be our filter, our prism, the perspective through which we see the world," Mark recalled.[29] As active participants in the women's movement in New York during the 1970s, Camhe and Mark could not help but be caught up in the feminist debates that characterized the time. Yet they perceived no contradiction between the nature of their work and the dictates of feminism, in large part because they saw themselves as artists in the tradition of visual art. The Western notion of "the artist" gave them permission to fly in the face of feminist taboos—the artist as rule breaker and groundbreaker, one who stands outside of societal norms.

This is not to say that Camhe and Mark naively considered their work as somehow unproblematic. In reflecting on the first festival some months later, reviewer Barbara Baracks shed light on at least one reason why a producer might have considered a women-only policy in 1980. She wrote, "The first time Camhe publicly presented her slideshow, it was to an all-woman audience, and she worried about what they would think of its eroticism, in which bodies and sweeps of costume in 'female' and 'male' are permitted the same texture as a face. Erotic photographs of women are so strongly associated with male pornography it was easy to anticipate feminist misinterpretations. As it turns out, the audience loved it. At a second showing, with an audience that included men, Camhe felt the women didn't permit themselves the same unguarded appreciation. The audience's own performance had changed."[30]

For Camhe and Mark, permission to make work out of step with prevailing ideologies also came from a belief in the empowering dimension of play. The two had taken a clown workshop in 1974 with Cheryl Gates McFadden, who went on to play the role of Dr. Beverly Crusher in *Star Trek: The Next Generation.* In McFadden's workshop they encountered a commedia dell'arte approach to performance. This allowed a creative, no-holds-barred form of play that would inform and shape their aesthetic. Like the tradition of stock characters in commedia dell'arte, workshop participants developed their own characters and then created a play through and around them. Out of these workshops McFadden founded a touring clown company called New York Theatre Commotion (1974–75). Camhe first invited women from this workshop to her loft to rummage through a trunk full of costumes and play dress up, re-creating themselves to be photographed. This early photo shoot marked the beginning of an ongoing tradition of what might be considered a form of private performance or salon theater.

Throughout the second half of the 1970s, Camhe and Mark would throw parties in their loft that revolved around performances. "Instead of bringing *presents,* we asked people to bring *presentations,*" recalled Camhe. "We made parties that were events." The loft had a piano, and they built a stage. Guests would arrive in costume or would pull costumes out of Camhe's trunk, inspiring impromptu performances. "Women did songs, they did readings," Mark added. "Pamela might show slides of her most recent photography." It was at such a party that Camhe first donned balloons and performed her "Failing in Love" song. Some parties had themes; guests were invited to come in costume and bring a theme-related performance. One party was a parody of television quiz shows. Camhe and Mark had rigged up lights that flashed and buzzers that sounded when a "contestant" triggered them. Some guests were invited to perform the TV show's commercials. A birthday party required all the guests to come dressed as Camhe herself. Silver sneakers mounted on a plaque were presented to the guest with the best impersonation. "Our friends were so talented and inventive," recalled Mark. "Some made puppets that looked like Pamela and made clothing to match." Camhe explained, "I was very eccentric in what I wore. I used to wear a mustache on the street all the time. It was made of small black stars. As a femme I always wore makeup and often a man's gabardine suit and my little mustache." Mark added that Camhe "did a lot of very personal street theater."[31]

In her 1988 book *Feminism and Theatre,* critical theorist Sue-Ellen Case has described Natalie Barney's early-twentieth-century salon theater as an example of a "personal theatre of sexuality."[32] Of Barney, Case wrote, "She invented the practice of women performing for women; . . . she introduced images of lesbian sexuality; she conceived of improvisatory performances relating to the talents of women performers; and she created theatricals which occurred in her private, domestic space."[33] The qualities Case attributes to Barney's performance practice could easily describe those of Camhe and Mark. "There were plenty of women our age who were developing their careers," Mark recalled. "We were playing. This fed us. Instead of elbowing our way into the art world, we were *making* our world."[34]

Unlike Barney, however, Camhe and Mark had the *choice* to perform privately rather than publicly. In the 1970s, though, this choice was a hollow one and existed more in theory than in practice. The rising stars then coming out of the art world were the artists Jenny Holzer and Barbara Krueger—known for their subversive use of text—and the photographer Cindy Sherman, who became known for her pointedly staged self-imagery. None of these artists shared anything resembling Camhe and Mark's aesthetic "bent." As Case has pointed out, "The traditional canon of art, literature and theatre omits almost entirely any images of lesbian experience or sexuality."[35] This was certainly true in the 1970s. The desire to rectify this erasure was one of the driving forces behind the creation of the WOW Café. The spirit, sensibility, and style of the work Camhe and Mark developed during that decade and presented at WOW's festivals in 1980 and 1981 would inform WOW's burgeoning aesthetic in important ways for years to come.

Strippers, Flamboyant Ladies, Terrorists, and Mountain Women

At one point we considered calling the festival WHOOPIE, as in Women Herald Ongoing Opportunities to Perform in an International Exchange, so that "Make Whoopie" would be our publicity slogan.

—JORDY MARK, 2001

Camhe and Mark's festival offerings were among four other examples of work that—it is generally accepted today—could not have been imagined let alone produced by feminists at the time. Shaw described one such seemingly anachronistic performance at the second festival as "strippers dancing on the bar." Go-go dancer Diane Torr had been performing in working-class bars in New Jersey when she enlisted two of her cohorts, and the three of them performed their striptease acts, unexpurgated, at the festival. Unlike their regular shows, however, in their festival performances the women reminisced about their work in the sex industry while they stripped. Calling her act "Diana Tornado and Her Dicey Dames from Passaic," Torr "wowed the packed bar," according to Prudence Sowers writing for the *Advocate*. "The three women talked to the audience about the life of a dancer: [these were] curiously moving stories about lying to parents and the total lack of regard club patrons show for dancers," wrote Sowers. "But at the same time, they were doing those dances, slowly undressing while they moved in erotic, salacious circles. . . . No one quite knew whether to be embarrassed, offended or turned on."[36]

Torr's piece was performed twice in two different spaces. One replicated the ambience of "dancing on the bar" with the dancers atop platforms scattered among the spectators. The other performance took place in front of the audience. Two-dimensional cutouts of painted male figures lined the back of the stage, arranged shoulder to shoulder as if the stage surface was the bar at which they were seated; live audience members were, by extension, cast in the role of patrons seated on the opposite side of the bar. The painted figures—all depicting men in varying states of drunkenness—were riffs on the barfly cliché. In her review for the *Villager,* the journalist Jessica Abbe described them as "hideous male cretins with lolling red tongues, stained armpits, leering grimaces and open flies."[37] In an interview conducted by novelist and playwright Sarah Schulman a year later for *Womanews,* Torr explained, "I was very curious to see how women would respond in a performance generally done for men. I was also interested in presenting a documentary of the dancers' backgrounds so that, instead of the myth of the go-go dancer, it would be the reality of these women's lives accompanying the illusion. Also, some of the dancers are really good and it's a shame that they should be seen only by men. . . . Well, some women responded just like men—cat-calling and giving us tips. Some women were really turned on."[38]

Twenty years after Torr presented her Dicey Dames at WOW's festival, third-wave feminists Jennifer Baumgardner and Amy Richards would cite go-go dancers performing for women as a new phenomenon in their 2000 book *Manifesta: Young Women, Feminism, and the Future.* They describe the girl culture of third-wave feminism as a "generation . . . predestined to fight against the . . . rigid stereotype of being too serious, too political, and seemingly asexual."[39] As evidence of this new culture, Baumgardner and Richards draw on numerous examples, including "the New York club Meow Mix and other joints with female go-go dancers getting down for women."[40] Grounds certainly exist for the stereotype Baumgardner and Richards invoke. Torr recalled an incident that occurred when "Go-go World" was presented at Amsterdam's Melkweg Women's Festival in 1982. She remembers the audience as being so demonstrably outraged by the show that someone cut the power, pitching the room into darkness and ending the performance. Torr and the other dancers were hustled to safety through the kitchen and out a back door of the building. "I realized," Torr recalled, "there were a lot of 'lesbians' in that audience who didn't actually sleep with anyone, and they were standing in judgment of our sexy performance!" Each time Torr's go-go dancers performed at WOW's festival, she remembered, "two or three women were offended and walked out in protest."[41]

The piece engendered a productive controversy that revealed differing sentiments. Writing about Torr's piece for *Womanews* in 1981, the feminist Joan Blair demurred, "How strip-teasing and feminism can be reconciled is beyond me. The dancers' insistence that because they are paid well for tits and ass display they are liberated women involves logic which evades me."[42] Writing about the same performance for the *Villager*, however, Abbe described women in the audience "whistling and cat-calling in the traditional spirit of a New Jersey night."[43] In the discourse of third-wave and postfeminism, the spectators who responded lustily and lustfully to Torr's work would be considered as existing *outside* of feminism, and alongside the women's movement rather than in it, while those women who were offended and walked out of her performance in protest would be cast as representing *all* feminists. In contrast, Torr has always considered "Diana Tornado and Her Dicey Dames from Passaic" a feminist piece.

Another challenge to the strictures of the era's cultural feminism was Alexis De Veaux and Gwendolen Hardwick's black women's theater company, the Flamboyant Ladies. The name itself is oppositional. "Ladies" by definition are not elaborately showy; they do not behave excessively. And black women historically have been excluded from the definition of "ladylikeness," as descended from the nineteenth-century notion of "true womanhood." That category was reserved for upper- and middle-class white women (chapter 6 explores this topic in depth). Because the word *flamboyant* had long circulated as a descriptor of gay men, especially drag queens, it is tempting to take the leap and claim gay male performance as a primary influence on the work of the Flamboyant Ladies. But De Veaux and Hardwick created the neologism "flamboyant ladies" as a reaction against the limitations of having to identify as either butch or femme in black lesbian culture and as neither in dominant feminist culture. In a telephone interview, De Veaux explained that "flamboyant" was meant to fly in the face of straight black culture's prescriptions for black women's sexuality by connoting "outrageousness—a sexual, racial, beautiful extreme."[44]

Founded in 1977, the Flamboyant Ladies Company was located in Brooklyn, and, like Camhe and Mark, De Veaux and Hardwick had created a salon for their friends and other artists. A 1980 press release for the troupe stated, "We are pleased to announce the opening of *Flamboyant Ladies Saturday Salon:* an alternative arts space that will nurture and support artistic endeavors and provide a gathering place for women to enjoy brunches, jazz, discussions, shows, as well as parties!" Another flyer announced a Flamboyant Ladies Theater Company benefit performance at 11:00 p.m. followed by a dance and "all night boogie."[45] The Flamboyant Ladies performed their piece *Reverberations* in the "Pasta and Performance" series at WOW's second festival. The production consisted of an ever-changing variety of short pieces, some of them with explicitly lesbian content. Even the artists themselves can no longer recall exactly which vignettes constituted *Reverberations* at the festival, and it is impossible to ascertain the dynamic and impact of the performance from the slight press coverage it—and other pieces by women of color—received.

Festival cofounder Shaw counted the Flamboyant Ladies' *Reverberations* among those pieces she remembered as "really hot." This sentiment supports

De Veaux's own description of the group's work: "As artists we could be very black, very erotic, very lesbian, and very political."[46] In a review of several of the festival's performances, the *Village Voice* writer Barbara Baracks briefly described one version of *Reverberations*.

> In *Masked Moments,* Gwendolen Hardwick's 30-year-old daughter attempted to communicate with her intransigent mother, played by Tommye Myrick. Hiding behind fans doubling as masks, the characters parry and eventually quarrel, as the mother refuses to discuss her daughter's age, sexuality, ideas and ultimately her desire to communicate. In *The Woman Who Lives in the Botanical Garden* [which Shaw remembers as "The Queen of Prospect Park"], De Veaux . . . begins an impassioned monologue: "The delicate spread of her branch, a thickly muscled arm . . . is named South Africa." She warns off would-be visitors to the garden with an M-16 rifle. . . . Judith Alexa Jackson's *Obstacles* completed the trilogy's movement from personal to global considerations. When the spotlight went on . . . a hand . . . crept into sight, wearing a white glove. . . . Not really "her" hand at all, the glove served as an image of all colonization, which at the piece's end, she managed to strip off.[47]

A production by the Flamboyant Ladies mounted at the All Craft Center between the two festivals was "so hot it cost us our space," Shaw and Weaver recalled. On March 1, 1981, the Women's One World Festivals presented De Veaux's *"NO!": A New, Experimental Work of Neoliterary Events, Political Messages, and Innovative Stories for the Stage.* De Veaux is a poet, and her theater work resonates with Ntozake Shange's style. According to Glenda Dickerson, who adapted *"NO!"* for the stage and directed it, "The production was woven from the following threads of Alexis De Veaux's writings: *Erotic Folktale #7;* a short story, 'The Riddles of Egypt Brownstone'; excerpts from a new play, *When the Negro Was in Vogue;* and poetry." Dickerson wanted to bring De Veaux's voice to the stage "in the varying forms she used to express herself: her poetry, her short stories, her political statements, her plays, her sexuality." But she admitted, "I found that I was scared to reveal the things she wrote about, things that should be kept 'under the rose' and not bandied about in the light of day." Dickerson described the process of directing *"NO!"* as one in which she "reclaimed the colors of shame."[48]

Following its showcase production at WOW, *"NO!"* moved to the Henry Street Settlement's New Federal Theatre, where it received a favorable review from *New York Times* critic Mel Gussow.[49] Gussow made no mention of the production's lesbian content, but an unnamed reviewer for *Big Apple Dyke News (B.A.D. News)* wrote, "De Veaux and Dickerson clearly view lesbian sexual activity as rich and sensual and the production conveys this beautifully."[50] The production was controversial in some quarters of the black community. According to Hardwick, the specific source of this controversy was *Erotic Folktale #7*—the explicitly lesbian part of the play. "It was only one part of the piece," recalled Hardwick, "but it was as if it were the whole piece."[51] Dickerson compared the show's New Federal Theatre run to the experience of producing the play at WOW: "For a while it seemed that we had moved upstairs. . . . But the rowdy '*NO!*' had sprung up from our own soil, from our own hands, and should never have left home. . . . '*NO!*' [had] reached its zenith at the WOW Festival. *The lesson we learned is that you can't wear your scarlet dress in Big Daddy's house.*"[52]

Had "*NO!*" attempted to return home, however, it would have found that the family had moved. The All Craft Foundation's contribution to the endeavor was its space, a place where women in the electrical, plumbing, and carpentry trades were trained. "One night the Flamboyant Ladies . . . performed a show that Weaver describes as 'very, very hot, very sensual.'" Shaw and Weaver explained to scholar and feminist critic Alisa Solomon in 1985: "'It was beautiful,' says Shaw, 'but a little too sexy for the Center.' It happened that near the end of the show there was a fire in the building next door that had nothing to do with the performance, but it caused some damage to the Allcraft [*sic*]. The next time the WOW staff came to the space, they found padlocks on the door."[53] Shaw believes that work both black *and* lesbian was too much for the women responsible for the All Craft space. Although this may or may not have been the case, "*NO!*" was actually the last in a series of straws that ultimately broke the relationship's back.

The women running the All Craft Center at the time had experienced difficulty with another theater troupe—the all-white Radical Lesbian Feminist Terrorist Comedy Group (RLFTCG). According to Camhe and Mark, the All Craft women had balked when a festival publicity flyer was distributed that included the All Craft name on the same page with the word *lesbian*, as it appeared in the troupe's name. The New Right of Reagan era politics in the early 1980s was building steam, and All Craft was concerned about losing the center's public funding. In her 1981 *Womanews* article "Lesbians Too Terrorizing for NYC," the feminist journalist Peg Bryon wrote, "Women's One World are standing by their decision to include the Radical

Lesbian Feminist Terrorist Comedy Group in their program at the cost of their home at All Craft Center. . . . Joyce Hartwell, who has charge of the large building and rents it from the city, told *Womanews* she was fearful of losing funding for her program. . . . 'She's really paranoid about the new right—the new Reich actually,' said [festival organizer] Pamela Camhe."[54]

Although De Veaux's piece *"NO!"* devoted just one segment specifically to lesbian sexuality, RLFTCG's work was saturated with in-your-face lesbian shtick. The group performed at both WOW festivals. Their shows were made up of a series of short spoofs in a revue format with titles like "I Was a Teenage Lesbian" and "The 'Bluefish Cove' Fan[atic]." In her review of the group's performance at the second festival, Baracks wrote, "For openers, Deborah Glick [subsequently a New York State assemblywoman] sleazed out in bathing suit, boa, and Donald Duck mask. 'I don't understand,' she told the audience, 'they told me to come dressed as a typical duck.' 'Not duck,' called a chorus of voices from behind the curtain, '*dyke.*'"[55] In another skit, "Lesbian Ms. America Contest," three women lined up across the stage for the talent portion of the contest. One contestant (played by Marge Helenchild) wore a basketball outfit, sunglasses, and a fright wig. Her talent was dribbling—and playing beer bottles, which she was actually good at. The second woman (played by Joan Goldman) sang "Lady of Spain" and played the accordion (badly) while wearing ice skates. The final contestant (played by Mary Anne Bollen) wore nothing at all but a bow tie, thigh-high stockings, and spike heels. Being naked is her talent—and of course she utterly upstaged the other contestants. When asked by "Beatrice Parks" (played by Margarita Lopez) what she would do if she won the contest, the naked contestant responded breathily, à la Marilyn Monroe, "I'd sleep with lots and lots of women so there'd be more and more lesbians in the world."[56]

In 1976 RLFTCG was launched by a group of white women who had come together out of a desire to write and perform. At a meeting to determine what they would call themselves, one nervous, closeted member made a comment that backfired: "Well, we can't very well call ourselves the 'radical' 'lesbian' 'terrorist' comedy group." The others thought it was a great title and the word *feminist* was appended.[57] Reviewers who have mentioned RLFTCG over the years have commented on the group's amateurism and the unevenness of the material. Jane Chambers, whose own play was spoofed in the "Bluefish Cove" skit, wrote that their "enthusiasm and occasionally brilliant lesbian/feminist material overshadowed their lack of polish."[58] About the troupe's following, Bollen speculates that "the RLFTCG audience didn't really come to see us; they came to see each other."[59]

The work of Camhe and Mark, De Veaux and Hardwick, Torr, the Radical Lesbian Feminist Terrorist Comedy Group, and the Split Britches troupe was original; and the productions were all quite different from one another. Collectively, these pieces stood out among dozens of other festival offerings as representative of a departure from the ascendant feminist aesthetic that had emerged out of the 1970s. The influences and radical impulses underpinning this work can be traced to different sources—none of them representing the dominant feminist party line. From the lesbian glamour of Camhe's photographs to the gender-bending eroticism of Mark's cabaret, from strippers, flamboyant ladies, and comedy terrorists to the mountain women of the Split Britches' play, these women ushered in alternative political and aesthetic sensibilities.

The *Village Voice* critic covering the second WOW festival predicted that the play *Split Britches* "when finally honed . . . will be an important contribution to contemporary theatre."[60] By 1987 theater professor and editor Linda Walsh Jenkins wrote in the second edition of the landmark *Women in American Theatre* that *Split Britches* was in fact "now considered a masterpiece of feminist theatre."[61] A fledgling version of the play was performed at the first festival under the auspices of the Spiderwoman troupe. It was directed by Weaver with Shaw in one of the play's three roles along with two other members of Spiderwoman, Cathy Gollner and Sylvia Beye. Still billed as a work in progress, *Split Britches* was presented again at the 1981 festival, but by then Deb Margolin had been brought in to rewrite parts of the script. Along with Weaver, Margolin herself joined Shaw in the cast. These three women would become the Split Britches Company. A number of established artists—Lisa Kron and Alina Troyano (aka Carmelita Tropicana) among them—have recalled seeing a production of *Split Britches* and consider the experience a turning point in their lives and work.

One of the reasons for the play's groundbreaking status in the early 1980s was its approach; unlike much women's theater at the time, *Split Britches* was political without being didactic or attempting to express something universal about all women. In this regard, the author and theater critic Laurie Stone articulated the significance of *Split Britches* in a 1983 review of the play for the *Village Voice:* "It's rare to see feminism on the boards without banners or goddesses."[62] In a 2001 interview Margolin further explained: "Rosa

Parks didn't say anything; she just took a seat. That's how we took on the political aspect—by having the nerve, by having the gall to let the lights come up and just stand there. . . . We were political by virtue of our refusal to directly address issues. Everything about us rose up against homophobia and misogyny. Just the three of us standing there was a radical act—this butch lesbian, this little femmie femme, this bizarre Jewish girl with no restraint—together we flew in the face of anything sensible to the community at large. Together we were not even remotely acceptable to prime time."[63] Poet and novelist Eileen Myles captured the essence of this kind of work at the festivals when she said, "The aesthetic was the politics."[64]

The play's rather peculiar specificity was equally remarkable for its time. Writing about *Split Britches* in 1989, feminist scholar Vivian Patraka described the company as "departing from both the universalizing rituals of cultural feminism and the documentary realism of representative women's experience, which so often was the core of earlier feminist collective performance."[65] Like the Women's Experimental Theatre, which also presented work at both WOW festivals, *Split Britches* took the experiences of women as its starting point. However, the Split Britches troupe did not mine these experiences to get at themes ostensibly common to all women across time, ethnicity, class, and other differences. In describing the piece the Women's Experimental Theatre presented at WOW's first festival, Chambers wrote, "*Electra Speaks* gives us a new look at the old myth from Electra's point of view, and although its form is so experimental that I several times lost track of the continuity . . . the piece speaks with an intelligent universal voice."[66]

Like *Electra Speaks, Split Britches* employed techniques developed in the experimental theater of the 1960s. But it used them to question the authority of "Truth" in the face of multiple, overlapping, and contradictory truths about particular women, thereby throwing representation itself into relief. The play made no claim to universality; it did not valorize women's experiences; and it did not mirror the contexts and conditions of its largely white, urban, middle-class audiences. *Split Britches* is about three isolated, disenfranchised rural women living in the Blue Ridge Mountains of Virginia in the 1930s—all of the characters are based on Weaver's own relatives. The play's title itself signals the content, tone, and politics of the piece, referring to a garment worn by women in agricultural regions and designed to facilitate peeing while standing in the fields. As Patraka has suggested, "*Split Britches* is about women too old, too poor, too dumb, too lesbian, or too insistent on controlling their own lives to be visible."[67]

On the work of the Split Britches troupe in general, Shaw explained in a

1997 interview, "Lois and I . . . established an aesthetic we had cultivated in Hot Peaches and Spiderwoman of vaudeville interludes, songs, genre-crunched stories, and flamboyant, ragtag sets and costumes."[68] Through the company's work, Margolin, Shaw, and Weaver explore the details of lives lived under particular conditions, in peculiar and sometimes fantasy situations. The resulting work riffs imaginatively on what emerges from this exploration. The characters they create represent extraordinary women, not in the sense of heroic accomplishment but in a very real, creative, and frequently fantastical sense of lives lived outside of the ordinary, outside of the expected. The play *Split Britches* is imbued with the kind of darkness that attends grinding poverty, yet much of the dialogue is humorous, and the action is interrupted by songs and bits of shtick in a mixture that characterizes the distinctive style of the troupe.

The action is set in the kitchen of a dilapidated farmhouse where, for example, Margolin's character—an octogenarian—leaves the scene at one point to gather wood and returns slowly dragging a huge tree trunk across the stage. Weaver's character, described in the script as "sweet, complex and shadowy but not quite right in the head," senses there is something more in the world out there and repeatedly wanders off. Shaw's character is a strong, butch mountain woman who takes care of the other two; she describes her lesbian desire as a fire that "can make ashes out of me if I ain't careful." A line this character delivers later in the play is an astonishing metaphor for a life lived in the closet: "I had a fire in my pocket. . . . I looked in my pocket, and there was the fire, lookin' up at me just cute and sweet as a pretty girl."[69] Throughout the production these characters are periodically framed by the light of an empty slide projector that breaks into the play's narrative nearly thirty times. The light catches the characters in a series of still-life tableaux reminiscent of tintype photographs.

The play was unlike most theater presented at the WOW festivals and more like the work of some visual artists in content, structure, and effect. Interestingly, Judy Chicago's *The Dinner Party* made its New York debut at the Brooklyn Museum the day before WOW's first festival closed, but the play *Split Britches* had more in common with work like that of the feminist artist May Stevens. Stevens's collage piece *Two Women* (created in 1976) echoed the sensibility of *Split Britches* in telling the stories of two specific women—Stevens's working-class, housewife mother Alice and the Polish German revolutionary leader and murder victim Rosa Luxemburg. The work is one in a series of pieces devoted to these same two women called *Ordinary/Extraordinary* (produced from 1976 to 1980). As a series of repeated images, *Two*

Women resonates not only with the ways the characters are drawn in *Split Britches* but also with the play's repeated phrases, retold stories, and series of tableaux vivants. The art history scholar and curator Jo Anna Isaak has described *Two Women* as follows: "Images of Alice and Rosa are juxtaposed— from their childhood when they look very similar, full of great expectation, to early womanhood . . . to the two women at the end of their lives: Alice old, overweight, legs swollen from years of hard work, sits silently in her room in a mental hospital; the last image of Rosa is a photograph taken after her bludgeoned body had been retrieved from the Lanwehr Canal, her open eyes staring directly at us. These are . . . two stories which Stevens tells over and over again in images and texts, the activity of telling and retelling undertaken as if the ritual would incrementally restore a subjectivity to these women."[70]

As Isaak has suggested, *Two Women* is not a commentary on all women; rather, it is an attempt to deploy the apparatus of art making to create subject positions for women overwhelmingly denied them, that is, to create active subject positions to counter the passive position of silent object traditionally reserved for women. In much the same way, the play *Split Britches* grapples with theater's meaning-making apparatus to give voice, visibility, and subjectivity to three of Weaver's rural, poor, silenced, and invisible relatives. "For some people," Shaw commented on such specificity, "you have to have a war to make the play important. . . . We're busy doing shows about all the little details of relationships."[71] Like Stevens's work (and unlike much feminist theater at the time), *Split Britches* does not replace one universal address (man) with another (woman). This move to position women as speaking subjects in their own narratives through the particular and away from the universal would have a profound influence on much of the work to emerge from WOW in subsequent years.

Snow White as Butch: The Difference Is Audience

Why do we go to a festival like WOW? The place was packed every night. The value is not only the work onstage but also the connecting within and between the minds of those going to see it.

—BARBARA BARACKS, 1980

If women form a punk-rock band, or put together an a cappella singing group, or chamber orchestra, or theatre piece which is all women, does that make it lesbian? Is an event that speaks to women a lesbian event?

—AUDREY ROTH, 1980

In her 1997 book *Re-dressing the Canon,* Alisa Solomon has discussed the many ways in which women wearing men's clothing can be perceived. She concludes that "the difference is audience."[72] Similarly the women who attended WOW's festivals contributed to the phenomenon—mirroring those performances that were erotically charged, the spectators informed every event. In an article describing a series of fund-raising events that preceded the first festival, the writer Bethany Haye observed, "For those who came along to the 'Summer Nights' performances with impressions of an all-female haunt straight out of *The Killing of Sister George,* a great surprise was in store. The audiences were as boisterous and chummy as a girls' hockey team, stomping and catcalling their appreciation . . . shouting alternative punch lines to the comics' bits. Not one pair of orthopedic shoes was spotted."[73] In her review for the same publication ten days after the festival, Baracks wrote, "For two-and-a-half weeks I ducked in and out of the 50 or so events going on. . . . Witches, nuns and ladies bearded in glitter kept dropping in. The performers had a hard time not being outdone by the feistiness of the audience."[74]

Evidence of audience desire can be found in the critics' comments when they speak for themselves as spectators. What Weaver has said about performers applies to spectators as well: "[P]erformance is sex in that it comes from that place of desire, that real deep-rooted desire to express yourself and to feel intimacy."[75] In a review of Edwina Tyler's African American women's dance and drum ensemble, the poet and essayist Donna Allegra wrote hungrily, "In the background, Kip Graves and Joan Ashley worked their rhythms up to a frothy lather. And then, there was Joan's leg peeking through her lapa (an African material wrapped into a skirt). I would give up being a vegetarian for even just a taste of that thigh."[76] Regretting the close of the second festival, critic Prudence Sowers wrote, "Second Avenue had finally emptied of the stunning European women who made walking down the street an almost unbearable pleasure."[77] In a review of *Snow White,* performed by a troupe from Holland and Switzerland, Deborah Proos, writing for *Womanews,* bemoaned the event's innocuousness: "Snow White Street Theatre could easily tour our public schools . . . [as] they seem very unthreatening and proficient—seductive children with colorful costumes and Shirley Temple grins." Bringing her own predilections to bear on the act of spectatorship, however, Proos described the character of Snow White, saying "she never looked butchier."[78] As audience members, these critics undoubtedly echoed the experience of other spectators.

The notion that spectators brought to the performances their own deep-rooted desire to express themselves and feel intimacy was also evident in the festivals' nonperformance activities. For example, some of the women-only dances held each night were followed by "massage parties" in the lofts where out-of-towners were housed. In a 2001 interview one of the important, indefatigable, behind-the-scenes festival volunteers, Sherry Rosso, described these gatherings as orgies. "'Massage party' was code for 'sex party,'" she explained, a signal for partygoers of what to expect.[79] Shaw said of these parties, "Yeah, I heard about them, but I was too tired from sweeping floors and counting box-office receipts to check it out."[80]

Looking back at the 1980 festival lineup, Shaw and Weaver perceive the beginnings of a queer sensibility in a troupe from London called Beryl and the Perils. Shaw described the group's sexuality as "mixed," to which Weaver added, "You couldn't pinpoint *who* they wanted to sleep with." Weaver recalled some of their lyrics: "Nothin' could be finer than to be in your vagina in the morning / Nothin' could be . . . [unable to recall the exact word] than a labia majora when it's yawning." This group was "the perfect representation of a kind of mad, anarchic, irreverent, radical, feminist, and lesbian work."[81] The identifiably lesbian status of the *specific* piece Beryl and the Perils presented at the festival is debatable, however. This raises an interesting point regarding how a performance addresses an audience and the ways individual spectators receive it.

Jean Grove, an active festival participant, attended all of the performances and wrote a letter to the producers briefly giving her impression of each piece. Of Beryl and the Perils she wrote, "Everything was about women's relationships with men. I was able to relate to their skits as a woman, but not as a lesbian."[82] In the *Soho Weekly News,* Baracks reviewed Beryl and the Perils, writing, "Like many . . . of the performers at WOW, they're accustomed to performing before mixed audiences. But more than the other performers, Beryl and the Perils make a point of addressing some material to men. 'The balls may be in your court,' notes one Peril, 'but the racket's in mine.'"[83] Weaver read the work as lesbian, while others did not. Perhaps what made Beryl and the Perils "queer" in its sensibility is precisely this ambivalence. The point is that questions of audience were as central to WOW's festivals as an understanding of what was presented.

Because the festivals were billed as "by, about, and for women," it is not unreasonable to assume that a mix of lesbians and heterosexual women were in attendance. The examples thus far of "audience desire" represent *lesbian* desire. Were the festivals open and inviting to heterosexual women as well? The answer to this question would be terribly important in terms of WOW's future. After the first festival Chambers wrote, "I was startled by the W.O.W. Festival . . . startled by the number and quality of the acts, startled by the packed houses. And, although the Allied Farces women are reluctant to state this, the fact is that 99 percent of those . . . audiences were lesbians. (The W.O.W. Festival aims to appeal to and attract *all* women, regardless of sexuality)."[84] As though in response to Chambers's perception, Proos wrote in *Womanews,* "Interestingly enough, certain critics have made the assumption that this festival is lesbian." And in the same issue Roth penned, "In a related problem, some of the press labeled the festival as lesbian, which threatened its viability as a festival for *all* women." Roth further asserted, "Both straight women and lesbians comfortably took part in the festival. Actually, most of the time, you couldn't justify making a distinction between lesbian and non-lesbian culture."[85] When Haye, a reporter for the *Soho Weekly News,* asked if the thrust of the first festival would be "gay as much as feminist," co-founder Camhe answered, "Definitely." But, according to Haye, Camhe emphasized that the festival was "for all women, which is why they decided to admit men accompanied by women, so as not to alienate straight women."[86]

Following the second festival, *Advocate* critic Prudence Sowers wrote: "Weaver said that WOW had wanted to establish itself as a female-gay theater concept. Once the point had been made . . . the producers could build from that reputation. Emphasis this year was less on creating an all-gay event." In terms of the producers' intent, however, Sowers misunderstood what Weaver had said—WOW's first festival had *not* been intended or designed to be primarily a "female-gay theatre concept." In the same article Sowers quoted Weaver as saying, "There is such a thing as a lesbian ghetto, where as long as you're politically right, your art is OK. And that's fine. It's nurtured a lot of people. But straight people can't look at the festival's schedule and write it off because it's all gay performers. We are artists. We want recognition for that first." The festivals' organizers were dedicated to woman artists as artists *in their own right* regardless of gender, national origin, race, class, or sexuality. Mining and performing the vagaries of gender would endure as pivotal not despite other categories of identity but by paying attention to where they collectively intersect. Sowers also wrote, "Most of the performances we attended were concerned primarily with women's (not necessarily lesbian) experiences."[87]

Cofounder Mark has maintained that "it wasn't a gay event, but we weren't going to hide the lesbians." Many of those who attended the festivals agree that, although the majority of the performers were not lesbian, the audience for both of WOW's festivals was primarily made up of lesbians. Whether this was true—it is impossible to prove in any case—is not the point. What is important about this debate is the intention and practice of the producers. Their approach opened the door for a certain kind of participation in WOW that would continue over the years. It opened the door for heterosexual women like Margolin, who thrived as an artist at WOW without feeling excluded or marginalized. Later this approach would open the door for participation by members of transgender communities. Had the festivals' producers imagined a primarily lesbian enterprise, WOW's future might have been quite different.

Writing about the WOW Café in the mid-1980s, Solomon has pointed out that the organization had, "if not by design, acquired a reputation for producing lesbian work." But WOW "made no deliberate attempt to appeal exclusively to lesbians."[88] Over the thirty years of its existence, WOW has never referred to itself as an exclusively lesbian theater. Sexuality is of course a central concern, but WOW has always insisted on keeping gender equally in the mix. "Interestingly," Case wrote about the Split Britches Company, the troupe "includes both these factions: the pro-sex lesbian one and the feminist one that is anti-woman-as-object, etc."[89] Similarly, at WOW the concerns of these factions are not considered antithetical or mutually exclusive. Of the artists who presented at the first festival, Baracks wrote in 1981 that many of them "don't necessarily identify themselves as gay or straight. . . . Their dialogue is with audiences who see issues of gender as central and political. For the women performers especially, the real context is feminism."[90]

But why didn't heterosexual women attend the festivals in greater numbers? There are undoubtedly dozens of answers to this question. Margolin has said that she would have skipped the festivals herself had she only heard or read about them instead of being asked to work on *Split Britches*. She would have thought the festivals were not about or for her. "I had just finished college as an English major," Margolin said, and then offered a graphic definition of what it means to be male identified: "The only authors I read were men. The only important people I encountered in literature and art were men. My idols were men. I thought I was a man."

Festival participant C. Carr suggested another reason why WOW's festivals—though intended to appeal to all kinds of women—were attended primarily by lesbians. "In some circles," she said, "'woman' was code for lesbian."[91] The historical moment of the festivals supports this contention. As cultural historian Alice Echols has explained, "Of course, some heterosexual radical feminists remained involved in radical feminist groups, but by 1975 the radical wing of the movement was predominantly lesbian."[92] This might be the crux of the matter. Feminist thought had produced an essentialist feminism preoccupied with what was considered essentially true about women and thus was common to them all and made manifest in women's culture and concomitant standards of behavior. But feminist thought also sowed the seeds of an oppositional, resistant feminism with its sights set on a radical critique of what in subsequent years would be described as "heteronormalcy."

Looking back, Margolin maintains that "anyone invested in heteronormativity would not have been comfortable at the festivals; but heteronormative people in general are not the people who are into inclusion." Ironically, lesbian feminism would adopt the essentialist features of heteronormalcy, which may explain why the lesbians who attended the festivals were largely of a different stripe. Of the heterosexual women who attended, Myles explained, "These were women who wanted to be among the girls; they put art first and weren't going to let fear of lesbians get in the way."[93] Even if Chambers's assertion that 99 percent of the festivals' audience was made up of lesbians is true, these were not by and large the androgynous, seemingly asexual lesbians of cultural feminism. It was as if all those policed out of cultural feminism during the 1970s showed up at WOW's festivals. Myles attributes this in part to the influence of European artists and the presence of significant numbers of their followers. Indeed, the producers had wanted to re-create what they felt was the sexier atmosphere of women's theater festivals abroad, where there was also less of a divide between heterosexual women and lesbians.

The festivals' producers sought work that was nontraditional in its style (such as the Women's Experimental Theatre) or over the top in its content (like the Radical Lesbian Feminist Terrorist Comedy Group). This was not the impulse behind the First Gay American Arts Festival, held the previous spring in New York where a production of Chambers's play *Last Summer at Bluefish Cove* had been prominently featured. Like all the plays presented there, it was realist in style. Carr attended that production. "It didn't interest me as a piece of theater," she recalled, "but I liked seeing it because there was little else about lesbians at the time."[94] It might be said that Chambers's work blazed the path and WOW's festivals turned the corner. The festivals were not about achieving equality for women in an otherwise unequal world; they were not about compliance and fitting in; they were not about a woman-centered counterculture. At heart, WOW's festivals were big and bold and ambitious. They were about imagining a different kind of world. They were about changing the social fabric and conditions of life and art for women.

Cultural Memory

We all wanted to be women. We were all impersonating women; but drag queens wanted to get it "right" and we wanted to get it differently.
—SHERRY ROSSO, 2001

The eclipse over the years of contributions by Camhe, Mark, Torr, De Veaux, the Flamboyant Ladies, and the Radical Lesbian Feminist Terrorist Comedy Group, however, does not alone explain all that was lost. The essayist and critic Wendell Ricketts wrote in 1995, "Many aspects of lesbian and gay life are still struggling to appear on stage. Lesbian theatre has demonstrated a certain unwillingness to look forcefully at sexuality . . . although notable exceptions include the work of Holly Hughes and the collaborations of Peggy Shaw and Lois Weaver."[95] This statement is a product of cultural memory as a process of forgetting. It stands as a testament to just how much feminist and lesbian history is missing. Lost is work from the 1970s by Ana Maria Simo and Medusa's Revenge, as well as work from the 1980s and 1990s by Lisa Kron, Madeline Olnek, Reno, Alina Troyano, and the Five Lesbian Brothers. None of these artists hesitated "to look forcefully at sexuality."

According to critical theorist Joseph Roach, "[C]ollective memory works selectively, imaginatively, and often perversely, . . . [and] selective memory requires public enactments of forgetting, either to blur the obvious discontinuities, misalliances, and ruptures or . . . to exaggerate them in order to mystify a previous Golden Age, now lapsed."[96] Far from mystifying or glorifying a previous period, the inability of participants to recall some of the WOW festivals' most salient features is the consequence of a process of maligning a previous age. Vilifying feminists and feminism as essentialist, assimilationist, and antisex had a totalizing effect. What was in fact a reaction against specific kinds of feminism effectively sealed off further consideration of other feminisms and their multiple sensibilities.[97] The resulting conviction—that "feminists didn't do that kind of thing"—is collectively held in cultural memory.

Echoing a conclusion drawn by other scholars, the cultural anthropologist Esther Newton has written about the 1990s as being a period of "widespread dissatisfaction with the excesses of lesbian-feminism and heterosex-ism in mainstream feminism." This, she explains, "caused many lesbians to look toward gay male culture for alternatives."[98] This move is not difficult to understand. Beginning with Newton's own important book *Mother Camp: Female Impersonators in America,* written in 1972, gay male culture has re-ceived far more attention than feminist or lesbian aesthetic production.[99] Newton's sense of what happened during the 1990s is reflected in the often-repeated anecdote about the origins of WOW's aesthetic in which Hot Peaches provided the costumes that brought Spiderwoman out of feminism's androgynous closet.[100]

In this narrative WOW's sensibility came into being at an intersection where women's theater meets gay male theater, where strident feminist/girl meets flamboyant drag queen/boy, with its oddly heterosexual overtones. This repeatedly published account is one of those "public enactments of for-getting," as Roach has suggested, that serve to blur discontinuities. In 1974, several years before Spiderwoman opened that trunk full of drag queen cos-tumes, Camhe opened a trunk full of hot, glamorous women's *and* men's clothing precisely so that women could indulge their fantasies and remake their images. What she described as "female drag" was aimed at representing women on their own terms, creating new possibilities and alternatives for women.

Regarding the emergence of a 1990s aesthetic sensibility, Newton wrote, "What I see happening . . . is a creative ferment arising from the synthesis of lesbian traditions—butch-femme and feminism—with gay male culture (queer identity, camp theatricality, and modes of sexual behavior and im-agery) in the context of *modestly expanding lesbian power.*"[101] I would argue that those characteristics Newton ascribes to gay male culture are not the ex-clusive purview of that culture; rather, they were operating in some corners of lesbian culture in the 1970s as manifest in the performances and spectato-rial practices of WOW's festivals. For many, an apotheosis of lesbian cultural production can be found in a 1990s queer dykehood that valorized gay male culture as the source of its liberation, sensibility, and politics. Queer dykes of the 1990s reacted against a particular strain of 1970s feminism and in so do-ing looked to gay male culture for what in fact feminist lesbian culture had been producing all along. Early radical feminism produced and became conflated with essentialist feminism, but it also generated alternative radical impulses that continued to operate in multiple contexts, WOW among them.

An eclipsed history led younger, girl-culture feminists to equate all previous feminism with essentialism. They overlooked the rich aesthetic traditions that had emerged out of feminist sensibilities from the get-go.

WOW is a historical, embodied example of what queer culture thought feminists had missed and gay male culture got right. As Camhe has explained, "More than anything else, no matter what group we traveled in, we saw ourselves as feminists first—even within the gay movement." The eclipse of work by such artists as Camhe, De Veaux, Mark, and Torr and troupes such as the Flamboyant Ladies and Radical Lesbian Feminist Terrorist Comedy Group helps to clarify a description of WOW's artistic approach that appeared in the *Village Voice* just four years after the festivals: "It's the triumph of the drag queen aesthetic."[102] Thus, by 1985 a significant dimension of the festivals' legacy had already been lost to cultural memory. Gay male culture has been an obvious and important influence on WOW's development, but it is neither the only influence nor the primary one. The aesthetic operating at WOW throughout its three decades is a direct descendent of a sensibility that emerged from 1970s feminism as manifest in WOW's founding festivals. Over time, that which made the festivals so exciting was lost in a process of forgetting that was necessary to the eventual emergence of an ostensibly new, queer dykehood and girl culture in the 1990s.

WOW's festivals featured drag performances complete with "the mustache," which ostensibly was the sole purview of drag king performance in the 1990s.[103] The festivals were saturated with an energy that was highly erotically charged. They included significant participation by women of color, which at the time was not always the case with events produced by white women. These distinguishing attributes were all reflected in WOW's twentieth anniversary event. For many if not most spectators that December night in 2000, it was inconceivable that the performances unfolding before them resonated with an event held twenty years earlier. When the sources of influence shift from feminism to gay male culture, feminism is reduced to a single dominant strain. What is significant about the performances at WOW's festivals is erased, and women's cultural production continues to be devalued. This is how important theaters like Medusa's Revenge and the Flamboyant Ladies become lost to cultural memory.

Writing for the *Village Voice* following the second festival, Baracks commented on the changes under way: "Feminist performers have, in the past few years, pushed aside a lot of boundaries—some of which were constructed by feminists. As Peggy Shaw said in the festival's closing revue, in her guise as

Gussie Umberger, lesbian shopping-bag lady . . . 'I've been to 37 women's festivals, and this is the only one that had go-go dancers.' "[104] Those who attended the festivals remember them as extraordinary because they were. Margolin, who at the time was new to both theater and feminism, described her experience: "It was exhilarating. I'd never been in a cultural community where the criterion for great theater was the passionate desire to speak. And here it was. I watched it roll in like the storm from the water. It was fantastic."[105] Similarly, an observation Jill Dolan made about the Split Britches Company applies to WOW's inaugural festivals as well. She wrote, "The founding of Split Britches . . . was an anomaly in an otherwise stagnant scene."[106] WOW's festivals appeared in these stagnant waters as the storm Margolin imagines, poised to launch many a ship.

Chapter 4

Feminist Space and a System of Anarchy: The Storefront

The lesson of the [Barnard 1982 "Toward a Sexual Politics"] conference is simple: there is no safe space unless we make one.

—CAROLE VANCE, 1984

Just as the infamous sex wars were heating up in the early 1980s, WOW was closing down the second of two successful international festivals and looking for a permanent home. The producers and volunteers were utterly exhausted, equally exhilarated, and did not want to lose the momentum the festivals had generated. How to sustain it was the question. Some wanted to begin immediately planning a third international festival with the idea that it would become an annual event like the Michigan Womyn's Music Festival. Others wanted to make their own theater work and felt the time commitment required to mount another ambitious festival encroached too significantly on this agenda. Monthly theme parties and performances had sustained momentum after WOW's first festival in 1980 and had garnered what little funding the next one could count on. But here, too, the energy needed to secure and maintain space for these events—which often required putting up and dismantling the entire stage and audience setup between every performance—sapped time and strength.

Because no one was paid for these Herculean efforts, dedicated volunteers squeezed in time between holding a job that paid the rent and living expenses while producing a major festival along with year-round fund-raising events. Those artists most intent on creating work believed the solution was to find a permanent space for WOW. They were not alone. Women who had participated in any number of ways over the months—and had found in WOW an experience like no other—imagined a place where they could gather regularly rather than periodically. They wanted to expand the social and community aspects of WOW. Within four months of the second festival, WOW had moved into a storefront space it could call its own at 330 E. Eleventh Street in the East Village.

But others valued WOW's itinerant nature and were wary of the move to permanent space. Eileen Myles was among them. "The festivals had a 'carnival tent' atmosphere in the sense of throw it up fast, do it cheap, let it collapse," she recalled. "It created urgency, like a traveling fair or the wildest of parties. There was a 'heat' about it. It was extravagant. It radiated energy."[1] Myles feared this new direction would domesticate WOW—hardly an unfounded concern. "Help WOW find a home" had been the fund-raising pitch for rent parties and performances. Historically, limiting women's access to space has been a powerful means of constraining their economic and political mobility, and associating women primarily with the domestic realm has been the most consistent means of containing them. For Myles it had been thrilling to watch women transform public sites across the East Village into spaces of their own, with the theatricality, humor, and faux razzle-dazzle of a circus and the down and dirty atmosphere of a carnival. Did they really want to go home? As it turned out, WOW's festivals would have a lasting influence on how the fledgling organization conceived of itself in its new space.

A City of Women

WOW is a thirty-woman collective with no one in charge. More than a theatre company, it's a community. If you're just interested in putting up a show, WOW may not be for you. Here you have to care about the collective.
—LISA KRON, 1990

In some measure WOW's festivals were exciting in direct relationship to the multiple venues they commanded throughout the East Village. Unlike most women's festivals in the United States at the time, WOW was not separated from the ebb and flow of everyday commerce either out in the countryside or existing solely within institutional walls made possible by a particular affiliation. The festivals had given women the opportunity to take up space, claim it, inhabit it, and manipulate it within and across an urban landscape. Large numbers of women had traveled from site to site and spilled onto the sidewalks outside the venues. The festivals also made the experience of continuity across time a possibility by providing places where people could gather before, after, and between events, from the daytime café and nighttime bar to festival-wide dances and private parties. *New York City News* writer Donna Allegra described the scene: "During the two weeks of performances and for the month preceding the festival, the café at the University of the Streets was like the town square of a blossoming lesbian village on the Lower East Side."[2]

This critical mass of women inhabiting and moving across urban space through and over an extended period of time inspired another critic to describe WOW as a city onto itself. "I'm spending my nights and days in a city of women," wrote Barbara Baracks in the *Village Voice*. "They fill large halls and small rooms, corridors, doorways, spilling out into the streets. Singles, in couples, trios, whole crowds of women."[3] The festivals' diverse offerings ensured that these crowds would consist of women from different walks of life with varied social and cultural histories. That WOW began as a kind of city would have deep-seated significance for its subsequent development as a community. The festivals can be seen as a microcosm of the "unoppressive city" that scholar Iris Marion Young would later theorize as an alternative to the ideal, libratory community of feminist imaginings and longings.[4]

Young has suggested that insofar as *community* refers to those people who identify with each other in a particular locale, the desire for mutual understanding, group identification, and loyalty will lead inexorably to implicit standards of commonality and conformity that exclude those with whom the group does not identify. Following this logic, a feminist community that aspires to some form of political efficacy will be defined not only in contrast to patriarchy but against potential allies as well—that is, those with similar political affinities and goals but different identities and practices. Indeed, the thrill of recognition that enthralled early women's theater practitioners and their audiences around a common experience of gender oppression led many white, middle-class feminists to turn a blind eye to those women who did not share their ostensibly universal experience, marginalizing women who experienced inequity in different ways. Or, as the title of a groundbreaking 1982 black feminist anthology cogently stated it, *All the Women Are White, All the Blacks Are Men, But Some of Us Are Brave*.[5] Young has argued that the urge for unity, wholeness, and belonging that *community* denotes underpins various forms of racial, ethnic, and economic chauvinism and segregation. Community and homogeneity, then, are two sides of the same coin.

In contrast, Young described city life as characterized by the "being-together of strangers" who may remain strangers in their encounters while tacitly acknowledging their proximity and the contributions of each to the whole. In these encounters "people are not 'internally' related . . . and do not understand one another from within their own perspective. They are externally related, they experience each other as other, different, from different groups, histories, professions, cultures, which they do not understand." If communities tend to be melting pots, cities are constituted in difference. From here Young envisions the unoppressive city as "openness to unassimilated otherness."[6]

Although she acknowledges that no widespread openness to difference currently exists in social relations, a look at how the unoppressive city's salient features played out in WOW's festivals opens a window on the perspectives and practices WOW retained and developed in its permanent home. Rather than abandoning one mode of operation to settle into another, life in WOW's new space grew organically out of its activities over the previous eighteen months. Even in this permanent home, for instance, WOW managed to retain the feeling of itinerancy Myles had so valued about the festivals. Shows ran only one to four nights, sometimes a different show was scheduled for later in the evening on the same nights, and one night a week was reserved for variety shows. Joni Wong, a lighting designer who was one of the first to infuse production values into WOW's aesthetic, has described the years in the storefront as " 'hit-and-run theater.' Put it up fast; then it's gone."[7]

What immediately struck festival participant C. Carr about the storefront space on E. Eleventh Street was the mix of women. "Everyone was there," she recalled, "middle-class women from the Midwest, working-class New Yorkers, women of color, bar dykes, straight women, butches, femmes, leather dykes . . . and nobody cared who anybody was or was not." Like many women who had attended the festivals, by the early 1980s Carr was bone tired of feminism's infighting and looking for respite from a fractured women's movement. "As soon as WOW opened its doors," she said, "I was right there."[8] Other women also appreciated this diversity. In a 2001 interview, the theater and casting director Heidi Griffiths remembered what first impressed her about the storefront: "I came from this feminist place where everything was very button-down, and here was a place where you could be whatever you wanted. You could be a butch or a femme or a straight woman who was married."[9]

At a time when feminists were squaring off against each other on the basis of differences among women, the impulse at WOW was for inclusiveness.[10] This was not formally decided or proclaimed but was embedded in the very nature of the festivals. They had been too large and decentralized for most of the participants to know each other in the face-to-face manner out of which most feminist communities typically emerge. The only previous experience of WOW for some newcomers to its new home had been an entirely mediated one; they had been following the festivals' activities in local newspapers. As the press release for the first festival stated, "The idea is to generate a *sense* of community."[11] WOW initially garnered a diverse following that would mark it as an organization with a propensity for inclusiveness.

WOW has never been a culturally homogeneous operation, but it has not always been a thoroughly diverse one either. Today the collective is remarkably and noticeably diverse across age, class, race, sexuality, and ethnicity—although this has not happened without effort, nor has it been unproblematic.[12] Endemic to WOW—as a consequence of its origins—is the possibility for what the author, activist, and public intellectual bell hooks has called a "space of radical openness."[13] Carr and Griffiths encountered just such a space when they showed up at the storefront. Indeed, "showing up" was the basis on which WOW membership was (and still is) built. Before each and every performance, a WOW member makes a brief announcement inviting any woman who wants to join the group to attend one of the collective's meetings (held every Tuesday night). Like city residency, "being there" constitutes membership. The collective does not interrogate current or prospective members for their motives, politics, or aesthetic choices. Participants move fluidly in and out of WOW. There are approximately thirty women active in the collective at any given time and hundreds of inactive or associate members.

But how can a space be radically open when it is largely exclusionary on the basis of gender? Men have attended WOW over the years and participated in its productions, albeit in statistically insignificant numbers. They have appeared in shows and on rare occasions have directed and written them. The 1980 festival excluded men not to celebrate the supposed superiority of women but to provide women with an opportunity to present their own work in one of the world's cultural capitals. In New York, theater is (still) created and produced overwhelmingly by men and primarily serves the ideological and institutional interests of white, heterosexual, middle-class masculinity. WOW exists to give women a chance to be in charge of the creative and operational process without having to make work that serves mainstream ideological and political interests in order to do so.

Even those critics most opposed to separatism as a political haven have acceded to the necessity, in certain instances, for marginalized groups to separate themselves from oppressive, constraining circumstances as a strategy for accomplishing important work. Some less than open attitudes and practices help to explain why WOW has been less ethnically and racially diverse during certain periods, but the need for strategic separatism on the part of women of color may be a contributing factor as well. The women of the all-black Flamboyant Ladies Company presented their work in WOW's new space, for example, but they did not join the collective. "WOW was great; it was deeply radical," according to Flamboyant Ladies cofounder Gwendolen Hardwick. "But there were other things we needed to be doing then."[14]

"Woman" is the sole identity category of WOW, not to elide differences but to allow them to remain in play. In the absence of funding, WOW's ambitious festivals depended on massive amounts of volunteer, cooperative labor and participation among women who were asked to support each other in mounting and attending women's theater. *Doing* something in common contributed as much to the palpable sense of unity that emerged from the festivals as did *being* something in common. WOW is essentially a band of women bound together by limited opportunities and committed to cooperative labor as the means of creating them. This is probably the reason why a showdown over its definition as either women's theater or lesbian theater did not occur until after WOW had reached the twenty-year mark in conjunction with a growing transgender membership.

The festivals' dual objectives of serving individual and collective agendas would also shape WOW's development. Whereas many collective organizations had been founded on subordinating individual desires to the aims and values of the group, WOW attempted to fulfill individual desires and aims *within* a supportive environment sensitive to the needs and interests of others. Not unlike a city, the collective supports self-interested competitiveness among individuals while attending to the often conflicting needs of the whole. It is an imperfect system that sometimes fails and, unlike a city, repeatedly attempts to be less rather than more of a system at all. Ironically, WOW adopted anarchy as the principle on which to organize itself. This, too, had to do with space in the larger sense, for in the 1970s a palpable sense of "anything goes" was the zeitgeist of the neighborhood that would become WOW's home.

A System of Anarchy

We want to be amateurs. We're into chaos not music.
—JOHNNY ROTTEN, 1970S

Like the punk rock vocalist Johnny Rotten, WOW was comprised of unabashed amateurs who were resolutely into chaos. Eileen Myles need not
have worried about the organization becoming domesticated. In a typically
"bent" fashion, WOW christened its new space a "home for wayward girls."
This home may have existed to (re)form girls but not in the sense of
"straightening" them out. The storefront was imagined as a kind of playground where bad girls could be as bad as they wanted—an asylum run by
the inmates if you will. Calling themselves "girls" was but one of many indi-
cations that WOW's feminism would be of a different stripe. This appellation
flew in the face of a decade-long struggle by feminists to be taken seriously in
part by insisting they be referred to as "women" and not infantilized as girls.
That WOW's participants self-identified as "wayward" was astonishing at a
time when so many feminists were promoting what they believed to be
women's natural inclination for goodness, along with an intrinsic capacity
for nurturing and nonhierarchical cooperation.

In both presentation and audience response, WOW girls behaved consid-
erably outside the bounds of mainstream and feminist decorum. This is
where WOW's neighborhood of origin came into play. If the festivals had created a kind of city, then the East Village was the palimpsest on which it was
mapped. Bohemia in the United States during most of the twentieth century
had become nearly synonymous with the progressive art worlds of New
York's Greenwich Village. "The Village" typically referred to an area radiat-
ing outward from Washington Square Park in Lower Manhattan. By the time
WOW was founded, however, the gentrification of the Village, with its sky-
rocketing real estate values, marked the neighborhood (particularly its west
side) as an upwardly mobile socioeconomic area. Artists living on the economic margins who were not already ensconced in rent-controlled apartments had moved to the Lower East Side, the northern half of which (between Houston and Fourteenth Streets) became known as the East Village.
Income disparities along gender lines meant more gay men lived in the West
Village while lesbians tended to migrate east.

Economics was not the only means of redistributing marginalized populations. Between 1980 and 1982, for example, three lesbian bars in the
Washington Square area—Bonnie & Clyde's, the Duchess, and Déjà Vu—
were forced to close. The State Liquor Authority (SLA) had canceled the
liquor licenses of two of the bars on the charge of "ceasing to operate a
bona fide establishment." The *Village Voice* writer Robert Massa pointed
to scores of gay male bars as evidence of the SLA's selective enforcement of

the law. Massa concluded, "It is gay women who are being discriminated against."[15]

Culturally, the East Village had long been marked by its immigrant populations primarily from Eastern Europe and Puerto Rico. By the 1970s it had become a mostly Jewish, Latino, and Ukrainian neighborhood. The area was characterized by its rows of tenement buildings. The kind of apartment in which most East Village residents lived consisted of one or two rooms, or a series of small rooms arranged in a line (known as a "railroad apartment"), with a bathtub in the kitchen. Many buildings included street-level commercial space or storefronts that landlords rented to businesses of various kinds. Despite the fact that New York City was experiencing a deep recession during the 1970s, buildings in the West Village were renovated and rents continued to climb. But apartments in the East Village remained inexpensive, and many storefront spaces were empty. WOW rented one of these storefronts, with a typical railroad layout—narrow and deep. For most of WOW's history its members have lived in the East Village, but rents in the neighborhood eventually became so high that today many members live in the Bronx, Brooklyn, and Queens.

By the 1980s ticket prices for alternative theater and music could be as much as five times more costly in the West Village than east of it. Although the West Village was considered far from pristine—with its gay bars, sex shops, and late-night sexual activity on the Hudson River piers—the East Village represented the seamier side of Greenwich Village. Drugs were dealt all over the city, of course, but the East Village became known as one of the neighborhoods where drug dealing took place on a grander scale. Until Mayor Rudolph Giuliani's reign from 1993 to 2001, New York's reputation in general was one of lawlessness, but the East Village was reputed to be especially dangerous. The aura of criminality was a by-product of local drug trafficking and was linked to the larger drug scene that characterized some East Village art worlds.

Contributing to the climate of danger was the presence of a flourishing punk rock music scene, which had existed alongside the traditional, multiethnic cultures of the East Village at least since 1973, when a club called CBGB opened under a flophouse on the Bowery. Initially called Country Bluegrass Blues and Other Music for Uplifting Gormandizers, what distinguished the club was its requirement that musicians play only original material. A huge festival in 1975 featuring more than forty as yet unknown bands captured media attention and put CBGB on the city's map as a center of "downtown entertainment."[16] Individual artists and groups in theater, music, visual art, dance, and poetry were active across the East Village throughout the decade, but punk rock iconography and sensibilities permeated the neighborhood.

Punk music's permissive, anarchical approach fostered an anti-institution, do-it-yourself mentality that did not privilege virtuosity and, in turn, encouraged participation. A band associated with the East Village music scene and CBGB, the Bloods, was one of the all-girl groups that would later participate in WOW's festivals. Although the Bloods themselves were five accomplished musicians, the group's guitarist, Kathy Rey, invoked a fictitious—but nonetheless representative—participant in the punk scene: "I've been playing guitar for three weeks and just wrote this cool song."[17] In a 2001 interview, Carr recalled that visual artists who did not necessarily play instruments (herself included) were asked to join bands. The well-known girl band the Bush Tetras was made up, according to Rey, mostly of painters. Insofar as punk was feminist, it was incidentally so. The singer-songwriter Patti Smith is considered the godmother of punk. She broke through the "girl singer" mold with what Tracey Tanenbaum of National Public Radio described as her "ecstatic blend of free-form poetry and three-chord rock."[18] But punk rock did not feature women in significant numbers any more than any other art movement or medium, with the possible exception of dance. Those women who did participate in the punk scene were considered "tough, opinionated, and hedonistic" in Rey's words. The wayward girls of WOW were not without role models.

The anything-goes permissiveness of punk was palpable beyond its own insular subculture because punk was performative beyond the clubs. Punk musicians and their followers performed their personas and accompanying styles and attitudes visibly in the streets. At the same time, a less visible subculture also had a role to play in the sensibility and modus operandi of WOW's new storefront space. According to New York State Assembly member Deborah Glick, "A culture came out of girls having fun—a certain percentage of lesbians were feminists back then and totally into having a good time. We poked fun at ourselves and at the lesbian feminist community."[19] This subculture was associated with bars like Bonnie & Clyde's, where femmes and butches were welcome, and also with the Gay Activist Alliance (GAA) when it was located in a firehouse on Wooster Street. "The gay community still meant gay men," however, recalled Glick. For example, "the GAA held a dance for lesbians on Friday night once a month and the Lesbian

Liberation Committee of the GAA was relegated to meeting on Sunday afternoons."[20] These meetings sometimes included poetry readings or panel presentations and were always followed by a gathering at Bonnie & Clyde's for a free buffet dinner, dancing, and partying. Not only was this group largely made up of the outcasts of lesbian feminism, but it existed on the margins of the gay community as well. It was subculture experiencing a dire scarcity of venues. Given these conditions, Glick was always surprised by the large audiences the Radical Lesbian Feminist Terrorist Comedy Group drew for its sporadic performances. This unmoored group of lesbians had carved out its own cultural space for its members to assert and experience their identity freely. It was a space in search of a place.

"The East Village made it all come together," said Rey. "Women taking power musically and artistically lived in the same community and were informed by the same stimuli and it all had an effect on everybody." The East Village was not for the faint of heart; it attracted and produced dissident voices. Rey recalled the "insurgence of European women" present at WOW's festivals: "You come to New York because wherever you come from you're a black sheep; you're ostracized. I thought they were looking for one other place on the planet where they might fit in."[21] At the festivals, feminism's bad girls were welcome and good girls could go bad. Some of what went on there represented the underside of women's culture. In those days the hot, punked-out, leather-jacketed Bloods associated with the seamy music world of the Lower East Side would not have been welcome at the Michigan Womyn's Music Festival. And some of the poets who participated in the festivals were reported to be "notorious junkies."[22]

WOW's activities had created a kind of space that both exceeded its festivals and preceded its home. In this sense a fledgling space characterized at base by its tacit feminism moved into a place. The festivals had created a social and cultural milieu that went so far beyond theater as an art form that WOW was billed as a "social club" on the flyer for the first big event to follow the second festival: "an X-rated Xmas party." Theme parties had long been a feature of the visual art scene at places like Club 57, which was located in the basement of St. Mark's Church in-the-Bowery. WOW had adopted this practice as well, throwing such parties as the Military Drag Ball, the Freudian Slip/Psychotic Underwear Bash, the Medical Drag Ball, Debutantes on Parade, and the I Dreamed I Paid the Rent in My Maidenform Bra party. Holly Hughes was a visual artist at the time and saw a flyer for the Christmas party. Perhaps because it was held at Club 57, she decided to go. It was only upon arriving that she discovered WOW had something to do with theater. The flyer Hughes saw captures the initial impression Myles had of WOW as "carnivalesque" and demonstrates how the spirit of the festivals was retained and expanded upon. The flyer read:

XX-Rated XMAS
FOR WOMEN ONLY
AN EROTIC EVENING
of hoochie cooch dancing, sensual
acrobatics, exotic tapping, high &
low comedy & wild abandon
BENEFIT FOR WOW SOCIAL CLUB[23]

As Hughes remembered it, the party took place in "this seedy basement that had been transformed into a kind of bordello called 'Noel's.' It looked like a cathouse at Christmas. It had a carnival atmosphere with kissing booths and racks of thrift store clothes—tuxedos, band uniforms, ball gowns with sparkly sequins, UPS uniforms, corsets—and all these sweaty women swirling around in bizarre getups doing impromptu performances." She was thunderstruck by the possibility of acting on desire and fantasy, which the party's mise-en-scène suggested and invited: "The idea that I could be more than a spectator was transformative."[24] These theme parties broke down the static performer/audience dyad, prefiguring theater in WOW's new home as so participatory that the line between performer and spectator would be blurred.

The way in which the festivals, the theme parties, and the neighborhood's prevailing sensibilities came together in WOW's storefront space was expansive. Women could remain whoever they were when they crossed the threshold, or they could create and enact their fantasies. Griffiths had arrived at WOW from London via Smith College, where she was getting a graduate degree in theater. She first visited WOW's storefront during one of its Sunday brunches. These were daylong events that included performances, and the atmosphere was raucous. Playwright and performer Claire Moed would show up decked out as Marilyn Monroe, for instance, and maintained that persona throughout the brunch. "But she was way sexier," Griffiths recalled. "She went out in the street accosting people to get them to come in for the show, wearing more lipstick than you ever thought possible and speaking in a sexy, breathy voice that was impossible to say no to. It was wild, very wild; it felt unformed but incredibly exciting." Subcultures, even radically alternative ones like punk, are conformist to the extent that members adhere to certain signs, symbols, and behaviors that identify individuals as part of the group. The premise at WOW was that all signs and symbols were available and anyone had permission to indulge her wildest fantasies. "You didn't feel like you were stepping on a land mine if you took a particular position," remembered Griffiths. "There was no censorship of sexuality and its expression." Moed concurred: "The heels. The makeup. The dresses. It was the only place in the world where I could wear those clothes and it could be lesbian."[25]

Having taken her Marilyn Monroe persona out into the street, Moed would return to a "kissing booth," where spectators could buy a kiss for a dollar. She then might appear onstage during a performance. Porous, permeable boundaries like those between the theater and the street, brunch and performance, and performers and spectators characterized WOW's storefront space. "Even those who weren't in theater threw themselves into it," Griffiths said. "Everyone was encouraged to participate." Alice Forrester, a stage manager who went on to become a drama therapy practitioner, agreed: "I'd say, 'Oh, come in and do *something*. You say you can whistle through your nose? Great!' And they'd show up dressed in a tuxedo and whistle through their nose."[26]

From the beginning, WOW accommodated a felt but unarticulated value for women simply getting up onstage. This impulse marks WOW as feminist. Whatever an individual's sexual practice, it was understood that she experienced oppression psychologically and socially as a consequence of gender imperatives and expectations. In chapter 2, for example, Jimmy Camicia described Peggy Shaw as reticent or habitually uncommunicative during her early years with Hot Peaches, illustrating the insidiousness of unconscious gender constraints. As Shaw discovered for herself, insofar as reticence is gender inflected or conditioned, getting onstage can be a powerful strategy for women who want to break through the silence.

This desire to empower women and promote their agency would ultimately lead WOW to embrace a number of practices antithetical to those of traditional theater. For example, anyone could get up and perform at weekly Variety Nights, anyone who wanted to be in a show could do so regardless of training or experience, and those who did not want to perform were repeatedly encouraged to "just get up there and do something." Even in amateur or community theater, those who want to be cast must endure the often excruciating process of auditions. At WOW, however, the opportunity to perform in a nonjudgmental, enthusiastically supportive environment inspired a great deal of creative thinking and innovative approaches to representation. Women were empowered to take a chance on expressing themselves. Although many of these experiences were mostly fun and perhaps therapeutic in nature, some led to the further development of pieces that ultimately became stand-alone evenings of performance. Women who had worked in theater solely as stage managers, designers, and "techies" found themselves onstage in the storefront. A few of them, like Forrester, ended up writing and performing in their own work at WOW. This is equally true of a number of women who initially had no interest in theater at all.

One of WOW's core commitments is to be a place where women can work out the dynamics of agency through whatever means. Every woman is encouraged to become her own leader, to find or develop a voice, to take matters into her own hands, and to assume the power needed to get the job done. When it comes to how the shop will actually be run, there are no followers in the group, only leaders. Hierarchy is sidestepped when everyone is presumably at the top. When played out organizationally, agency as practiced at WOW will lead to chaos even when anarchy is not the express goal. This nonhierarchical approach to collective organization represents the influence of the women's movement in general and women's theater collectives specifically. However, the sociocultural landscape of the East Village in the late 1970s had the most significant influence on the shape WOW would take because anarchy was explicitly identified as the organizational foundation on which WOW would be constructed. "The inbuilt system of anarchy still exists; it's very hard to build in a 'system' of anarchy," Shaw has explained. "Everyone wants to make something *something*. Everyone, at one time or another at WOW, has wanted to make it into a functioning Off-Broadway theatre. We as a group have fought it because the roots are anarchy."[27]

This is not to suggest some naive notion of a theater that somehow manages to operate without structure; rather, as Shaw put it, the group fights to pull the operation back to its roots in an ongoing battle to thwart the formation of rigid structures. The image of "a fight" is fitting, for, like anarchy historically, WOW's notion of governance is one that is absent *force* but not absent *confrontation*. "It's not polite. It's not pretentious," Moed explained. "It's not phony. It's not 'touchy-feely.' It's real."[28] The emphasis is more on stepping up and fighting for what you want than on getting along, which is in keeping with anarchy as a kind of philosophy of nonsubmission. Anthropologist Esther Newton has pointed out that anarchism is also "an ideology of permanent rebellion."[29] In this sense WOW's process of organizing itself is a never-ending one. Current WOW member Jen Abrams said it this way: "We structure ourselves so that we are required to agree on as little as possible. We can disagree about almost everything and still get it done."[30] Rather than repeated attempts to reconcile differences, WOW has organized itself so that resolution does not have to take place for the group to move forward. The system of anarchy is an ever-evolving one.

Forrester recalled an incident shortly after the move to the storefront that demonstrates how the space operated then. "There was a debate about what color to paint the ceiling; and in the middle of the night those who wanted it a certain color just came in and painted it. That was a core characteristic of WOW—you could do whatever you wanted if you had the energy and you just did it." She remembers that "the techies were the backbone of the space, but there was a real team feeling of 'we're all in this together.'" Hughes agrees with this assessment: "Decisions were hashed out and made at weekly staff meetings. So much was happening in the space that everyone basically pitched in and did everything." The sheer joy of having a space of their own fueled this enthusiasm, which in turn fueled an intensity that at times could be characterized as "over the top." Forrester recounted her first engagement with WOW to emphasize how all consuming an experience the enterprise could be in its early years. She had met Weaver and Shaw after WOW's first festival, when they had taken *Split Britches* to a women's theater festival in Boston where Forrester was stage-managing. She had returned to New Jersey and was living with her boyfriend when she got a call from Weaver. "I told my boyfriend I was going into the city to talk to some women about stage-managing a festival and that I'd probably be back late," Forrester remembers. "I took the train into the city and never made it home. I never went back."[31]

At the end of that first summer in the storefront, the Split Britches troupe went abroad on tour for three months, taking Forrester and another member active in the space along with them. Camhe and Mark ran the space until they were invited to produce and perform in an event called Decadent Night at the Melkweg Women's Festival in Amsterdam. Hughes had not been at WOW very long at this point, but in keeping with the spirit of the place she picked up the ball and began managing it. "The books were a mess when everyone returned from tour," Hughes recalled. "My idea of bookkeeping was to throw receipts in a paper bag."[32] Record keeping was not a priority at WOW. Many participants believed that filling the space with activity was more important than accounting for expenses and that the effort required to manage the funds was energy better spent elsewhere. "We knew there were times when one person or another had their 'hand in the till,'" Weaver remembered, "but it was never much and some people were really poor. We just figured when someone took it, they needed it."[33]

An already vast scope of activity was taking place at WOW, and Hughes brought in more. There were as many as three shows a week plus an open mike Variety Night. The comic Reno curated late-night stand-up comedy shows on Friday nights. Hughes herself curated art exhibits and brought artists in to show slides and talk about their work. More than one event was going on every night. Before long Hughes was exhausted, and Susan Young—who would later become an award-winning designer—stepped in to manage the space. Under Young's stewardship, a group called the Asian Lesbians of the East Coast began holding meetings and events (films, videos, poetry readings, music) every Sunday night.

Soon a predictable pattern of successive burnout became apparent. Just as some members wanted to attend to their own work rather than run a festival, they did not want to run a space either. Operating the storefront eventually fell to whoever was willing to pour her heart and soul and labor into it. Everyone agreed that this was unsustainable, so the group sat down to talk about what it really wanted to accomplish. This was the prototype for what would become the tradition of WOW's annual retreats. At one of these retreats what became known as "the fantasy circle" was initiated, a practice that also endured. Sitting in a circle, each woman would articulate her fantasy for WOW: what she herself most wanted to do in the space, what she most wanted WOW to be, and how she envisioned WOW in the future. Each member also articulated what she did *not* want individually and what she did *not* want for WOW. It became clear that no one wanted to host the work of women from outside the group any longer. Women with no stake in the space too often left behind a mess and sometimes broken equipment. From the fantasy circle exercise grew the outlines of how WOW would function without becoming an institution. It would operate on the basis of shared labor and giving something back to the space.

To this day, Tuesday night meetings are the structural center of WOW. A volunteer facilitates each meeting, beginning with a "go-around" to break the ice. The facilitator poses a question like "What's your favorite Halloween costume or the best one you have ever seen?" Each woman in turn states her name, preferred gender pronoun, and answer to the question. The facilitator then asks who has an agenda item for discussion. Hands are raised and the meeting's agenda is generated on the spot. Although the number of women present at these meetings ebbs and flows, members are motivated to attend by a long-standing agreement that whoever shows up makes the decisions. There is no waiting to consult with members who are not in attendance. In recent years, though, decisions deemed of great import might be postponed until a following meeting, giving a greater number of members a chance to show up. Conversations and debate may take place via e-mail, but decisions are made on Tuesday nights. The power is shared so that no single person has the final say about anything relevant to the group as a whole.

WOW is a chaotic organization to the extent that something like the following can and has occurred. At one meeting the question arose as to whether groups outside of WOW's collective could occasionally use the space. It was decided that yes, they could—as long as a WOW member agreed to present the group by assuming the role of the show's producer. But then let's say a WOW member produced an outside group whose play was written and directed by men and the production was of such a nature that it could have been produced at any number of other venues. This might lead to an agenda item at a future meeting and a decision that outside groups are no longer allowed to use the space. This would become policy until someone raised the issue again, and then a different decision might be reached.

The experience of playwright Madeleine Olnek provides a case in point. Olnek became a member of WOW's collective in 1988 and produced a number of her plays there over the following ten years. She maintains, "WOW will always be the great place where I learned my craft as a playwright, where I was given a production slot in advance of writing the script, where I had total and complete artistic freedom, and where my thoroughly and uniquely lesbian plays were embraced."[34] Olnek remains enthusiastic about WOW despite what she describes as a minor, but nonetheless "schizophrenic," episode. She was asked by the collective to fill a time slot in a particular season with one of her plays. The collective was aware that Olnek had engaged a man to direct her play—a not unprecedented move—when it invited her to produce. Still, this choice prompted an agenda item for the collective's next meeting, and shortly thereafter Olnek learned that her play was being withdrawn from the slot she had been asked to fill. Had a different mix of members been present at the meeting, perhaps a different decision would have been reached. Indeed, at a subsequent meeting the decision was reversed and Olnek's play was presented. Understandably, Olnek found the initial rejection upsetting. Some WOW members have opted out of the collective altogether as a consequence of such operational ambivalence. Olnek eventually got beyond her justifiable anger, chalking up the experience to the nature of the beast that is WOW.[35]

After three decades, it seems incredible that WOW still does not have a clear policy on the participation of men in the space. The first conversation on the topic took place in 1980, but there would be many others. In the spring of 2002 performance artist and collective member Susana Cook was staffing a show when a couple of male actors showed up. She was on her knees cleaning the toilet when, in her words, they "dropped their backpacks and said, 'We're here to perform.'"[36] The incident sparked an agenda item. For many collective members it seemed that men had become more and more involved at WOW. The ensuing conversation went on for weeks via e-mail about this issue, as well as ticket prices—another ongoing debate—which had climbed to twenty dollars for some shows.[37] Significant, knotty issues related to class and gender privilege were acknowledged during the exchange. The e-mail correspondence was passionate, thoughtful, and occasionally vitriolic and mean-spirited. It revealed what appeared to be massive confusion about the collective's mission. One member pondered the contradiction of men playing central roles in a lesbian theater. Some members were surprised to learn that WOW was a lesbian theater; they thought of WOW as a women's space. Another woman was surprised that WOW was considered a women's space and wanted to know what was meant by that term. After two decades of uninterrupted operation, how is it possible for the fundamental tenets of an organization to be so unclear to its own members? The short answer is that this very ambiguity is what has sustained WOW over the years. From its inception WOW has been organized in ways that retain fluid meanings and avoid ironclad definitions. Even when consensus is reached and resolutions result, WOW's organization ensures that most issues will eventually be revisited.

More often than not, a heated debate ends in parody rather than resolution. For example, a series of e-mail messages wrapped up the "men in the space" exchange by playing on the title of *Naked Boys Singing,* an off-Broadway play that was currently running in the West Village billed as "*Oh Calcutta* by a *Full Monty* gang.'"

Subject: My secret

Okay—I'll come out with it, the reason I defend the right for Wow women to work with men is that I have a beautiful vision for my next project. . . . I want to do *NAKED BOYS SINGING* at Wow. ALL BOYS! ALL NAKED! ALL THE TIME! NAKED! SINGING! Whaddya all think?

Responses:

Can I be a naked boy singing please?!

GOOD FOR YOU—Coming out is sooo healthy.

Yeah, yeah—as long as you cast all women as the naked boys—Toys in Babeland [a local erotica shop] will have a run on their stock of strap-ons![38]

In typical WOW fashion, the issue was not resolved, but the message was sent and heard. Men would not be prohibited from participating, but members would be more circumspect in keeping the spirit of WOW in mind when making decisions about their individual productions. Two e-mail messages in particular from this exchange captured WOW's modus operandi. "I'm not pro-men-in-the-space; I'm anti-policy," wrote one member. Another marveled and celebrated the fact that following such a contentious debate "we always manage to come out whole." To emerge whole as a collective without resolution is an accomplishment WOW repeated many times over many years. Not all debates concluded as amicably, however.

The first major discussion around issues arising from WOW's growing transgender membership took place at a summer retreat in 2002. No resolution was reached, and the issue dominated e-mail discussions and debates for two years. Membership in the collective is based on self-identification; if a person self-identifies as a woman, she is eligible to become a member of the collective. Those who self-identify as men can participate in the same ways men have participated in WOW productions over the years. Members of the female-to-male transgender community particularly objected to an understanding of WOW as "women's space." They felt that invoking gender as a basis for inclusion served to reinforce binary gender constructions and thereby contributed to the oppression transgender and transsexual people experience in the world at large. The counterargument held that those who carry the gender mark of "woman" are in need of opportunities still overwhelmingly denied them.

The debate became so heated that some members of the collective called for a vote to decide the matter. A statement was drafted and a vote was taken on September 14, 2004. The collective resolved that "WOW is a women's space. We welcome all women, including (but not limited to) women of all races, abilities, ages, economic backgrounds, and women of trans experience." Although there was confusion about what the statement meant and further debate ensued, the issue gradually subsided. For many members the resolution was unsatisfactory, however, and a number of them left the collective as a consequence of this action. The collective did not emerge whole in this case, but it did emerge. What transpired in this instance serves as a reminder of the painful consequences of insisting on resolution and formulating policy, particularly policy perceived as exclusionary.

The Promise and Tyranny of Structurelessness

WOW was a respite from the ugliness of the outside world; it was about respect. I loved it there, but I was afraid of the collective aspect and ill-at-ease amongst those folks.

—RENO, 2001

Looking at WOW in the early 2000s is instructive regarding what Griffiths has called its "hiccups" over the years and what others would call its "failures." In late 2001 a group of eight women representing a diverse mix of WOW's membership gathered for a conversation.[39] Most said they were at WOW because "we fell for the pre-show talk," although two of them had sought out WOW after learning about it in college from work that had been published by and about WOW artists. All agreed they had been surprised to find no one in charge when they showed up for their first meeting. Basically, the operation runs on sweat equity, which in its simplest form means "if you work on my show, I'll work on yours." The group explained that "people show up for the people who have shown up for them."

For years WOW has operated on a list of procedures that fit on a single sheet of paper, a spirit that continues today. Each show has a designated producer, a role that must be filled by a woman. The producer is responsible for every aspect of the show except managing the house (box office, ushers, and so on), which is provided by the collective. Each producer takes 50 percent of her show's box-office receipts to cover production expenses and returns 50 percent to the collective (for rent, utilities, insurance, and other shared expenses). If the producer brings in an outside show, the producer receives 10 percent of the box-office receipts, the outside group gets 40 percent, and 50 percent is returned to the collective. Thanks in part to the city's secondhand shops, Dumpsters, and an organization called Material for the Arts (MFTA)—where nonprofit arts organizations can "shop" for and acquire new and used supplies for free—a typical WOW production can be mounted for roughly seven hundred to a thousand dollars. The space operates on a budget of about fifteen to seventeen thousand dollars a year.

Time is WOW's most precious commodity, time for artists to present work in the space. Each summer over the Fourth of July, WOW holds a three-day retreat consisting of long meetings during which production time for the coming season is allocated and other major decisions are made. For many years the retreat was held about three hours outside of Monticello, New York, on land known as Beechwood—the former home of the late Barbara Deming, a renowned lesbian peace activist. Active and inactive members alike are welcome to attend this retreat, including new members who have just joined the group. As many as twenty-five members typically take part. They pitch tents, work hard, and play avidly. The schedule for the upcoming season is determined on the basis of two criteria: a collective member's seniority and the amount of sweat equity she has contributed to productions in the past. A selection committee is made up of those who are not requesting production time for the coming year. Proposals are submitted before the retreat that list preferred dates, amount of time requested, and past contributions. A member may request four weeks in April, for example, but get two weeks in February, her second or third choice. Those members who are allocated production time are then assigned house management responsibility for the same number of weeks on other shows during the season.

Productions run back-to-back at WOW from Thursday to Sunday nearly year-round. In keeping with its origins, the season typically includes a festival of new work that might be coproduced by two collective members and usually runs for three to four weeks. Festivals provide opportunities for those members not allocated a time slot in the regular season to present work. After-hours cabarets and late-night shows like "The Service Economy Vaudeville Cabaret" and "HyperGender Burlesque" are scheduled at 10:30 and provide further opportunities. On the first Friday of every month a cabaret called "Rivers of Honey" features primarily the work of black women and transpeople of color. A Latin cabaret on Saturday nights features primarily the work of Latinas, and a drag cabaret is presented on the third Friday of every month.[40] During the 2001–2 season, for example, more than a dozen productions were presented in addition to two festivals and two regularly scheduled late-night cabarets.

In more recent years shows have typically not been presented in July and August because the weather is too hot and the air conditioner too noisy, although weekly meetings continue, rehearsals for fall shows begin, and outside groups might perform. There is a rule of thumb for the amount of rehearsal time a production is allocated in the space before it opens, but, like other guidelines at WOW, this is negotiable among producers. Rehearsals in the space must end by 5:00 on show nights; current shows have priority on Wednesday nights for a pickup rehearsal; and Tuesday night rehearsals cannot begin before 8:00, by which time the 6:30 meeting of the collective will have concluded. To the greatest extent possible, each producer has final decision-making power regarding her show. She is expected to attend Tuesday evening meetings for six weeks before her production opens, as well as during the run of her show and the week after. Each producer is responsible for leaving the space in better shape than she found it, which includes a "producer's gift," which can take the form of sewing the blacks (curtains), fixing equipment, painting the ceiling, or purchasing an item for the space from the collective's wish list. At every retreat the group reflects on what worked and did not work operationally during the previous season, but as a general rule they do not critique individual shows on aesthetic, political, or any other grounds.

Traditionally, this is the sum total of WOW's operating procedures. WOW functions as a single venue in which a series of independently produced events are presented. Shows have often closed on Saturday so the next show has a day to load in, allowing for more ambitious sets and higher production values. Because many of the same people work across productions, opportunities abound for creative cross-fertilization. Throughout the season and during retreats, WOW members build bonds with each other and partnerships emerge—some would call these "cliques." During the 1980s, for instance, each member of the Five Lesbian Brothers arrived at WOW independently, and the company grew out of affinities that developed through working together in a number of contexts over time. An environment that attempts to remain as judgment free as possible fosters collaboration. One of the first dimensions of WOW's anarchic impulse was to resist exclusionary practices. Although this goal has never been perfectly met, and over the years some women have felt that WOW let them down, there exists a desire and continual recommitment to operate as supportively and nonjudgmentally as possible. Nevertheless, an abundance of opportunities for making and showing work also means ample occasions for conflict to arise.

During the group interview with eight members of the collective in late 2001, WOW's overall atmosphere was described as supportive, upbeat, lively, and fun, but the group admitted to occasional "blowups" at meetings. When this occurs, they explained, the collective takes an immediate time-out. The parties involved might engage a mediator, separate from the meeting, to help them work through the issue. The collective keeps a list of available mediators from among the collective's membership for these occasions. Mediators are members who have undergone instruction in the mediation process, provided by a group called Volunteer Lawyers for the Arts, which offers free training workshops in mediation skills. Members feel that "the group mind gets healthier" over time through this practice—that is, fewer "poisonous agendas" arise. The group can then focus on the common bond that unites them, which they described as "a basic commitment to the survival of the space, acknowledging its history while imagining a future."[41]

Poisonous agendas were defined by the group as encompassing any issue that serves to alienate people by stirring things up for the sake of stirring them up. For instance, someone might bring an agenda item to the table masquerading as an issue that is really intended to fill an unconscious, emotional, attention-getting, or power-wielding need. The group recalled one meeting at which someone "fled the room in tears." Following the outburst, there was a minute of heartfelt silence. Someone said genuinely, "That was deep." Then someone else asked, "What's next on the agenda?" In other words, moments like these do not paralyze the collective. Instead, there is a commitment to problem solving and mediation, but when that is not possible the group moves forward. As choreographer and performer Jen Abrams put it, "WOW is more of an organism than an organization. You have to surf it." Another member agreed, noting, "We manage to reach an amazing amount of consensus."[42]

A member can receive a penalty for not meeting her responsibilities as a producer or house manager. She might lose a few weeks to produce in the following season or she might lose her slot to produce altogether.[43] Determined at retreats, penalties are rare, however. They are meted out only for egregious lapses like showing up to house-manage drunk or treating spectators poorly. "You cannot be penalized for being a pain in the ass," the group agreed, "but you can be penalized for not meeting responsibilities." The group also agreed that members "may decide to leave the collective, but no one can be kicked out." This was not always the case. In the mid-1980s, the collective's insistence on minimal rules proved inadequate to address a complex interpersonal situation and brought to light the dynamics underpinning a vacuum in leadership. WOW's anarchical approach had failed its members in a particularly unfortunate episode that revealed the potential for injustice embedded in a notion of nonhierarchical "structurelessness" as an ideal.

In 1973 the feminist author and activist, Joreen (aka Jo Freeman) published an essay entitled "The Tyranny of Structurelessness" in an attempt to debunk a widely held belief within feminism that an organization could operate without anyone or any group in charge. The idea of leaderless, structureless groups had been the foundation of consciousness-raising and eventually evolved to the point where structurelessness became the dominant organizational principle of the women's movement. The essay argued that "structurelessness becomes a way of masking power" and maintained that in any organization there is always someone or some group implicitly if not explicitly in charge.[44] The group interviewed in 2001 confirmed that certain members are "listened to more" than others, but all agreed that this is simply a function of longevity and expertise. In their words, these are "pillars of the community" that have the longest history with WOW (which could be as few as three years). Such "veteran" members are the ones to whom new members turn for mentoring, which is described as "going on all over the place." They admit that those who assume an inordinate amount of responsibility at any given time are perceived as having more power, but in fact they have no more say in decision making than any other member.[45]

The ability of WOW's structureless approach to succeed in a sustained way has evolved. The commitment has always been there, but for a variety of reasons the collective's lack of formal structure has not always been productive. As two of the four original founders, Weaver and Shaw played unarticulated leadership roles during the 1980s both behind the scenes and more publicly—some would say by design, while others would say by default. Hughes remembers that the two played a pivotal role in the decision-making process: "Lois and Peggy were persuasive at meetings. There was a collaborative sense to it, but a pure cooperative model it wasn't. It may have been complicated and murky, but it worked!" All four of WOW's original producers were "first among equals" in the new space; the storefront's lease was in Pamela Camhe's name. Of the founders, Hughes recalls, "They were like one word exhaled in a single breath, 'Jordy-Pamela-Peggy-Lois.' "[46]

Camhe and Mark eventually withdrew from the organization. The reasons for this outcome are complex, but one of them had to do with a nuanced understanding of what WOW was and should be. For Camhe and Mark the emphasis was slightly more on the social aspects of WOW in the sense of it being a community center, a café, or a club that included performances. For Shaw and Weaver WOW was centered on performance, with a community revolving around it and emerging from it. The conflicts that arose among the founders as a consequence of differing visions were in many ways typical of any organization as power dynamics evolve and shift over time. Camhe and Mark decided that it was better for WOW to survive than for it to end because of conflicts among the founders.

Camhe and Mark's decision to withdraw allowed Shaw and Weaver's perspective to prevail, but there were other reasons Shaw and Weaver were perceived as leaders. According to stage manager and producer Alice Forrester, Shaw and Weaver operated out of an especially demanding work ethic and contributed an extraordinary amount of labor to the organization. For example, in 1985 when escalating commercial rents forced WOW to move from the storefront into abandoned factory space, Shaw had taken on the crucial, arduous responsibility for identifying and acquiring new space. Betsy Crenshaw was a new member and had dropped by to take a look at WOW's new theater. "I thought Peggy and Lois were two of the most extraordinary artists I'd ever seen perform," she remembers. "And there they were just head-to-toe covered with filth, up to their elbows scrubbing the place down. It made a real impression on me—I had thought these were the *stars* of WOW."[47]

In addition to their labor, by the time WOW had settled into the storefront in 1982, the Split Britches troupe (Deb Margolin, Shaw, and Weaver) had established a reputation beyond the collective. Their play *Split Britches* was an acknowledged critical success, soon to be widely recognized as a turning point in feminist theater, and the troupe had already mounted its second play, *Beauty and the Beast,* at another venue. Lighting designer Joni Wong worked extensively both with Split Britches and at WOW. "They had the vision," she recalled of Weaver and Shaw. "The vision was in their theater work, which inspired the work of others. They were leading by example, not imposing an aesthetic."[48] A number of WOW artists have agreed that the work of Split Britches influenced their own developing aesthetic; many looked to Weaver and Shaw as role models and mentors.

Weaver was also central to one of the practices at WOW that fostered creativity and innovation throughout the collective and beyond—teaching. Workshops had been offered during WOW's first two festivals and in the months between them, a custom that continued in the new space. For example, the stand-up comic Margaret Smith, who had already headlined major clubs and appeared on the *David Letterman Show,* taught a class at WOW in comedy writing. Established writers and performers like Smith were brought in from time to time, but Weaver herself offered workshops and classes on an ongoing basis in performance strategies and techniques. Of her teaching, Weaver has said that she is committed to creating "a space where women feel safe enough to create. It's about encouraging people to believe its okay to explore any little impulse that opens up expressiveness." Weaver offered workshops on a variety of topics. "I did a workshop called 'acting on impulse,'" she recalled. "It was all about freeing up the associative part of the brain and the associative creativity within us . . . you could work on impulse and out of image. You didn't have to work on a cognitive idea of text . . . or psychological aspects of character."[49] Because most of WOW's participants have studied with Weaver over the years, her influence has been widespread. Weaver's approach is so individual and open that the work that has emerged from it is often quite unlike her own. Once a student of both Weaver and Margaret Smith, Hughes is an example of an artist who developed her aesthetic in a different direction and subsequently offered her own writing workshops at WOW. Shaw was also central to the development of new work. As an endlessly enthusiastic cheerleader—"Come on, step up. You can do it!"—she encouraged women to perform and make their own work. It was in this spirit that Shaw first pushed Alina Troyano onstage, where Carmelita Tropicana was born.

Shaw and Weaver may not have wanted to run the show, as it were, but in many ways they did by the very nature of their talent, experience, and contributions. Most would say that Shaw and Weaver resisted throwing their weight around and that any power attending the roles they played had been accrued by default. But other members have argued that Shaw and Weaver welcomed their unspoken status in the collective and manipulated that power. Ultimately, WOW has survived and thrived in large part because of Weaver and Shaw's initial vision, their early contributions, and their ongoing attention. However, the strength, leadership qualities, and mentoring activities of WOW's many other participants cannot be glossed over and devalued. After all, WOW continued to operate productively when Shaw and Weaver were away on tour for months at a time during the early years. And the theater continued to be enormously productive as Weaver and Shaw gradually became less active members during the 1990s. For WOW's twentieth anniversary event in 2000, Shaw and Weaver returned to perform. Weaver cohosted the evening with Alina Troyano, and Shaw helped move equipment, furniture, and props on and offstage between acts.

Wong believes that the ways in which Shaw and Weaver were perceived as leaders during the early years had something to do with the expectations people brought to the space. "If you saw WOW as a 'home,' " she explains, "which it could be, then Lois and Peggy were parents." Forrester agrees with this assessment: "Peggy and Lois were generous and warm, but if you thought of them as parents then they could be encouraging, loving parents or rejecting, disapproving parents depending on what you brought in terms of expectations." When Shaw dropped into a rehearsal for *Queer Justice*—a production Weaver was directing in 1990 with other collective members—one of the performers, Babs Davy, happened to be rehearsing her song in the show. At the end of the rehearsal, Davy recalled, Shaw gave her some suggestions that Davy found especially useful.[50] She appreciated Shaw's help as a supportive colleague and mentor, but other performers might have interpreted it as arrogant or intrusive or as indicating disapproval. Kathy Rey has referred to WOW as a "mom-and-pop operation," and it is easy to imagine how Weaver and Shaw might be considered its femme/butch matriarchs.

Sarah Schulman, a talented artist who would become an important and widely published writer and novelist in the 1990s, spotted the potential for tyranny in WOW's structurelessness. She was not alone in her concerns and wanted to do something about it. "There was discomfort at times around Lois and Peggy's undefined leadership roles," Hughes recalled. "It was anxiety making for people because the rules weren't explicit. Sarah had a persuasive argument. She wanted to make it explicit that they were the leaders and vote on it or vote to rotate leadership depending on who was running a particular production." In the end, however, Schulman—who had three of her plays produced at WOW—was dropped from the collective's membership. According to Griffiths there was no mechanism in place to deal with major conflicts. "Sarah and a couple of others had really, really rough passages," she recalled. "What happened to Sarah was complicated, and WOW was not set up to deal with complexity."[51]

In retrospect, Schulman views WOW as what she calls "a psychological cult" where loyalty and a particular aesthetic were expected and demanded. "If you didn't spend every minute there," she said, "you would be ostracized."[52] Given Forrester's anecdote about walking away from her former life and never going back, it is not difficult to imagine how WOW could be considered all consuming. Schulman's theory of WOW as a cult resonates with the notion of WOW as a family, and she makes an important point in this regard. In 1992 she wrote, "I think lesbian vulnerability to group-think, gang mentality and conformity arises from our profound rejection experiences from our families. Ten years later, I can see clearly why lesbians would get caught up in that kind of group mentality—some kind of combination of self-loathing and the desire to be accepted by a family."[53] In other words, not all of WOW's wayward girls were wayward by choice. WOW's collective celebrated every holiday as a group in part because so many members had nowhere else to go, no family to return to.

Like many others, Schulman was caught in the crosshairs of WOW's ever-changing position on issues. "My problems with WOW began in 1985, when I was chastised for having a man in my play," she wrote. "My second problem arose when I was criticized for not writing in the WOW style."[54] She saw the cumulative effect of such conflicts as a means of keeping members in line. "There are long lines of lesbian artists who have been bullied, slandered and damaged by WOW. The group dynamic there is dependent on human sacrifice—there is a kind of victim-of-the-year mentality required to keep the hard-core cult members bonded, first by ganging up against someone and feeling superior to them and united against them and second by reaffirming the lack of aesthetic tolerance and variety."[55] Of course, every member's experience of WOW is legitimate. Following the collective's 2002 retreat, long-time WOW member Sharon Jane Smith complimented members of the "new generation" on their mediation process and pointed out that it was an improvement over the kind of "pack action" that had sometimes existed in the past.[56]

There are as many interpretations of what happened in Schulman's case as there are collective members who were involved. At the time, the collective believed—perhaps erroneously—that it was in the position of having to choose between Schulman and another member of the collective. "It was a case of the work and people's personal lives getting kind of muddy," Griffiths recalled. "None of us had the tools to figure out how to separate them and the best way to deal with what happened."[57] Whatever the specifics, the situation made clear the need for WOW to establish a mechanism to facilitate mediation, something that would not happen in a formal way for several years. Until then, in the spirit of consciousness-raising, special meetings were called from time to time to air and "process" difficulties among members.

The playwright Terry Diamond also had a difficult experience with WOW. She had served on the productions of several other members of the collective, but when she was assigned a slot for her own show in 1991 only one member stepped forward to work on it, Babs Davy. Diamond decided to mount her play anyway. She ran an ad in the trade publication *Back Stage* and brought in people from outside the collective to perform, direct, and provide labor. This "outside" director caused problems for Davy, however, so she eventually quit the production. The show went on, but after it closed Davy asked for a special meeting of the collective to address and process what had happened. Diamond felt the purpose of the meeting was primarily to condemn her, so she decided not to attend. The meeting focused, yet again, on the issue of outsiders participating in productions. Shortly thereafter Diamond self-selected out of WOW and walked away from the collective. In a 2002 interview, Diamond reflected on the events. She did not believe WOW was a cult or that an aesthetic had been imposed on her, but she did feel that Shaw and Weaver were pulling strings behind the scenes. "You had to make an alliance with Peggy and Lois," she recalled, "and if you couldn't then you were screwed and treated shabbily." As Diamond described it, "There was a pecking order, a hierarchy, and stars. Lip service was paid to collective action, but it didn't feel like collective action."[58] Even those organizations that are formally structured typically have informal, behind-the-scenes processes through which alliances are formed and things are accomplished. For whatever reasons, WOW's organizational structure did not work for Diamond.

The playwright Madeleine Olnek remains enthusiastic about WOW despite her own wrenching experience when the collective asked her to fill a slot and then decided to cancel her show. Over the years many women have had their difficulties with WOW, but ultimately they have found the collective worthwhile enough to continue to work there or to return after a hiatus. Eventually women have moved on—the collective's membership is continuously in flux. The scholar Amy Robinson has pointed out that "Acts of betrayal have been and will continue to be a part of feminist collaborations. In part it is to perform the costs of feminist alliance in the same space as their possibility, to refuse the fantasy of an 'outside' to a space of collaboration."[59]

A Collective for the 1980s and Beyond

The Cuts grrrls are thrilled to be bringing their heartfelt piece of theatre to WOW, a women-run collective that has been nurturing queer and feminist performance since before some of the cast members were born!
—*She Cuts Herself/She Likes to Write*, PRESS RELEASE, 2001

Although respect and tolerance for ideological conflict was a more or less conscious goal from WOW's beginnings, this was not always the case among the collective's members when it came to emotional distance or maintaining emotional boundaries. WOW is about desire—desire for autonomy, desire

for voice, desire to play, desire for community, desire for sex, desire to create—and developing a capacity to act on desire. On this subject the scholar
and critic Alisa Solomon quoted Shaw in the *Village Voice* following WOW's
twentieth anniversary celebration in 2000: "'Desire isn't enough by itself,'
says Shaw, recalling why WOW sought out a permanent location in the first
place. 'You have to have space where desire can be formed.'"[60] Of her initial
experiences with WOW, Hughes echoed this notion: "I don't know who I am
yet—I'm not a performance artist—nevertheless, I am determined to express
myself. I'm sure that here at WOW I'll be able to develop a self worth expressing. WOW isn't sure who she is yet, either."[61] In contrast to the sup-
pression women experienced in dominant, mainstream society, WOW
fulfilled so many desires that a certain amount of emotional overinvestment
is understandable.

Maintaining emotional boundaries was further complicated by the fact
that so many of WOW's members were having sex with each other. This in itself was unusual and daring during the 1980s, a time when even within some
feminist circles sex for women was assumed to be less central to their lives,
less focused on orgasm, or of a more spiritual nature. WOW women were
acting on sexual desire with a vengeance, and those who were not acting on
such desire could not help but be swept up in the erotically charged atmosphere. "I didn't think of what I was doing as theater," Hughes wrote. "Theater was something that happened in a different neighborhood. . . . What I
thought I was doing was falling in love. With about twenty-five women at the
same time. I did this theater thing because that's what they were all doing. If
it had been skeet shooting, I'd be out there screaming: 'Pull!'" Forrester explained it this way: "You didn't have to be a lesbian or sleep with another
woman, but you had to buy into the idea of it as a possibility."[62] What
emerged from this practice was not only an over-the-top emotional invest-
ment on a personal level but a perspective that came to typify the world of
WOW, influencing work on an aesthetic level. There is an enduring adage at
WOW: "They come for the girls and stay for the theater."

For some WOW participants, the collective provided the social closeness
and comfort of community. Because WOW is structured more like a city—
where it is possible for multiple cultural expressions to be in play—doors remain open for those who do not feel an absence of community among
women in their lives and do not seek community through WOW. Hughes
may have joined WOW for the love of women and been as happy to engage

in skeet shooting as theater, but it is entirely possible for women to join WOW primarily to make theater.

In the broadest possible sense of the term, *theater* is what WOW has always been about. *Theater* presumes both the physical space of an embodied event and the symbolic, discursive space of performance. But like the use of the French military term *avant-garde* to describe progressive artwork, a definition of *theater* as space might most appropriately be a military one. Just as "the European theater" designated all continental land, sea, and air where military operations were carried out during the world wars, WOW's theater designates an urban site of cultural production where the operations of agency are played out among women. It is through this notion of theater that WOW has created feminist space wherever it is located and whatever its activities—be they theme parties, festivals, meetings, performances, or simply hanging out.

As they muddle through WOW's complexities, celebrating its triumphs and enduring its struggles and failures, the collective engages in an activity that constitutes a crucial condition of WOW's productivity and longevity—play. To cite but one example, in June 2002 the theater held a Second Chance Prom, otherwise known as "the prom you wished you'd had." The event was billed as a "pan-queer, gender-radical party. All women, men, and others welcome! Bring your friends! Bring your enemies! Sir Real and special surprise celebrity guests will be performing throughout the night. Don't miss the crowning of the King and Queen!"[63] Performing both its costs and possibilities, WOW has worked and played its heart out in ways that have been both painful and hopeful over its three decades.

Chapter 5

Staging the Unimaginable: New York's East Village Club Scene

The mind . . . shouldn't be able to make up anything that wasn't there to start with, that didn't enter it from experience, from the real world. Imagination can't create anything new. . . . It only recycles bits and pieces from the world and reassembles them into visions. . . . [I]t's really only the same old ordinariness and falseness rearranged into the appearance of novelty and truth. Nothing unknown is knowable.

—TONY KUSHNER, *Angels in America*, 1992

For many women at WOW, the storefront on E. Eleventh Street in the East Village was the equivalent of Virginia Woolf's "room of one's own." Desire is not enough. As WOW cofounder Peggy Shaw has reminded us, "You have to have a space where desire can be formed."[1] But desire and space alone are not enough. Woolf was also calling for space of a different kind for women—that is, representational space, a place in the world of signs and symbols where women can be players *on their own terms*. Historically, limiting women's access to public and private space has been a powerful way of curtailing their desires and ambitions. But by far the most effective means of undermining women's capacity as individuals for self-realization and their right to self-governance has been eliding their agency as speaking subjects, as opposed to silent objects, in representation. "Humanity is male," the philosopher Simone de Beauvoir wrote more than half a century ago, "and man defines woman not in herself but as relative to him; she is not regarded as an autonomous being. . . . He is the Subject . . . she is the Other."[2] Woolf described the instrumental nature of this "otherness" in an image that captures woman's unique position in representation as being ubiquitously present and utterly absent. "Women have served all these centuries," wrote Woolf, "as looking glasses possessing the magic and delicious power of reflecting the figure of man at twice its natural size."[3]

Ideologies of gender and racial difference have produced a paradox in which women are simultaneously visible and invisible, overrepresented and underrepresented, an egregious convolution that feminists from de Beauvoir to the poet and essayist Audre Lorde have worked to expose and rectify. WOW makes a contribution to this project, which is what makes the theater's work so important—as important as work recognized and included in the legitimizing canons of both mainstream and avant-garde performance. Establishing a place to make work was exciting, presenting pieces by and for women was thrilling, but opening a space in representation for women as speaking subjects and thereby making it possible for women to represent themselves on their own terms was breathtaking and groundbreaking. As Harvard scholar Robin Bernstein has put it, "Work coming out of WOW made it possible to think thoughts previously unthinkable."[4]

Sociological versus Aesthetic Significance

NYC, downtown, the eighties. . . . Clubs and art galleries flourished. It was the best of times: Art was more about process than product, more about esthetic edification than career, more about transgression than mainstream assimilation.
—ALINA TROYANO, 2000

By 1984 WOW was attracting attention by association with a novel and exciting development in its neighborhood—the opening of several bars as performance venues known collectively as "the East Village club scene." An aura of intrigue surrounded the clubs in general, which had as much to do with economics and geography as aesthetic production. East Village rents were low, but the cheapest rents could be found east of Avenue A, where the Pyramid Cocktail Lounge (1981), the Limbo Lounge (1982), 8BC (1983), Darinka (1984), and Club Chandalier (1984) were located. Known as Alphabet City, the easternmost part of the East Village spans Avenues A, B, C, and D to the East River. In the early 1980s the area exemplified urban blight; much of it was in ruins, with nary a block free of crumbling, burned-out structures and vacant, boarded-up buildings.

Late in 1984 a scholarly publication devoted to avant-garde performance, the *Drama Review* (*TDR*), became interested in what was going on in Alphabet City. The journal sent a number of writers out on a single night to cover the clubs for a special issue devoted to East Village performance. Through this experience I was introduced to a wholly new kind of women's theater. Like so many others stumbling on WOW for the first time, I had never seen anything like it. In his introduction to the issue, the editor, Michael Kirby, questioned the status of East Village performance as "a new and significant artistic movement in theatre." He concluded, "It may be, however, that the sociological aspects of this performance phenomenon are more important than the aesthetic ones."[5] Kirby was right in the sense that the aesthetic emerging from the clubs was not significantly different from, for instance, Theatre of the Ridiculous and the work of such established avant-garde artists as Jack Smith or groups such as Hot Peaches.

What eluded Kirby, though, was the way in which an intersection of sociology and cultural production representing heretofore elided subjectivities might produce in WOW an aesthetic significantly different from that of other East Village venues. By the time the issue was published in the spring of 1985, some of the clubs had closed. Most were gone by the end of that year. WOW endured, its fleeting association with the clubs a mixed blessing. On the one hand, it is entirely possible that in the absence of the club scene WOW would have continued to operate under the radar of spectators who might otherwise have missed it altogether. On the other hand, because of its status as a player on the club scene, WOW was subsumed within critical circles by a larger, more recognizable aesthetic that diminished its roots in the previous decade's feminism.

When critic Don Shewey's hopefully titled article "Gay Theatre Grows Up" appeared in 1988, the East Village clubs had long since closed. He wrote, "Holly Hughes emerged from New York's East Village club scene, which has nurtured art stars . . . as well as any number of young performance artists who mix dance, theatre, music and video with outspoken gay content."[6] Specifically, Hughes emerged from, was nurtured by, and grew up at WOW, but her legitimacy is granted by virtue of an enterprise deemed weightier than women's theater, her entrée to the category of "gay theater" secured through her association with the clubs. This shift in perspective "disappears" the singular aesthetic developed at WOW in the early 1980s and has profound consequences for understanding WOW's larger significance.

Ten years after Kirby suggested that the East Village club scene's sociology might be more significant than its contribution to the aesthetics of avant-garde performance, the theater critic Clive Barnes came to the following conclusion in his New York Post review of a production by the Five Lesbian Brothers: "The whole farrago is mildly amusing, but for most non-lesbian brothers, sisters and other family members it is likely to be more rewarding as a cleverly expressed social phenomenon than an artistic event."[7] In calling the performance a "farrago"—a confused hodgepodge—Barnes demonstrates his inability to read the performance on its own terms. The play he reviewed, *The Secretaries*, is one of the most important pieces in the repertoire of the Five Lesbian Brothers. Aesthetically it is one of the most significant productions in the annals of contemporary theater production overall, as well as what theater scholar David Savran has called the new American queer theater.

Virtually everything that characterized the East Village club phenomenon was also true of WOW. An "anything goes" ambience permeated club performances made by a generation of artists weaned on television sitcoms, talk shows, soap operas, and commercials. Performances commented on mainstream culture through riotous, scathing, yet loving parodies of its popular forms. Performers adopted personas that they sometimes played both on- and offstage, and most performers felt no compunction about dropping character altogether to comment on the persona itself. Unlike much avant-garde theater at the time, club performances returned narrative to the stage and in such a way that the most serious content could be fodder for outrageous comedy. Performers explored and exploited the furthest reaches of "not for prime time" material, mining forbidden, taboo subject matter for its inherent and often hilarious contradictions. They treated the prevailing culture's most sacred symbols and institutions with wild, irreverent abandon. One identifying characteristic of the club phenomenon *not* endemic to WOW, however, was a preponderance of men in drag—both gay and straight—descendants of the theatrical traditions of Andy Warhol's Factory, Charles Ludlam's Ridiculous Theatrical Company, and the work of Hot Peaches and Jack Smith.[8]

The clubs featured fringe artists performing for a largely fringe East Village audience until media attention began attracting what was caustically referred to as the B&T (bridge and tunnel) crowd—sophisticates from New Jersey and Long Island in search of the latest, most obscure, and hippest trends. Some of the better-known performers on the scene included Charles Busch, Ethyl Eichelberger, John Jesurun, John Kelly, Beth Lapides, Ann Magnuson, Tom Murrin (aka the Alien Comic), and John Zorn. Before landing off-Broadway, Busch's *Vampire Lesbians of Sodom* played the Limbo Lounge. The clubs typically mounted several different performances a night as spectators hopped from bar to bar and show to show until the wee hours of the morning. Many performers traveled as well, playing the early show at one bar and the late show at another.

WOW performers also traveled to perform in a number of clubs, and their audience followed them to these venues. For several reasons WOW's storefront space, however, was not a destination for barhoppers on the club circuit: first, it was not a bar but rather a theater masquerading as a "café"; second, it was located on the edges of Alphabet City; and, third, it was considered "women's theater." As a performance space devoted to and marked by women's theater, WOW remained on the margins of this marginalized scene, a ghetto within a ghetto. Nonetheless, it was very much a part of the overall scene. The Limbo Lounge presented a festival entitled BOW-WOW co-curated and coproduced with WOW in 1983. Hughes's infamous play *The Well of Horniness* played a series of one-night stands at nearly every East Village club with its all-WOW cast, and performance artist Alina Troyano's persona Carmelita Tropicana was a regular at Club Chandalier.

By the summer of 1985, a few months before the club scene was exhausted and relegated to history, a celebratory article appeared in the *Village Voice*. The journalist Kathleen Conkey described East Village performance in general and WOW's aesthetic in particular as "the triumph of the drag queen aesthetic, but new and improved! Once the province of a gay male fringe, drag is influencing a new generation—male and female, straight and gay."[9] The role that 1970s radical feminism had played in launching WOW's sensibility and politics had already been lost to cultural memory. Enormously frustrated by Conkey's assessment of WOW, Shaw wrote a letter to the editor in an attempt to set the record straight. "Conkey based her description on the sick premise that we feel free enough to adopt the men's drag scene," she wrote. "That is not what WOW, a performance space by and for women, is about. We're not uptight about being associated with drag queens—we're all in this together . . . but drag is not our aesthetic. Conkey hyped up the Café into a drag club, ignoring the fact that we've produced hundreds of shows."[10] Shaw made a forceful claim for what WOW's aesthetic is *not*, but she did not articulate what in fact made it so different from drag performance in the clubs—a task that would have been far from simple.

As C. Carr, a major chronicler of the club scene for the *Village Voice,* put it at the time, "There is simply no precedent for much of the work I've seen at WOW Café over the years."[11] Like any phenomenon that exceeds the boundaries of current critical understanding in the Foucauldian sense of that which "disturbs what was previously considered immobile," it takes time to develop the framework and vocabulary necessary to adequately describe it.[12] As performers in the East Village explored and performed forbidden, taboo subjects, WOW pushed the impulse further, opening up an as yet unimaginable representational space. WOW was staging *as subjects* those who embody an otherwise gendered status as objects, rescuing them from their position in representation as solely in relation to something or somebody else.

To get at what was being staged at WOW during the heyday of the club scene, I'll describe my own initial encounter with it in 1984. How can the ephemeral experience of performances attended decades ago be salvageable when recent events have already been lost to memory? Partly because they are documented in the *Drama Review* but also because the experience of WOW engendered in me an epiphany of sorts. Like details experienced in slow-motion clarity during a life-threatening event, it may be that life-altering ones also remain somehow more readily retrievable. A decade earlier, in 1973, I had experienced an equally transformative performance when I saw Charles Ludlam's play *Camille*. I followed the original production as well as its periodic revivals from venue to venue, taking along everyone who came to town to visit, including my then teenage sister. (Years later this sister, Babs, would join WOW and become a founding member of the Five Lesbian Brothers.) I compare my first experience of Ludlam's work with my first encounter with WOW to differentiate WOW's unique aesthetic and make the case for its significance.

Ludlam's work was clearly an influence on much of the performance that took place in the East Village clubs. The work created and produced at WOW has repeatedly been compared to Ludlam's theater. For instance, in 1994 Barnes wrote, "Unfortunately, *The Secretaries,* for all its topsy-turvy logic and good humor, does miss the vitality and ludicrous genius of Ludlam and his motley crew."[13] Invoking Ludlam's artistic approach here helps to illuminate the ways in which WOW's aesthetic is both like and unlike "East Village performance." More than ten years separated my viewing of *Camille* from the night I crossed WOW's threshold. Because audience response is inseparable from the meanings any performance elicits, it is important to note that as an only recently out lesbian at the time, I experienced WOW from essentially the same psychosocial perspective as I experienced *Camille*—that of a straight, white, middle-class woman. By the time I took a seat at WOW, however, I had attended a wide range of alternative theater work. I was keenly aware of the ways in which practitioners of the avant-garde had been grappling with how the experience of performance might productively alter ingrained patterns and habits of thought and emotion with an ultimate goal of altering consciousness itself. By the end of that first evening at WOW, at some gut level I felt this tiny women's theater had blown the lid off this project.

Because by definition performance is constituted in the dynamics of a mutual encounter in place and time, I attempt to capture here some semblance of the performances themselves. I read them back through an admittedly different sensibility, marking with broad brushstrokes my social positioning and concomitant state of consciousness at the time—the feminist critic as spectator, to invert Princeton scholar and author Jill Dolan's illustrious phrase.[14] Others seated with me in the audience certainly experienced these performances differently. The following section maps the contours of reception, unpacks the way an aesthetic "works," and in the process hopes to demonstrate the genius that is both WOW and Charles Ludlam.

"Chick Chat" versus Camille

Lesbian desire is a country without a language of its own.
—HOLLY HUGHES, 1996

The theater is a humble materialistic enterprise which seeks to produce riches of the imagination, not the other way around. The theater is an event, not an object. Theater workers need not blush and conceal their desperate struggle to pay the landlords their rents. Theater without the stink of art.
—CHARLES LUDLAM, "Manifesto: Ridiculous Theatre, Scourge of Human Folly," 1975

On the evening of November 30, 1984, Jill Dolan and I set out for the East Village, where, along with a number of others affiliated with the *Drama Review,* we were to witness and document performances in the clubs.[15] We started at WOW, where I had been assigned, then headed to the late show at Club Chandalier, where Dolan was covering something called *Carmelita Tropicana Chats.* As someone who did not travel in WOW's circles, I had found it challenging to determine if a performance was being offered at all on the designated night. I had checked listings in the local press—not there; directory assistance was a dead end—no phone. Word of mouth was WOW's primary vehicle for publicity along with flyers distributed around the neighborhood. One of my colleagues recalled that WOW referred to itself as "WOW at 330," and another thought it was located on E. Eleventh Street. Eventually I walked by the theater; without the street number, I would have been stymied. An unadorned announcement of coming events was handwritten on a piece of cardboard and taped to the inside of the storefront's picture window. On November 30, *Heart of the Scorpion* would be playing, "written, directed, and starring Alice Forrester"; the show was billed as "a Harlequin romance for the girls."

What appeared to be utter chaos that evening turned out to be typical of WOW. No one seemed to mind. As well-mannered theatergoers, Dolan and I arrived ten minutes early for a show scheduled to begin at 8:00. No one was outside the storefront, and the door was locked. In response to my knock, a woman poked her head through a crack in the door and explained that a rehearsal was going on; the show would begin at 8:30. When I asked if it would be alright to take photographs during the performance, she said she would have to check with the director. "No, no!" a voice from behind her barked. "The stage manager handles that." "Okay," the woman behind the door said. She turned to head back into the space, stopped, and asked, "Who's the stage manager?"

Women began to congregate on the sidewalk, smoking and chatting until the theater finally opened at 8:30. Dolan and I were the odd girls out—everyone seemed to know each other. We entered the dark doorway and paid five dollars admission at a slip of a table lit by a bare, glaring lightbulb. Apparently not everyone expected the show to begin on time; some arrived just before it actually did start at 9:00. WOW operated on what I would later learn is referred to as "lesbian time." The tiny space was crammed with about twenty-five women sporting a mishmash of sartorial styles from butch and femme to leather dyke to retro flower child. Everyone was chatting and waving acknowledgment to each other across the seating section—a space about ten feet wide and twenty feet deep. Gray metal folding chairs in rows of four each had the names of ostensibly supportive donors printed on their backs in block letters—"Katharine Hepburn," for example—a small conceit marking the theater as self-aware of its institutional status by commenting on its lack thereof. Although no food or beverages were served in this "café," an intimate, social club ambience permeated the space.

According to the evening's program notes, which were printed on hot pink paper, the play was about "romantic notions," described as "every mother's wish for her little girl . . . to find that perfect woman . . . run away to the Greek islands . . . and live happily ever after." The sound of traditional Greek music signaled the start of the show and provided background for a short film shot as though the viewer is looking out the side window of a car traveling down a tree-lined street. In the accompanying voice-over, a woman recited a corny monologue wistfully and longingly about the meaning of "home." The car reached its destination, and the camera panned from a house to a full-length shot of a white horse in the yard. The horse walked directly up to the camera, its mouth moving in such a way that it appeared to be delivering the monologue. As its nose filled the screen, the film ended.

The moment the camera panned from house to horse, the image was met with knowing laughter from the audience over the constraints of home versus every little girl's fantasy of having a pony and the abandon that image portends. Or it could have been a reference to romantic notions of home and domestic bliss juxtaposed with the sexually potent metaphor of a horse galloping wildly between a woman's legs as the image might be drawn in the annals of lesbian lore. This is but one example of several references culled from lesbian subcultural sources, all of which I missed in that first encounter. Ultimately, however, my inability to read the show's subtext would not prove disabling. As it turned out, Forrester had put the subculture on the stage, presenting it as constitutive of the status quo.

The performance wittily riffed on the formulaic genre of the romance novel presented in television soap opera style. Fittingly, an upended, steeply raked, twin-size bed was the focal point of the stage, nearly filling it. The plot focused on a college student, Annabelle, and her unrequited love, Ran. The story was frequently interrupted by romantic subplots in a series of short scenes that took place in several locations—a lawn chair indicated the deck of a ship, for example—all played in front of the set with the raked bed looming over every scene. Forrester herself is a strikingly beautiful, large woman who, by virtue of her size alone, dwarfed the stage space. When two other performers joined her onstage, it looked like a crowd scene. The acting was purposely bad and consistently sloppy, which drew laughter from the audience in and of itself. Performers occasionally fished for their next line of dialogue and, once found, delivered it in an exaggerated version of soap opera acting. Film was imaginatively used to set some of the scenes until the Super 8 projector broke down midway. Before long, it was clear that absolutely all the characters in this love story were women and all of the couples were lesbian.

As a spectator, I typically abhor audience participation and routinely sit in the back to avoid it. But there was no avoiding it during *Heart of the Scorpion,* even though no one singled me out or asked me to do or say anything. The space was set up for typical voyeuristic proscenium viewing, but it was far too small and the lighting too primitive for there to be much separation between the audience and the show. Some of the spectators turned out to be performers themselves, making their entrances and exits from their seats. This was not an avant-garde strategy designed to make the audience feel more a part of the action by literally crossing through the fourth wall's invisible divide. Although that was the effect, it was simply a result of conditions—there was little room for the performers to be anywhere else. At one point during the show I heard rustling and turned to see a near-naked woman noisily changing her costume by the door to the street. Later my attention was drawn to the same woman in the lap of a spectator passionately and urgently kissing. One performer emerged from the audience decked out in full, butch, S/M black leather regalia—definitely a feminist no-no at the time. Spectators called out to her encouragingly and appreciatively as she mounted the stage. Her costume did not match the character she was there to play, which suggested she was wearing her street clothes and was in fact a member of the S/M community.

The performance's incongruities and fits and starts were part of the bawdy hilarity that swept me up in its raucous energy. Riding the wave of the show's outrageous comedy was a palpable sense of desire circulating onstage and in the audience; the room was unmistakably sexually charged. The space was so small and the line between performers and audience so terribly blurred that it was nearly impossible not to become part of a roomful of demonstrably engaged, desiring women. I was enthralled. But the source of this exhilaration had little to do with "being" a lesbian. Like every identity, "lesbian" is an ongoing, learned process, and I had barely breached the starting gate at that time. Everyone jumped in with enthusiastic applause at the curtain call and stayed afterward to mingle with performers. The room was abuzz with talk of a show an hour later at the Chandalier, where, it was said, WOW girls were scheduled to perform.

A few blocks away, on the second floor of a building with the street number taped to the door, spectators were waiting for the show to begin at Club Chandalier. When they ventured forth to the bar at the far end of the club's long, narrow room, they were greeted by "New York's meanest bartender," who yelled at one unwary customer: "J&B on the rocks? What do you think this is, the Mayfair Hotel? This is Avenue C!" Dolan described the scene: "A small glass chandelier that looks slightly dusty and yellowed hangs low above the bar and seems to provide the club's name. The bartender . . . is a woman wearing black lipstick, a black leather short skirt, fishnet stockings strategically ripped, and a deep-plunging, black sleeveless top with thin straps. A snake tattoo crawls up from between her breasts, and her cleavage is marked by a seashell. Her neck is ringed by a studded black leather collar. In an unabashedly loud New York accent, she seems to be the night's warm-up act: 'You just passing the time of day, or do you want to order?'"[16]

When forty or so spectators settled in and the lights dimmed, Carmelita Tropicana's entrance was met with wild applause. She was introduced as "part-time talk show host and feminist." In her *Drama Review* piece, Dolan wrote, Carmelita "appears in a low-cut, flaming red evening gown covered with large black and green printed flowers. A black feather boa is draped around her shoulders. She wears a flower behind each ear and dangling earrings that look like miniature disco balls."[17] Carmelita broke into a medley of her favorite tunes, like Doris Day's classic "Que Sera, Sera" and Debby Boone's hit single "You Light Up My Life." She sung them full out and unabashedly off-key with a heavy Cuban accent. The audience—made up largely but not exclusively of lesbians—adored her. Like Dolan and me, a number of spectators from the earlier show at WOW were there.

Applause, whistling, and catcalling greeted Carmelita when she walked onstage and continued during her opening act. Dolan described audience members playfully yelling out come-ons like "I love it when you talk dirty." A woman seated between me and her boyfriend got into the spirit of the moment and joined in, yelling out, "Take it off, Carmelita."[18] After a couple of minutes of this, a woman named Lou, wearing a buzz cut and a tie and sitting in front of her, turned around, looked her square in the eye, and said, "Now, that's outta line." I remember this moment the way you remember something you hope someday to understand. To me, at the time, the woman's remarks seemed entirely in keeping with the down and dirty catcalling of other women in the space. What follows is an attempt to explicate this specific moment.

Before bringing on her first guest, Carmelita gave a cooking lesson on Japanese Cuban cuisine, using a recipe for "chicken sushi." She explained that "the way to a woman's heart is through her stomach." Dolan wrote, "A raw chicken is used for the lesson. Carmelita insists you have to become friends with the chicken . . . and she dances with it a bit before she hacks it up with a large, Samurai-type knife. She asks for a 'beautiful audience helper' to accompany her rhythmically by banging on a pot while she garnishes the chicken with paper parasols."[19] In this opening scene and as she interviewed guests throughout the show, Carmelita addressed her prime-time television viewing audience—and by extension everyone at the Chandalier—as if all were lesbian all the time.

Carmelita's first guest was Tammy Whynot, Lois Weaver's persona of a famous country and western singer—an amalgam of Tammy Wynette and Loretta Lynn with the requisite down-home, twangy country accent. Carmelita brought Tammy "on camera" for some "chick chat" about her "life as a womans" and rise to stardom from white trash roots, as portrayed in Tammy's recently published autobiography. "Tammy wears a tight sequined gown," wrote Dolan in her accounts, "and her hair is piled into layers of blonde white curls. [She] reads a poem from her book, dedicated to her children. It chronicles events in their childhoods that Tammy missed while she was touring ('Mama was out of town'). Delivered with saccharine sentiment in forced rhyme, the poem parodies the mainstream opinion of the working mother's dilemma."[20]

Like Troyano's Carmelita Tropicana, Weaver's Tammy Whynot is performed empathetically, albeit eccentrically, and without a hint of condescension. Their chick chat concludes with a hilariously off-key duet followed by a plug for their upcoming TV special. This echoes the famous televised pairing of Carol Burnett and Julie Andrews, replacing them with another kind of entertainment world team—a trailer trash "coal miner's daughter" and a pre-revolution Havana nightclub Cuban dyke. Troyano and Weaver layer stereotype upon stereotype in what becomes an obvious and at the same time loving comment on them—a commentary completely absent derision. They are what might best be described as "eccentric subjects" who construct concomitant subject positions that willing spectators can take up.[21]

Watching Troyano perform *Carmelita Tropicana Chats* in the context of a mixed crowd at the Chandalier, I was struck by what had been so compelling about *Heart of the Scorpion*. It had played as if all Harlequin romance novels and all television soap operas are peopled exclusively with women. No particular attention was drawn to this, no overt point was made; a world of women was taken for granted—*indifferent* to the category "man," not in *opposition* to it. Like *Carmelita Tropicana Chats,* there was something radically different about the way the performance imagined and addressed its audience. Reading any performance on its own terms means accommodating the way the performance constructs its audience. On that night in the East Village, I entered a newly opened space in representation; something in the paradigm was shifting.

In the summer of 1973, I sat in the audience of the Thirteenth Street Theatre on the west side of Greenwich Village, waiting for Ludlam's production of

Camille to begin. The play was subtitled *A Travesty on La Dame aux Camélias by Alexander Dumas fils*. Ludlam's version closely followed the text of the original nineteenth-century romantic tragedy, but the performance itself was permeated with gay male subculture references, most of which I missed. Some of the action and segues between scenes were accompanied by the score of *La Traviata*, Giuseppe Verdi's opera based on the Dumas fils narrative, for instance, and at the time I did not understand the significance of opera in gay male culture. Like my first encounter with WOW eleven years later, I experienced Ludlam's production from the psychosocial subject position I occupied, what the French author and theorist Monique Wittig has so aptly called "the straight mind."[22] Gay men undoubtedly experienced the production differently. And much has been written about the pleasure heterosexual men have taken in flirting with the erotics of drag performance from the anonymous, passive position of spectator.

The Thirteenth Street Theatre was small and cramped, with no air conditioning on an unusually humid night. The space accommodated sixty-five spectators, and every seat was filled. In the oppressive heat the usual preshow chatter was subdued, and the production started late—hardly a propitious environment for an evening of comedy. But when the curtain finally rose and Ludlam swept onstage in full period costume and wig to play the role of the doomed heroine, Marguerite Gautier, he was so magnificent only the most stolid spectator could resist being seduced. Throughout the performance the actors' exaggerated makeup bled down their necks and into their heavy gowns and frock coats while sweat seemed to pour off the audience and trickle down the aisle. Still, no one left during the show's two intermissions except to cross the street and guzzle liquids from the local bodega. At the end of the three-hour-plus show, the audience cheered the cast on to a seemingly endless series of curtain calls. Played by Bill Vehr, Armand, the young, lovestruck, romantic male lead, carried the tragic Marguerite in his arms across the stage; she removed a long-stemmed plastic rose from between her teeth and blew kisses to her adoring fans. In their final sweep across the stage, however, Marguerite carried Armand.

Camille was the product of familiar and long-accepted traditions of gay male drag performance, and, as evidenced by the show's growing and sustained popularity, it was entirely possible to enjoy it from the vantage point of the straight mind. The show's campy gay male overtones were one thing, however, while the characters' urgently played homoerotic desire for each other, costumed and played as heterosexual couples but embodied as men, was quite another. The production's undertones referenced another world to which only some spectators had access. Four years after the Stonewall riots, an illicit desire separate from that of *Camille* played just beneath the surface onstage. What it alluded to had subversive potential to make the experience a transformative one for the audience.

The moment Ludlam set foot on the stage, his hairy chest was clearly visible above the cut of his gown, signaling his status as male. His performance of Marguerite conjured Greta Garbo's version of the character from the 1937 film. In his review of *Camille* for the *New York Times,* the critic Clive Barnes called Ludlam "a completely convincing Camille."[23] In playing Marguerite, Ludlam negotiated a position somewhere between a distanced, Brechtian presentation of the character and an illusionistic portrayal.[24] In an interview I conducted with Ludlam during a subsequent run of *Camille,* he located his portrayals of women in the great tradition of transvestism in the classical theaters of the Greeks, Elizabethans, and Japanese. "This is nothing new," he explained. "It has nothing to do with homosexuality. I use it as a theatrical device. It distances the performer from the role. It takes more art to play a role that is very unlike yourself. You must use everything; you must use your imagination to the utmost to create the impression."[25]

Although he played Marguerite for comic effect, Ludlam also portrayed her earnestly when necessary to milk the pathos of a scene, hushing the audience. He seduced viewers into "seeing" a woman as a kind of setup for moments when he dropped the character altogether to deliver a line or two as his actor/playwright/gay male self. In the final act, for instance, Marguerite on her deathbed, now a penniless consumptive, calls to her faithful maid, "I'm cold. Nanine, throw another faggot on the fire!" Nanine replies, "There are no more faggots in the house." Dropping character, Ludlam sits bolt upright, surveys the audience skeptically, and asks plaintively, "No faggots in the house?" Returning the character to her deathbed, he says, "Open the window, Nanine. See if there are any in the street."[26]

Ludlam does not represent homosexuality by writing plays about gay couples; instead, his actors signal their desire for each other through texts he constructs out of pieces of classical and popular narratives. They portray the heterosexual couples that inhabit these scenarios, flaunting and thereby presenting the gay male under, alongside, and outside of the straight male and female characters valorized in these canonized texts. Ludlam opened a window in representation, taking the faggots he saw in the streets and putting them on the stage, making visible their desire for each other—for those who are looking. "Although a lot of gay people do see it," Ludlam said of *Camille*, "an enormous number of straight people also come—couples clutching each other and weeping at the death scene, hugging each other all the closer." The piece worked for both gay and straight audiences alike, he explained, because "it transcends gay. It's a love story. It's the story of Adam and Eve. It's the romantic ideal questioned and rethought."[27]

This capacity to "transcend gay" while simultaneously performing it is what separates the boys from the girls. Arguing emphatically for two seemingly contradictory positions in his performance, Ludlam maintained that his rendering of *Camille* is *not* an expression of homosexuality but at the same time represents a form of coming out. This powerful sleight of hand is possible by virtue of Ludlam's whiteness and maleness. White gay male performance has access to a network of signs and symbols that produce what mainstream culture recognizes as a universal voice without fully objectifying and thoroughly erasing the marginalized, queer voice within it. Critics never singled out Ludlam's work as "homosexual theater." Two decades later, on the other hand, the theater critic John Simon ended an otherwise positive review of the Five Lesbian Brothers' *The Secretaries* with a backhanded remark that distinguished and thereby separated it from "heterosexual theatre." He wrote, "Any day now I expect heterosexual theater in New York to become a minority affair, which I salute as the only way to make it eligible for generous public and private subsidies."[28] And, although Simon compared the acting style favorably to that of Theater of the Ridiculous, he used gender-inflected descriptors like "distaff" and "slatternliness" to put the piece in its proper place. Commenting on how *The Secretaries* was generally received, Maureen Angelos, one of the Brothers, said, "It's that old problem of men not seeing a story about women as universal."[29]

Stanford scholar and theorist Peggy Phelan has written about the intense hatred gay men elicit from homophobic culture because it "implicitly 'feminize[s]' all men."[30] This is instructive; to think or feel intensely about gay men as supposedly "feminizing all men" is to be able to imagine the site of that alleged feminization—the forbidden sexual acts of "the sodomites." Ultimately, what made Ludlam's theater work so radical was the illicit desire manifest onstage and what it portended offstage. His making visible of homoerotic desire signaled homosexual *practice,* the subversive site of all that homophobic culture attempts to suppress, contain, and eradicate. As the gender and queer theorist Eve Kosofsky Sedgwick has put it, "The most significant stakes for the culture are involved in precisely the volatile, fractured, dangerous relations of visibility and articulation around homosexual possibility."[31] For all its campy, glitzy, hilarious comedy, Ludlam's *Camille* posed a very real underlying threat.

Could the same be said of a *Camille* cast with lesbians? Would it be possible to evoke from the culture at large an "offstage" site of forbidden, foreboding, dangerous lesbian sex? No. Any such image would be a well-ingrained scenario of women-on-women sex framed by a long tradition of straight pornography and made palatable through its lens. Male sexuality is visible everywhere. This is what makes it possible to imagine that offstage site of male homosexual practice. The nature of same-sex object choice functions as a destabilizing force that has an impact for sure, but men as autonomous agents acting on their desire is not new. And if some imagined lesbian production of *Camille* could manage to reference a site of lesbian sexuality, what would such an image connote for mainstream audience members aside from castration or what lesbians presumably do to and for men? Lesbians and heterosexual women are not represented on their own terms in accord with their reality; instead, they are constructed in terms of what they are not. This is summarized most succinctly, perhaps, in a line delivered to one of the lesbians in the 1985 Donna Deitch film *Desert Hearts*. As he watches a woman leave her cottage one morning, a ranch hand says: "How you get all that traffic with no equipment is beyond me." For him, female sexuality is inconceivable apart from his own.

In comparison to gay men, Phelan has written, "Lesbians are not as overtly hated because they are so locked out of the visible, so far from the minds of . . . the New Right, that they are not acknowledged as a threat."[32] This formulation of the relative visibility of gay men in contrast to lesbians is telling. As the English literature scholar Terry Castle has asked, "Why is it so difficult to see the lesbian—even when she is there, quite plainly, in front of us?" The answer: "In part because she has been 'ghosted'—or made invisible—by the culture itself."[33] This is where "lesbian" comes smack up against the gendered construction "woman," the sex that is not one, the sex maintained under conditions of erasure in dominant symbolic regimes. As autonomous, speaking subjects with agency, all female-gendered bodies are in effect ghosted by mainstream cultures to the extent that they are primarily encoded *as* body—that is, as *objects* rather than *agents* of desire (see de Beauvoir's Other and Woolf's looking glass as examples). Although fierce attempts to silence gay men have historically constituted standard practice, discursively white gay men can access a speaking subject position nonetheless—a feat made possible at the intersection of a debased sexuality and privileged race and gender positions. Lesbians and heterosexual women, however, occupy a gender category defined overwhelmingly by a condition of silenced and silencing embodiment.

Describing her own and other WOW work, performance artist Holly Hughes has said, "The camp frame lets the piece be judged really differently. People are laughing at lesbians and we're laughing at ourselves, too." But, she continues, "It's different if you ask the audience to really think about the reality of lesbians. If they stop laughing for two minutes, then they start to stampede out."[34] When a straight audience stops laughing for two minutes at a lesbian production, when you ask them to think about the "*reality* of lesbians," as Hughes suggests, they do not stampede out. They might flee if lesbian sexual practice could be imagined, but they stay put because mostly it cannot. As the feminist scholar and essayist Marilyn Frye has contended, "There is nothing women could do in the absence of men that could, without semantic oddity, be called 'having sex.'"[35]

I am reminded of a moment in 1997 following the curtain call for the Five Lesbian Brothers' production of *Brides of the Moon* at the off-Broadway venue New York Theatre Workshop. A man sitting in front of me turned to his companion, presumably his wife, and said without rancor, "What was *that?*" In the mind's eye of mainstream culture, lesbian sexual practice is different from lesbianism. Peg Healey, another Brother, has explained it this way: "Lesbianism is more threatening to the mainstream than gay men, because it shows women without men. Men without women isn't a big deal—women are the ones missing, and they aren't as important."[36] Exploring lesbian sexuality, then, might prove fertile ground for locating these missing women.

Like *Camille,* the WOW productions *Heart of the Scorpion* and *Carmelita Tropicana Chats* referenced a real world. Unlike Ludlam's work, however, for its desire to be enacted and made visible, for its subterfuge to be read, WOW had to open a space in representation and create a "there" to inhabit. What made the work coming out of WOW so important was the way it unflinchingly took on and grappled with this deeply troubling conundrum in the interest of women in general and lesbians in particular. As playwright and performer Lisa Kron has suggested, "The breakthrough part of the WOW aesthetic is the exploration and theatricalization of lesbian sexuality."[37]

A Productive Indifference

A very queer, composite being thus emerges. Imaginatively she is of the highest importance; practically she is completely insignificant. She pervades poetry from cover to cover; she is all but absent from history.

—VIRGINIA WOOLF, A Room of One's Own, 1929

Art enables us to imagine ourselves out of current situations. We have only begun to imagine the potential for women's work in theater.

—LOIS WEAVER, 1998

Unlike Ludlam, WOW artists Alice Forrester and Alina Troyano put an alternative world onstage explicitly and addressed their audiences as if all were born and bred citizens of it. In so doing, they referenced an offstage site of lesbian sexual practice—a sexuality by, about, and for women. For this site to register in the realm of the symbolic, however, requires a shift in the foundational terms of representation, the opening up of an alternative representational space through which previously unthinkable subject positions are constructed for willing spectators to take up. The pleasure for audience members comes from inhabiting these subject positions and engaging with the work on its own terms. This is precisely what the woman sitting next to me at the Chandalier had failed to do when she joined in the melee of catcalling. She lowered her voice and took on a kind of stereotypical "Joe Sixpack" persona, making her entrance into the audience exchange with Carmelita by way of this impersonation. The representational frame of reference her impersonation invoked appropriated and recuperated Carmelita's performance back into familiar, stereotypical scenarios like, for example, "girl-on-girl titillation for horny men." The catcalling of this particular woman inserted a desiring, heterosexual male gaze into the frame, skewing it, putting her version "outta line." She had misread the dynamic circulating throughout the space or, perhaps more accurately, she had assumed the only desiring position with which she was familiar—the only position from which she could *imagine* acting upon desire.

Forrester's and Troyano's narratives and acting styles actively and insistently thwarted the tendency to project onto characters and identify with them in heterosexual romantic ways. Forrester's Harlequin romance—that paragon of white, heterosexual dating and mating—is inhabited solely with lesbians who represent not only bourgeois college femmes but also S/M dykes and working-class butches. "Lesbian" is as fluid and diverse an identity category as that of any other group, built on multiple social and cultural positions. Although *Heart of the Scorpion* is built around a traditionally structured plot, there is no attempt at verisimilitude within the logic of its story. The narrative's women are all virtuous or fallen or rescued in a romance Forrester has manufactured with all the intrigue, sin, sex, and salvation the genre requires—not in opposition to the gendered category of "man " but indifferent to it. It is out of this indifference that a powerful intervention is activated and launched.

Feminist film scholar Teresa de Lauretis has theorized sociosexual (in)difference, a paradox in which lesbian representation is unwittingly caught.[38] I suggest that indifference to (in)difference, enacted within specific sociocultural contexts, is a productive step out of the morass. "It would be putting it mildly to say that the lesbian represents a threat to patriarchal protocol," explained Castle. "Western civilization has for centuries been haunted by a fear of 'women without men'—of women indifferent or resistant to male desire."[39] This is the source of heterosexist panic and rage around lesbian possibility and what sets up lesbians as targets when their presence manages to register on the radar screen of those who would do them harm. It also constitutes the source of charges like "dyke" and "feminazi" against heterosexual women who threaten just a little too much independence.

WOW artists embrace the very attribute that inspires fear and hatred—indifference—and deploy it as an aesthetic strategy. This, in turn, produces work that accomplishes a principle aim of the avant-garde. Understandings of what constitutes the avant-garde vary historically, and the work of both Ludlam and WOW artists clearly met the criteria of its time. About his rethinking of the romantic ideal through *Camille's* narrative of forbidden love, Ludlam has said, "I think it's presenting a positive image. I think it's coming out on a certain level. But I don't think it's 'gay.' It's a matter of being able to see the story freshly, without prejudice. It's a matter of giving the audience *a new vision instead of reinforcing fixed habits of thought.*"[40] This kind of intervention constitutes the promise of the avant-garde, but WOW artists faced a unique challenge in delivering on this promise.

Women occupy a different position within the confines of a foundational social contract whose ideology masks its own operations as a specifically *heterosexual* contract. This contract is utterly dependent on normative gender configurations. As de Lauretis has asserted, "[T]he heterosexual contract . . . is the very site in which the social relations of gender and thus gender ideology are reproduced in everyday life."[41] WOW productions set out to address women in ways that release them from a prescribed "in relation" status to the representational category of "man." Like the dynamic of the butch/femme couple scholar Sue-Ellen Case has theorized, representation coming out of WOW played *on* dominant cultural symbolic systems not *to* them.[42] Ludlam's work, however, played both *on* and *to* dominant systems because it could.

Working from an impulse not unlike the one that had propelled Ludlam's *Camille,* coproducers Alice Forrester and Heidi Griffith mounted a production at WOW in 1988 of the eighteenth-century playwright Richard Brinsley Sheridan's *School for Scandal.* All the roles were played by women, including the male characters, which were played by women in drag. In his review for the *Village Voice,* critic Robert Massa bemoaned the fact that the production inadequately commented on the play's sexism, "as if the point of women's theater were simply to cast, not to recast." He said that, as a spectator, "you soon forget all the roles are played by women." In the final line of the review, Massa maintained that "even the ones playing female characters appear to be in drag."[43] In other words, it was possible to read this *School for Scandal* as cast entirely with men. Why do women tend to be subsumed in male impersonation? Unlike female impersonation, male impersonation has no familiar institutionalized paradigm for reading it in such a way that women impersonating men says something about women. As I have argued elsewhere, camp parody does not serve lesbians in the same way it serves gay men. Camp's flamboyant performance style is, paradoxically, grounded in nuance—a place where women and lesbians tend to get lost.[44]

In the introduction accompanying the published version of her play *The Well of Horniness,* Holly Hughes speaks to the issue of agency for women. For those who intend to mount their own versions of her play, she explained that in the original staging "All the performers were, and still are as far as I know, women. I'm pretty tough about this part. No men in *The Well,* okay? I don't care if you're doing a staged reading in Crib Death, Iowa—no men."[45] Hughes has nothing against men, of course; she merely acknowledges that for women to realize agency attention must be paid, explicitly, and all promising devices employed aggressively. Even when a play is cast entirely with women, as *School for Scandal* demonstrates, mainstream discourses and contexts work to privilege the male voice and elide women as speaking subjects.

The so-called commonsense operations of representation tend to preclude and foreclose visibility for different kinds of social subjects. Therefore, a different kind of approach is required. In the case of Ludlam, for example, a certain subtlety is both possible and productive. His *Camille* is not "gay" inasmuch as its address is not exclusively homosexual; rather, within the dynamics of the production homosexuality surfaces, "comes out," and is rendered visible in the pockets, gaps, and fissures of an ultimately less than monolithic heterosexual configuration. The making visible of lesbian desire demands a far more explicit approach, however, a form of literalness that is far from banal.

Hughes's *Well of Horniness* exemplifies an aesthetic in service to an explicit, productive rendering of lesbian sexuality. In the play's text and many productions, Hughes stages what became known as "the pussy-eating scene." I describe it here in part because it is just so much fun, but also because *The Well* played nearly every club during the heyday of East Village performance. The scene creates a powerfully suggestive image that lived on notoriously in the local lesbian community long after the play had ceased to be performed. The following WOW girls appeared in *The Well* cast at one time or another: Maureen Angelos, Peg Healey, Lisa Kron, Deb Margolin, Claire Moed, Reno, Peggy Shaw, Sharon Jane Smith, Alina Troyano, Lois Weaver, and Susan Young.

Hughes's *Well of Horniness* is based loosely on Radclyffe Hall's classic novel of fraught lesbian sexuality, *The Well of Loneliness*. What little plot exists is broken repeatedly by a narrator's commentary, mock commercials, announcements, and a plethora of sound effects—all of which conspire to keep spectators firmly in the realm of the presentational. In a send-up of *Our Town* style, a narrator establishes the scene: "The setting, a peaceful New England town, just a town like many others . . . where every winter day is a white Christmas (*humming "White Christmas"*). . . . But beneath the apparently serene breast of new-fallen snow, a whirlpool rages . . . (*sucking noises*) sucking the weak, the infirm, the original and all others who don't wear beige down . . . down, down. As carrots in the Cuisinart . . . (*blender*) so are souls in the Well (*scream*) of Horniness! Meet Georgette."[46] Georgette, a "well-groomed word-processing trainee" and onetime member of the "Tridelta Tribads" sorority (also referred to as the "sisterhood of sin"), meets her brother, Rod (in the sense of "packing a rod" and referring to more than a gun), and his wife-to-be, Vicki, at a restaurant, only to discover that Vicki is someone Georgette knows from her past in the "sisterhood." They are introduced and "stand frozen . . . in near-embrace." Georgette orders dinner, but Vicki does not; instead, she stares longingly at Georgette, prompting the following lines.

Georgette: Whatsamatter honey? You sit in a puddle, or are you just glad to see me?

Waitress: Excuse me, Miss, are you gonna order anything or are you just gonna eat hers?

Narrator: As Vicki's fork clatters to the ground, something darker than etiquette draws Vicki down. . . . What began innocently enough, takes a turn for the worse underneath the table. Vicki finds no cutlery, but Georgette's legs, two succulent rainbows leading to the same pot of gold.

As Rod delivers a lengthy monologue in which he ponders the itinerary of his coming honeymoon, his fiancée is under the table with her head between his sister's legs. This scene was staged in many East Village clubs explicitly, with Georgette responding elaborately while Rod prattles on obliviously about honeymoon hideaways. As "the rod" reproduces and reinscribes the patriarchal construction of marriage, his fiancée is under the table busily disrupting it through her sexuality.

Vicki emerges from under the table, announces that she is feeling "a little hot," and heads for the restroom. Rod turns to Georgette and says—in the context of a play permeated with references to fish that signify lesbian sex—"Something's fishy, I can't quite put my finger on it, can you?" Georgette replies, "I'm working on it." Only four pages into the script and lesbian sexuality is established not merely as a theme but as the raison d'tre for whatever else transpires in a representational economy that abounds with references to fish, muff divers, bush leagues, eager beavers, tribads, bosom buddies, and the Stowed Finger Lodge, where two girls meet for a tryst. The metaphoric potential of "seduction under the table" for lesbian existence in homophobic culture is vast.

C. Carr recalled the premier of *The Well* "at the tiny Limbo Lounge on Tompkins Square [where] a cast member ended up on an audience member's lap during one cramped scene." She captures the disruptive dimension of the piece in another of its particularly "dykey" images, remembering the performance as ending "dramatically that first night when the door to the Limbo banged open and a woman stepped in off Tenth Street, announcing, 'Stella Bruce. Lesbian detective.'"[47] Perhaps this striking image was the impulse behind Carr's inspired notion of *dyke noir,* a term she coined to describe Hughes's work. Hughes had appropriated the genre of film noir as a vehicle for her subsequent venture, replacing Stella/Bruce with Lady/Dick. The detective Carr described appears in *The Well* as "a gorgeous gendarme who loves girls almost as much as she loves murder"; she reappears in *The Lady Dick* as "a woman who likes having a mystery around more than she likes solving them." The woman is "Garnet McClit, Lady Dick."[48]

Hughes took film noir's femme fatale and in a brilliant move constructed and *played* her as the neologism lady/dick. The way she approached this was quite explicit. Played by Sharon Jane Smith, *Lady Dick's* detective opens the play wearing a green strapless cocktail dress circa the end of the noir era. She holds a man's suit, also from the noir era, on a hanger in front of her. Stroking it, she sings:

> *A butch is a woman*
> *Who looks like a man*
> *Depending how close you look.*
>
> *A femme is a female*
> *Sometimes she may be male*
> *Sometimes she don't want to cook.*
>
> *A femme can be fatal*
> *A butch be prenatal*
> *But everyone knows a dick.*
>
> *Some walk like their moms*
> *Some walk like their dads*
> *It's never too late to switch.*

With the suggestive, boozy sound of an onstage saxophone as background (played by Peggy Shaw), Smith delivers a monologue about growing up queer in a town that never changes while she puts on each piece of the dick costume over the strapless cocktail dress. A crucial dimension of the piece was the continuous presence throughout the performance of the femme dress underneath the classic butch detective garb.

The lesbians who populate the play *Lady Dick* are not nice girls. There is no subterranean appeal to dominant culture for understanding and tolerance. The characters are bawdy, sinister, and sinful, as well as aggressive, sexy, and dangerous—no nurturing types here. Like most WOW shows, the spectator who looked into the mirror of the production in search of positive images and politically correct role models was thwarted. In a sense WOW productions liberated lesbian and feminist theater from the "good-girl syndrome" in its many mainstream guises, as well as its feminist ones. Women in the world of *Lady Dick* are overtly sexual and on the prowl—for other women. It is in and around this "over-the-top sexuality" that *Lady Dick* plays. In appropriating film noir as the playground for her lesbian romp, Hughes gestures toward a position both within and beyond the specificities of lesbian subjectivity. Through the familiar figure of the classic femme fatale, Hughes manages to stage an autonomous sexuality that is at the same time both lesbian and heterosexual.

Of the genre Hughes parodies, the film and media scholar E. Ann Kaplan has written, "Film noir *expresses* alienation, locates its cause squarely in the excesses of female sexuality ('natural' consequences of women's independence), and punishes that excess in order to re-place it within the patriarchal order."[49] *Lady Dick* stages but does not punish this excess of female sexuality, allowing it to float untethered across the production's mise-en-scène. The setting is a seedy, no-name lesbian bar frequented by "love's leftovers." Unlike *The Well,* in which lesbians are contextualized in familial relationships and surface as desiring and sexual according to the dictates of plot, *Lady Dick* is permeated with signifiers of desire that circulate lavishly among a series of "drifters," itinerants who undermine the totalizing characteristics of identity. In playing Stella/Bruce, Lady/Dick, and femme/butch all together in the same Bogart-like suit and hat, the production invokes the seamy world of classical Hollywood film noir in which the femme fatale's visual and narrative position (i.e., female sexuality as independent, sensual/sexual, aggressive, and ambitious) undermines a reductive reading of her status as solely an object of male desire. Hollywood's femme fatale epitomizes the potential for indifference to a heterosexual social contract, and as such she is dealt with accordingly within the genre's narratives. *Lady Dick* reconfigures and (re)presents the classic femme fatale and gives her free rein over the play's erotic landscape. The production addresses and engages its spectators as occupying a position of autonomous female sexuality and subjectivity; in other words, you do not have to be(come) a lesbian to play.

In their attempts to grapple with "woman" and allow her to speak, most practitioners of the women's theater movement during the 1970s and 1980s put the experiences of women onstage, usefully exploring and exposing the nature of gender imperatives through women's experiences under patriarchal regimes. In this sense experience is understood as something individuals *have.* If, however, experience is understood as that which *makes* individuals, then by staging their dreams and fantasies WOW artists gave shape to alternative subject positions for women. Rather than making visible the experiences women have—which ultimately indicate that psychologically, socially, and culturally "they've been had"—WOW practitioners devoted themselves to creating a world, a feminist space, that suggests alternative ways of being in the world for female-gendered bodies.

Queer theorists would point out that all this attention to identity categories such as "women" is precisely the problem, further propping up the very constructions that oppress women. But queer's anti-identity position and inclusive, universalizing move vis-à-vis fellow-traveling outsiders has a tendency to, once again, ensure that certain social subjects will remain locked out of the visible. As the literary theorist Fredric Jameson put it, "Every universalizing approach . . . will from the dialectical point of view be found to conceal its own contradictions and repress its own historicity by strategically framing its perspective so as to omit the negative, absence, contradiction, repression, the *non-dit,* or the *impense.*"[50] While undeniably important and enormously productive, the propensity of queer is to make of feminists and "old-time" gay and lesbian activists its negative, its absence.

If at base the aim of avant-garde performance is to somehow alter consciousness—replacing fixed habits of thought with new visions, as Ludlam explained it—then it is an achievement of significant proportions to open a space in representation where female-gendered subjects operate out of indifference to that which largely informs and gives shape to the conditions of heterosexual normalcy in the world. "[A] true avant-garde theatre," wrote theater historian Arnold Aronson, "must seek an essential change in audience perceptions that, in turn, will have a profound impact on the relationship of the spectator to the world."[51] Indeed, "to produce the conditions of visibility for a different social subject" is a move de Lauretis identified in 1984 as a kind of bottom-line feminist project.[52] WOW work accomplished this by way of an aesthetic similar to that of the East Village club scene but with compelling differences.

Ultimately, there are no conditions that guarantee the specificity of theatrical address and audience reception. No performance controls its readings, even within lesbian theater space itself. Nonetheless, and particularly during the East Village club years, work at WOW aggressively and persistently pushed at the symbolic and conventional boundaries of performance as a meaning-making apparatus to challenge and eschew male sexuality as the universal norm. This is what so frustrated Shaw in 1985 about WOW's aesthetic being described as the "triumph of the drag queen aesthetic." WOW artists were triumphant on their own terms but in a symbolic landscape that could not yet be articulated. WOW was staging the as yet unimaginable. At the intersection of sociology and alternative aesthetic production, a foundational paradigm of representation had shifted and with it the potential to transform "the relationship of the spectator to the world."

Chapter 6

Challenging Whiteness: The Fourth-Floor Walk-Up

WOW has always been miles from the lesbian/feminist "aesthetic." Too rude. Too raunchy. Too self-mocking and downright gay.

—C. CARR, 1985

The work produced at WOW made important contributions to understanding the dynamics of race and class, as well as gender and sexuality in representation. In Alina Troyano's *Carmelita Tropicana Chats,* for example (described in chapter 5), Carmelita hacks up more than a raw chicken. Her medley butchers songs made popular by singers like Doris Day and Debby Boone, songs inseparable from the avatars of respectable white womanhood who originated them. In Carmelita's heavily accented, off-key rendering of Boone's "You Light Up My Life," Troyano appropriates a paragon of white good-girlness, exposing the ideal of white womanhood, setting it up and sending it up by marking her own minority status and therefore her distance from it.

By the fall of 1985, when the collective relocated from the storefront to the fourth-floor walk-up space on E. Fourth Street, Troyano and Joni Wong were WOW's only women of color. This was troubling because women of color had been so much a part of WOW's founding festivals and had continued to present work in the storefront in the early 1980s. Once the collective formed, however, participation among women of color waned. A pragmatic reason for their relative absence may have been the very nature of the collective's organization in that women of color would be required to work on the shows of many white women in order to secure time in the space to produce one of their own pieces. As discussed in chapter 4, women of color who had performed in the festivals and participated in the storefront, like Gwendolen Hardwick of the Flamboyant Ladies, felt there were things they needed to be doing separately as a group in those days. In response, WOW decided to dedicate three to four weeks a year in the walk-up space to a festival of work by women of color, which the collective staffed.

The poet and novelist Jewelle Gomez had been active in New York's black theater movement in the 1970s and a regular audience member at WOW from its inaugural festivals throughout the 1980s. At one point Peggy Shaw asked her to write something for WOW, but Gomez declined the invitation because the request came at a time when she had made a conscious decision to move away from theater. "My own issue and terrors about getting involved with a group of ostensibly white women prohibited me from doing anything except being in the audience," she later explained.[1] Gomez grounds her hesitancy to get involved at WOW in her own issues as an individual, not necessarily those of all black women. Still, the statement serves as an explanation for the absence of at least one woman of color. Her description of WOW women as *ostensibly* white is particularly telling.

Troyano has voiced a similar sentiment: "To say 'white' already means, to me, up there in the mainstream. WOW is such a subculture that even when you're white, you're not getting a piece of the pie; well, it depends, but you're almost not white anymore."[2] She is emphatically *not* suggesting that WOW's white women are somehow women of color; rather, she claims for them a certain distance from institutionalized whiteness as a racial category. They are "ostensibly white." Like Troyano, Gomez has suggested that this discrepancy has something to do with class: "I felt it was really exciting to go someplace and watch women writing and acting imaginative fantasies. I kept coming back to WOW because of the potential; it is incredibly precarious financially and organizationally, and in that precariousness is its potential to be open, inclusive, and flexible, both in terms of diversity and artistic work as well."[3] This description resonates with the cultural theorist bell hooks's concept of a "space of radical openness" and indicates that there was something about the "imaginative fantasies" onstage that inspired Gomez to keep coming back.[4] At the very least, WOW work was not focused solely and unconsciously on the narrow worldview and preoccupations of middle-class white women. Something else was going on.

Issues of race at WOW are not confined to the composition of the collective or the bodies of women of color onstage; instead, race is always performed at the intersection of every other identity category, even when it is unmarked, as in the case of whiteness. Like Troyano, some WOW artists took on the ideologies underpinning white womanhood in ways that are instructive; for it is in the construction of white womanhood that the meanings of "whiteness" as a racial category reside. This is not to suggest that WOW practitioners and their critics examined whiteness openly and consciously in the early years. Rather, I mean to argue for this dimension of WOW's aesthetic production as more than merely an after-the-fact claim of relevance. Race in general and whiteness in particular were not wholly uncontested categories at WOW.[5] The putative invisibility of whiteness is so ingrained in mainstream culture that it might be said a chapter focusing on it is not about race. On the contrary, whiteness is a racial construct, a dynamic force producing conditions every bit as compelling in their privileges for white people as the dynamics of discrimination are for people of color.

This chapter begins with a production called *Saint Joan of Avenue C*, the opening show at WOW's new space. The show's title promised great things, reflecting German playwright Bertolt Brecht's *Saint Joan of the Stockyards*. The production was less than successful, however, demonstrating not only the pitfalls associated with generating material collectively but the consequences for a piece of theater when it is created by a collective unaware of the ways whiteness generates its own meanings in performance. *Saint Joan of Avenue C* is worth examining here for these reasons and also because it was the product of a particularly fraught moment in WOW's history. The play was driven by serious concerns over the changing socioeconomic climate of the East Village. In the end an overt political agenda overrode aesthetic considerations.

The Vagaries of Race: Saint Joan of Avenue C

Because no one else cared about what some crazy dykes on East Fourth Street were doing every night, we made work that was unself-conscious and vibrant. We got to make theater that felt like it mattered.
—LISA KRON, 2006

Although the move from the storefront at E. Eleventh Street to an abandoned doll factory in a fourth-floor walk-up on E. Fourth Street gave the collective more space in which to mount shows, that was not the primary reason for the move. The collective had lost its lease on the storefront and was forced to relocate, a victim of the gentrification gripping the East Village by the mid-1980s. The neighborhood's economy was turning around, and no one had the means to save the storefront in the face of exponentially rising rents. *Village Voice* writer Kathleen Conkey had penned a celebratory article on the club scene that captured the dynamics of WOW's neighborhood in the throes of gentrification. The article had appeared during the summer WOW was forced to move, and Shaw's response to it was particularly fierce. "Conkey's article stands out as one that can do damage to our work by trying to gentrify the Café into some kind of Steve's Ice Cream of lesbian theater," Shaw wrote. "We want audiences; all performers do. But Conkey's hype can only attract people who come to the East Village to be cool. The East Village is in the midst of horrifying changes, and WOW is in the midst of the East Village. Conkey's article can only contribute to the expansion of white surface consumer voyeurism."[6]

Conkey's piece is helpful in understanding what happened and why at WOW during this time. It begins with a description of Ciao WOW Day, an event that had taken place in the storefront location shortly before the move to E. Fourth Street. Ciao WOW was designed as an awards ceremony to clear out old props, bits of costume, and other discarded items and close down the Café. "Emcee Claire Moed wears a purple prom dress," Conkey wrote of the event. "Besides giving out awards (an electric frying pan, a spool of fishing line 'to catch a girlfriend with') she administers a voluptuous well-placed kiss to each winner and then meticulously freshens her lipstick."[7] In keeping with the spirit of WOW in the storefront, Ciao WOW was a funny, sweet, camped-up event but a bittersweet one nonetheless.

Conkey continued with an analysis that makes the collective seem somehow complicit with the gentrification that was forcing WOW out of its home. "Whether in crinoline or leather and hardware, these women bring a neofeminist attitude to their act. WOW's casual collective has helped add this new flavor to the neighborhood's traditional drag performance scene," she wrote. "The new look can be seen everywhere, in the store windows, on the streets, as well as on East Village stages. It's the triumph of the drag queen aesthetic, but new and improved!"[8] At the very moment when East Village "coolness" was precisely the reason WOW found itself on the street, Conkey described the collective's aesthetic as a "new and improved" commodity, a "new look" that could be merchandised and sold in store windows. By conflating WOW's work with the neighborhood's drag queen aesthetic, WOW became linked with several statements on the apolitical nature of East Village performance made by other performers quoted throughout Conkey's piece. For example, Alan Mace, manager of the Pyramid Club, insisted that "politically, we don't have anything to say. Right when we first opened we started dancing on the bar and dressing up. It was fun, that's all."[9]

WOW's storefront performances were definitely lots of fun, but they were also decidedly political, although the work may not have fallen within traditional definitions of political theater. Conkey's article ended with a nod to "economic encroachment," pointing to the opening of Steve's Ice Cream, which sold "$2 cones," as evidence. "Real estate values are creating something of a counterrevolution," Conkey wrote, "and lesbians claim they are getting hit the hardest."[10] Lesbians were in fact getting hit hard. In her response Shaw decried not only the economic changes taking place in the neighborhood, changes in which WOW was unavoidably caught up, but also the way association with the club scene in general was erasing WOW's unique aesthetic and political contributions.

In a 1985 interview, Shaw and Lois Weaver described plans for WOW's new home and the collective's vision for the opening show. "This is going to be about the neighborhood," Shaw said. "Carmelita is going to play Saint Joan as a lesbian. We needed a hero so we came up with Saint Joan . . . she's going to win in the end."[11] Much of the work produced at WOW is based in narrative, but it parodies those narratives in ways that are not necessarily linear in structure and rarely if ever didactic. With *Saint Joan*, the impulse was to be absolutely clear about the story and its message. Weaver stressed the importance of WOW's opening show as a form of community theater. "When you don't get trendy," she said of this kind of experience, "that's the feeling of community theater I have, along with the notion that anyone can play a part . . . whoever shows up for rehearsals gets to be in the play."[12] It is as if WOW's response to the "horrifying changes" taking place in their newly trendy neighborhood was to stage an aesthetically untrendy production. If WOW had been perceived as apolitical in the storefront, then it would come out in its new space as overtly political.

In *Saint Joan of Avenue C,* the collective set out to stage its version of the counterrevolution Conkey had alluded to in her *Village Voice* article. The show's program notes declare "LOWER EAST SIDE FIGHTS BACK!" followed by a brief description of the message underpinning the plot.

> This afternoon, citizens of New York's lower East Side scored another victory in its ongoing battle against luxury development of the neighborhood. Led by Juanita Loisaida, an ex-city office worker, the residents occupied lots slated for high-rises, buildings marked for demolition, and Tompkins Square Park. Donna Trumpet, a wealthy developer . . . said she was not in the least disturbed by today's occurrences. "They're just a bunch of dykes and derelicts," she said. "Obviously, the city will not negotiate with people of that ilk." But

Juanita and community organizer Dunois said they will not give up the fight until all people are guaranteed adequate shelter.

Like all WOW shows, *Saint Joan* was a community effort. Deb Margolin, Peggy Shaw, and Lois Weaver had written it in collaboration with the company. Susan Young designed the costumes, Joni Wong did the lighting, Shaw created the sets, and Diane Jeep Ries did hair. Alice Forrester was the stage manager, Alisa Solomon served as dramaturge, and Weaver directed the production. Alina Troyano starred in the role of Juanita Loisaida, a name that marked the East Village as a haven for artists and as home to a large Latina/Latino community. Pronounced "Lo-ee-SIDE-a," the character was the Lower East Side's Saint Joan. The cast included Ana Maria Simo, a founding member of WOW's precursor, Medusa's Revenge; filmmaker Ela Troyano (Alina's sister); and women who would go on to develop substantial work of their own at WOW, including Lynn Hayes, Lisa Kron, Claire Moed, and Susan Young.

Saint Joan of Avenue C did not quite come together, perhaps because of its rather flatfooted approach to politics. Another reason had to do with the group process as a means of generating material in the context of community theater. This long-standing if intermittent practice had been used during the storefront years to develop a piece called *A Tennessee Waltz*—all those who had responded to the open call developed their own material based on characters from the plays of Tennessee Williams—as well as an adaptation of Hans Christian Andersen's *The Snow Queen* by a group that billed itself as the Working Girls Repertory. Heady with the proposition of performing in a larger space and in keeping with the spirit of WOW, every member of the collective was encouraged to be in *Saint Joan*. The resulting cast of eighteen performers managed to fit on the stage if not in the dressing room. Looking back on the production, Troyano explained the process: "*Saint Joan of Avenue C* was real community theater. Everybody got to write their parts; we did a lot of exercises to develop dialogue and monologues. Everybody wrote their own stuff, but then to integrate them all into one thing was hellish to say the least. And a lot of people had never acted before."[13] Shaw said of the acting, "A couple of people in *Saint Joan* were really bad; it's always true in WOW shows. When people started complaining, Lois [Weaver] said, 'Listen, get over it! This is community theater. Anybody can be in this show.'"[14]

Uneven acting had always been part of WOW's charm. What undermined

Saint Joan, however, was having eighteen performers generate their own material. So why engage in this practice and continue it into the future? Because the experience of finding a voice from which to generate original material, learning techniques for developing it, and having the wherewithal to get up and perform it in front of an audience was important in and of itself. It was also productive for WOW's future development. Many of the women who participated in these productions went on to make significant work. Four of the Five Lesbian Brothers, for instance, had performed in one or more of WOW's early community theater productions. Considered a direct descendent of the Split Britches troupe, the Five Lesbian Brothers employed the techniques and strategies culled from these experiences in developing their own work, as did many of those working in WOW's second home. But not all WOW artists worked collaboratively. Holly Hughes, Cheryl Moch, Madeleine Olnek, Sarah Schulman, Sharon Jane Smith, and Alina Troyano, among others, are primarily writers who do not necessarily employ collaborative methods in the development of their scripts. All WOW shows are community efforts, but not all are community theater.

Despite *Saint Joan's* unevenly crafted, heavy-handed parable of good versus evil, there were moments when WOW's signature wit bled through. In an attempt to explain her woeful lack of hero potential, Juanita Loisaida cries, "I come home and watch *Cagney and Lacey.* On Saturday nights, my girlfriend and I do Latin disco!" Troyano consciously wrote and played the lead role as a Latina, while a kind of uninterrogated color blindness marked the parts written by white women. Troyano's acknowledged and simultaneously unacknowledged position as a woman of color in the piece affected the narrative in unanticipated ways. Critic Laurie Stone's review for the *Village Voice* panned the production: "The problem here is that they're too smitten with Joan to tinker with the story. . . . A large portion of the script is rally rhetoric. . . . Harnessed to a sacred cow, the group's fine outrage on behalf of the dispossessed and exploited goes loping into the dust."[15]

There were a number of reasons why the show did not work, but shyness over deconstructing a saintly saga was not one of them. Stone was right in sensing that *something* was wrong. Watching Troyano play the lead in a cast made up overwhelmingly of white women—without a whisper of her well-known alter ego, Carmelita Tropicana—made manifest what was amiss. The hesitancy Stone sensed in the production was not about fear of tampering with Saint Joan's story as a sacred cow—WOW artists are nothing if not fearless—but of a woman of color in the leading role of a narrative that called for her death as a sacrificial lamb. In describing the play's heroine, Stone stated matter-of-factly, "[H]er fervor shames and wearies her followers, and she's eventually sacrificed."[16] This means that *in performance* a cast made up overwhelmingly of white women turns on a woman of color. The company may have ignored this issue altogether or more or less consciously tiptoed around it.

When *Saint Joan* closed in the fall of 1985, whiteness remained a wholly unmarked and yet to be theorized dynamic in performance. A year later, however, a very different production opened WOW's second season in its new home—*Memorias de la Revolución*—a play that consciously took on white womanhood. Again, WOW would be in the forefront, staging that which was—if not unimaginable then—as yet unarticulated.

Taking on White Womanhood: Memorias de la Revolución

Out of the experience of being totally ignored and invisible, hilarious comedy erupted. The great gift of WOW was that lesbians were taken for granted. Plays didn't have to explain anything.
—MADELEINE OLNEK, 2002

The performance studies scholar José Esteban Muñoz developed a rich analysis of Troyano's Carmelita Tropicana persona in his 1999 book *Disidentifications: Queers of Color and the Performance of Politics*. Muñoz considers the strategies Troyano deploys in her work as exemplary of *disidentification*, which he defines as "a mode of performance whereby a toxic identity is remade and infiltrated by subjects who have been hailed by such identity categories but have not been able to own such a label."[17] Or, as the journalist C. Carr put it, writing about WOW performance in general, "What keeps me coming back is the energy of people who are publicly redefining the thing that labels them."[18] Muñoz invokes the Cuban notion of *chusma* as both a general quality and a type of individual to describe the particular kind of parody Troyano enacts. "The *chusma*'s life is *pure performance*," wrote Muñoz. "It is about studied excess and overblown self-fashioning. It rejects constraints on the self that are mandated for the 'good immigrant' by Anglo culture."[19]

In the earnest, straightforwardly scripted context of *Saint Joan of Avenue C*, the character of Juanita can be understood as the good, self-sacrificing immigrant. In the dialogue of the unpublished script, the character describes herself as follows: "Ladies you have not looked at me. I'm just a city office worker. I live with my mother, I support her. I go to work and I go home. I've learned to make a life for myself with these small things. I have a lover who's pretty and funny, and I like to eat Fried Clams. That's all. That's what I am."[20] The lesbian Latina protagonist of *Saint Joan* was played out in the tension between a toxic identity and the legendary stature of a historical figure. "Disidentification for the minority subject," writes Muñoz, "is a mode of *recycling* or re-forming an object that has already been invested with powerful energy. It is important to emphasize . . . the transformative restructuration of that disidentification."[21] The guileless production style of *Saint Joan* rendered the lead character unworkable in the absence of those reforming, transformative strategies that constitute Muñoz's concept of disidentification.

In her own work, however, Troyano addresses the complexities of her positions in enormously complex ways. The piece *Memorias de la Revolución,* for instance, enacts what the subtitle of her book *I, Carmelita Tropicana: Performing between Cultures* proclaims, consciously and pointedly "performing between cultures."[22] Born in Cuba and raised mostly in the United States, Troyano mined the boundaries of national identities for *Memorias,* extending her experience of living between cultures to an exploration of multiple border crossings. The piece exemplifies the project of disidentification in the case of the play's several stereotypical Latina/Latino characters, but it also mines the terrain of mainstream identities, representing and critiquing white womanhood in particular. Troyano "outs" institutionalized whiteness, particularly that of the United States as it is oftentimes *seen* internationally. In *Memorias,* Troyano builds on WOW's aesthetic principles, creating her own inspired and expansive vision. Multiple intersections of gender, sexuality, ethnicity, nationality, class, and race abound, but none is privileged. For this and many other reasons, *Memorias de la Revolución* was a groundbreaking work in WOW's production history.

The show's press release announced a "multi-media, comedy extravaganza with music and a cast of ten lovely beauties, in English, that presents the personal memoirs of the daughter of the Cuban revolution and star of stage and screen, Carmelita Tropicana." The play revolves around two nightclubs: the Tropicana in 1955 Havana, where Carmelita incites a revolution, and the Tropicana-a-Go-Go in 1967 New York, where she triumphs over the play's villain and sends up the period's feminism. *Memorias* uses a lush palette to paint a landscape of multilayered, intersecting identities. A cast of nine women each play more than one role: some characters are Cuban, some

American, some German; some are women, some are men; one plays a tomboy who passes as a man. The dialogue is in English, as promised, but interwoven with much Spanish, as well as German and Yiddish. The cast's tenth "lovely beauty" was played by the show's coauthor, Uzi Parnes, who made his appearance on 16 mm film as an apparition of the Virgin Mary-cum-Jewish mother, who appears to Carmelita in the dead of night as she flees Cuba by boat.

Troyano and Parnes managed to put multiple identities into play without reducing Carmelita or any other character to any single one. As nightclub proprietor, diva extraordinaire, and burgeoning revolutionary, Carmelita falls in love with a German gunrunner and spy, Lota Hari, granddaughter of Mata Hari. Lota is played by Diane Jeep Reis as a dead ringer for Marlene Dietrich. In a sub-subplot the couple adopts a little German girl, naming her Carme Lota Nota Hari ("Lota taught her spying, Carmelita singing").[23] She grows into a Joni Mitchell–type folksinger, dedicating her deadpan version of "Eve of Destruction" to "meine mutti."[24] In a play on Oscar Wilde's infamous character Dorian Gray, the Virgin tells Carmelita that in exchange for lifelong youth she must never let a man touch her. Carmelita responds delightedly: "Believe me, to Carmelita Tropicana Guzman Jimenez Marquesa de Aguas Claras, that is never to be a problem."[25] Turning to the audience, she winks conspiratorially.

Repeated references are made to economic conditions, calling attention to the excessive cost of things, and at one point Carmelita's baby brother speaks of the high-class people who live the high life and consider him "low-life *chusma.*" By simultaneously putting into play national, religious, and entertainment figures from disparate historical periods, identity categories lose their meaning as reliably fixed entities within the narrative. In *Memorias* identity is not the psychic property of individuals. Instead, identities are performed and come across as fluid, contingent, and historically and socially situated. The intersections of gender, race, class, ethnicity, and sexuality that produce identities are performed and critiqued in *Memorias* in ways that resist the trap of privileging and reaffirming stable identity categories. *Memorias* is inhabited with one-dimensional caricatures that bespeak multiple dimensions.

Carmelita herself is at the center of the play's Cuban revolution; she is the brains behind "Operation Fry the Banana," an assassination attempt on Havana's evil chief of police, Capitan Maldito. The characters rendezvous at "the fabuloso nightclub Tropicana, a place for art, revolution and political intrigue," where the Tropicanettes perform the show's big musical number,

"Jes, We Have No Bananas," with "large fruits attached to their costumes on their rears."[26] This is tremendous fun and provides an excellent example of disidentification at work, but it also functions to set up a critique of white women. In the audience of this decadent prerevolution floor show are the requisite bourgeois American tourists, Brendah and Brendaa, two white, similarly dressed "American girls." They symbolize what Shaw described earlier in her letter to the *Village Voice* as "white surface consumer voyeurism."[27] It is not an accident that in *Memorias* such symbolism is rendered in gender-specific terms, nor is the "duh" in the girls' indistinguishable names an oversight. White womanhood is the warehouse where vacuous consumerism and white supremacy are stored and from which their meanings are deployed. Brendah and Brendaa are multilayered caricatures that have no emotional depth but are packed with a plethora of meanings.

The Americans are present at the invitation of Carmelita's brother Machito, an incorrigible flirt. In a hilarious bit typical of the shtick that permeates the show, Machito takes the girls on a "quick tour" of the island; they run furiously in place while scenes of Cuba's tourist hot spots flash by on the screen behind them. Brendah and Brendaa are smitten with Machito and his sidekick, Marimacho (who is later revealed to be a woman passing as a man). The women chase them across Havana in hopes of landing a couple of "sexy, virile, Latin men" and returning home with rocks on their fingers. This send-up of voracious femininity focused on the ultimate goal of a trip to the altar highlights white women's presumption that Latin men are a kind of commodity somehow more sexed and sexual than their white counterparts and available to be shipped home.

As tourists, Brendah and Brendaa are voyeurs who serve as bookends to the play's action, witnessing events from beginning to end. They are essentially interchangeable in their indistinguishableness and suggest, by extension, that all white women and white tourists are as well. Preoccupied with their own concerns and mouthing inanities throughout, these twin tourists represent North American ethnocentrism and imperialism. When an especially violent incident in the revolution takes place in the nightclub, the two sit at an adjoining table completely engrossed with a matchbook on which a few lines of Machito's romantic poetry are written. Oblivious to the historical events unfolding around them, they busily steal ashtrays off the tables along with every other souvenir they can get their hands on. Brendah and Brendaa are so entirely out of sync with the rhythm and action of the play that they stand out as self-interested, greed-driven, particularly white sore thumbs.

Her assassination attempt thwarted, Carmelita flees Havana by boat—a tableau staged to resemble the famous nineteenth-century painting of George Washington crossing the Delaware with Carmelita posed nobly as the figure of Washington. The ensuing dialogue parodies the melodramatic scene from the 1944 Hollywood classic *Lifeboat,* when the character played by Tallulah Bankhead sacrifices her diamond bracelet as fish bait for the starving crew. *Memorias de la Revolución* repeatedly draws on images, narratives, and songs from various historical periods, classical works, Hollywood films, and other forms of popular culture, layering the piece with wildly disparate references. This mix resonates with the ways in which the characters' multiple identity categories intersect in both predictable and unpredictable ways. The Virgin Mary figure is played by a white Jewish man in drag. She appears to Carmelita following a life-threatening storm at sea to convey the message that Carmelita's *art* will be her revolution. Performing between cultures, identities, and mediums, the Virgin's lines are delivered via film: "Your art is your weapon. To give dignity to Latin and Third World women: this is your struggle."[28] Although the play is outrageously theatrical and hilariously funny, there is a kind of gravity underpinning many of its moments. The boat scene, for instance, is reminiscent of those Cubans who have made, or failed in their attempt to make, the dangerous crossing to the shores of Florida.

Laurie Stone gave the show a rave review, but her one criticism is telling: "the omission from the piece of the actual Cuban revolution—Castro and Che are never even mentioned." Stone attributes this lack to "fuzzy thinking" on the part of the playwrights, but it is she who has missed the point. "It's impossible to tell what Tropicana thinks of Castro's regime," Stone wrote, "but since her character simultaneously turns away from men and Cuban politics, an impression is left that Castro is abandoned because he's a man."[29] Here Carmelita's lesbianism is reduced to turning *against* men rather than *to* women. The agency of a woman, in this instance Carmelita, is once again eschewed by the claim that she can only make sense in relation to the category of "man," in this case Fidel Castro. Troyano is not against Castro and Che Guevara; she is indifferent to them for the purposes of her story. She is not indifferent to the historical revolution in Cuba; rather, she plays on it to portray a different kind of revolution—one that gives voice to the politics embedded in stories never told, the histories missing from history books.

In one scene, for example, Capitan Maldito brags about being so macho he has two cocks: "One's named Adolph, for Hitler, and the other Rudolph, for the reindeer."[30] He then harasses the club's chanteuse, Rosita, forcing her to sing a song and brutally dancing with her, repeatedly throwing her across the dance floor, grabbing her by the hair, and finally dropping her to the floor. Rosita sobs throughout the rest of the scene. As performed by the actors Kate Stafford and Lisa Kron, this dance was outrageously funny and horrifying, its alignment of macho with violence against women unmistakable. Those who have seen *Memorias de la Revolución* might well be tempted to paraphrase Troyano's description of her own experience when she first saw the play *Split Britches:* "It made me cry in one eye and laugh in the other."[31]

Memorias not only reflected progressive, cutting-edge thought; it reached beyond it. In the arena of performance, casting white women in Latino roles and playing them as men is but one example of this. Troyano's own male impersonation took the form of "Pingalito Betancourt"—an especially inspired character. "If a title hooked an audience, a name fed the imagination," Troyano later wrote. "When I heard the name Pingalito . . . little Dick, a typical macho Cubano, sauntered off the page with guayabera and cigar."[32] Her performance in full male drag was extraordinary in its portrayal of masculinity, particularly in contrast to her rendering of Carmelita. She utterly reined in the performative excesses of her better-known spitfire persona to portray a different kind of *chusma,* or overblown self-fashioning, in the form of an arrogant but endearing Cubano who hijacks the frantic pace of the production, taking up space and time in a comment on the condition of "macho."

As the conductor on Havana's M15 bus route, the character Pingalito is equal parts narrator, tour guide, and philosopher. He strolls onto the stage wearing a fashionable 1940s man's hat unfashionably; the top is stylishly pinched, but the brim is spread wide with conductor's tickets tucked in the band. He wears nondescript men's eyeglasses with a little bulge of rolled white tape holding the bridge together over his nose and a loose-fitting guayabera-style shirt hanging untucked over his trousers. Pingalito is a compact, self-possessed, self-assured, opinionated Cuban man—"the Socrates of the M15 bus route," as he proclaims. Cigar in hand, Pingalito addresses the audience directly, taking his time as he recounts anecdotes and imparts wisdom on a number of subjects—a kind of Cuban George Burns. "In order for you to enjoy the show tonight," he tells the audience midway through his monologue, "I will give you my own perspective of Cuba—from history, geography, and culture."[33] Reaching into his pocket for an "audiovisual aid," he pulls out a place mat with the title "Facts about Cuba," a document, he explains, that he picked up in a Miami restaurant.

Pingalito reads from the place mat, providing commentary and scratching his crotch periodically along the way. For instance, Fact #4 states, "Three-fourths of all Cubans are white of Spanish descent." To which Pingalito adds, "And a lot of these three-fourths have a very dark suntan all year round."[34] Troyano makes whiteness explicit as a social construct when Pingalito marks this bid for whiteness on behalf of Cubans as articulated on an ersatz document of Miami origin. The furtive nature of this cultural imperialism is foregrounded by cycling a Cubano perspective back through a Miami perspective on Cuba.

Cocreators Parnes and Troyano felt strongly that the characters written as men should be cast with women and played in male drag; they wanted the show's aesthetic to resonate with this doubling. Of Parnes as a director, Stone wrote that he "guides the performers handily, letting the women who play men exult in the pleasures of cross-dressing—hitching up their crotches, narrowing their eyes at women."[35] The doubling that cross-casting promises, however, is harder to sustain in male drag than it is in female drag. In his review of *Memorias,* the critic Kevin Grubb wrote, "So adept are some of the actors playing men that we search our programs in vain for the male actor who must have escaped our first reading."[36] Women tend to disappear in male drag because, as gender studies scholar Judith Halberstam has pointed out, "Within the theater of mainstream gender roles, femininity is often presented as simply costume whereas masculinity manifests as realism or as body."[37]

In other words, femininity is understood as artifice while masculinity is perceived as "the real thing." If femininity is artifice—a costume, an "act"—then *any* body can wear and enact it; if masculinity is perceived as the natural condition and sole property of male bodies, women who enact masculinity tend to pass as men, disappearing into the perception, the gestalt, of male bodies. Like Grubb, some audience members perceived the women in male drag as men, but others read them differently. Of Maureen Angelos's portrayal of Machito, "a macho among machos," Troyano later wrote, "Angelos was wonderful at male drag and cut a dashing figure that made both straight women and lesbians swoon."[38] Some swooned over Machito as a man, others as a butch lesbian.

Race is in large measure what makes male impersonation in *Memorias de la Revolución* readable. Halberstam is talking about the "theater of mainstream gender roles" or the way symbolic systems circulate within dominant cultures. White women tend to disappear into impersonations of white men. In his study of how race is performed in classic Hollywood film, the cinema scholar Richard Dyer has described performances by white people as so reined in, so severely unexpressive, that whites represent a pure or disembodied abstraction. "Whites," he suggests, "are the living dead."[39] Halberstam concurs with this notion but contends that such contained, nonexpressive performances characterize white masculinity in particular. Dyer describes the roles played by people of color as representing more "life" than roles played by whites, more emotion and sensuality derived from a presumed closer proximity to nature; thus, in this view people of color are positioned to represent backwardness, irrationality, chaos, and violence. In mainstream representation, then, people of color are constructed as somehow more embodied than white people and therefore more animated.

So, while a character like Pingalito is much less expressive than Troyano's rendering of Carmelita Tropicana, he is far more expressive than portrayals of his white, bourgeois counterparts. Halberstam has argued that genteel white masculinity is virtually nonperformative. This logic would suggest that it is easier to impersonate a working-class Joe Sixpack character like Dan on the long-running sitcom *Roseanne* than the father figures on *Leave It to Beaver* or *Father Knows Best*. Stereotypical expressivity does not flow naturally from Latino masculinities; instead, men of color—as well as other "others"—are aligned in the symbolic realms of mainstream culture with the supposed weaker boundaries of nature, signaling a wider range of expression in the social. Stone has described women playing Latinos as *exalting* in "hitching up their crotches, narrowing their eyes at women."[40] When such expressiveness is performed onstage and in the street, it reaffirms the supposed naturalness of it, marking its distance from bourgeois propriety.

Parnes and Troyano's desire for women to be visible *as women* impersonating men is in part about the ever-present scarcity of such portrayals. Spectators who occupy subject positions outside of mainstream forms of representation are hungry for experiences with which they can identify. As Holly Hughes put it at the time, "Women's sexuality is a tortured area. Whether it's gay or straight, it's always in the closet."[41] WOW productions engaged in butch/femme's seductive play on gender in an attempt to keep women visible in all the characters they played. As Hughes described male impersonation at WOW, women played men "in quotes."[42] Thanks to work like Halberstam's, today it is possible to understand and articulate these performances within and through what she has called "female masculinity"— enacted by women who refuse to agree that masculinity belongs solely to male bodies, wrenching masculinity away from this misperception and claiming it as their own. In the mid-1980s, however, women disappearing into male roles *felt* like women's sexuality returning to the closet. But this is precisely how Troyano pushed at the boundaries of what was conceivable at the time. In performance, *Memorias de la Revolución* gave women free rein over the performative landscape of Latino masculinities, and, as Stone saw it, they exulted in the pleasures of cross-dressing. In this and many other ways, Troyano's work imagined an alternative to the limitations of mainstream representation—a more expansive symbolic landscape for unrepresented, underrepresented, and misrepresented subjects.

Confronting Heterosexuality: Voyage to Lesbos

We don't kill them because they're bad. We kill them because we're bad.
  —*The Secretaries*, 1993

In a 1993 interview the novelist Margaret Atwood said, "We're tired of being good all the time. When you deprive women of any notion of threat, it pretty much puts them back in the Victorian age—all innocent without power, except the power of being good."[43] This otherwise innocuous statement demonstrates the not uncommon supposition that women are fundamentally defined in terms of goodness and innocence; it presumes "good-girlness" as a baseline condition of *all women.* That Atwood specifically references the nineteenth century is also apt because "the good girl" is a direct descendent of that century's amalgam "true womanhood," the ideological site where enduring notions of ideal femininity were fleshed out and circulated within what historians have described as the "cult of true womanhood."

As explored in previous chapters, the operating principles of WOW's space and the work produced there were informed by a strong desire to thwart good-girlness in its many manifestations. From its inception WOW was conceived as a site where good girls could go bad. At the same time, however, the historical processes and meanings that produce the good girl paradigm are inescapably called forth and manifested in the very act of thwarting it, giving rise to the question of who has access to a state of presumptive innocence and goodness in the first place. In performance, do *all* female bodies conjure ideal womanhood's constellation of images and meanings against which the bad girl is rendered legible?

Just as Troyano's *Memorias de la Revolución* depends on mainstream readings of ethnic and racial stereotypes—performing them in ways that refigure and transform them—so, too, does the work of white women at WOW. In mainstream Western culture, the good girl is understood as straight, middle-class, and white; she emerges at the intersection of gender, sexuality, class, and race. The point of transformative cultural work is to intervene in these symbolic systems insofar as they diminish whole groups of people who live under a cluster of limiting, prescribed meanings and concomitant constraints. Differing symbolic constructs call for differing modes of intervention. Dominant symbolic systems ascribe meanings to the bodies of women of color that are different from each other, as well as different from those attending the bodies of white women.

Although Troyano's work certainly engaged sexuality in resistant, oppositional ways, it was not preoccupied with sex in ways that characterized the work of at least some white women at WOW. These artists performed sexuality in specific, over-the-top, excessive ways that worked oppositionally because they were played out on the bodies of white women. For instance, in her review of the piece *Queer Justice,* the critic Alisa Solomon described two of the ten solo pieces that made up the show: "A woman introduces herself as a 'lesbian truck driver extraordinaire' and croons a country-western paean to life on the road, an eighteen inch vibrator dangling from her belt. 'Driving my truck is like a good fuck,' she sings. 'What do you say we set cruise control? We can rock till we drop and continue to roll.' The audience hoots, and swoons playfully in response to this open celebration of a sexuality that is represented rarely. . . . [A] woman in a short tight, black leather skirt gyrates and grinds, curling her ruby-red mouth into baby-doll kisses as she lip-synchs along with a recording of the old pop tune, 'Pretty woman, walking down the street. . . . ' As she twists toward the floor, her skirt hikes up her thighs, revealing red satin panties. Once again, the audience hoots, howls, and swoons."[44]

The sexuality rarely represented, as Solomon puts it, is produced in the exchange of desire between performers and spectators.[45] This hooting, howling, swooning audience is made up principally of women responding to the seductive overtures of the performers. In a mainstream venue these performances would be read quite differently; lesbian desire played out excessively as an oppositional strategy would be lost outside the context of WOW. The subversive potential of *Queer Justice* depends almost entirely on the production's subcultural context. Still, there is no mistaking this truck driver and pretty woman for good girls. A certain defiance of cultural norms remains in play. Moreover, the ability to read these performances as representing bad girls depends on a backdrop of all that constitutes proper womanhood, which is decidedly equated with white womanhood. The challenge for WOW's white performers is to retain a subversive edge, not merely a defiant one, in both subcultural and mainstream contexts. This is the challenge the Five Lesbian Brothers take on. Many WOW practitioners illuminated the machinations of white womanhood in the 1980s but none quite as fiercely as the Five Lesbian Brothers did in the 1990s.

Maureen Angelos, Babs Davy, Dominique Dibbell, Peg Healey, and Lisa Kron are the Five Lesbian Brothers—or "the Brothers," as they call themselves. Emblazoned across the troupe's T-shirts and letterhead is the tagline "Commercially viable yet enchantingly homosexual." With each production a number of artists and reviewers associated with the downtown theater scene believed that the Brothers were the lesbian troupe that would finally achieve commercial success. And they did. Four of the Brothers' five shows were produced off-Broadway. That they have not managed to sustain commercial success has nothing to do with their skill as performers or the ingeniousness of their scripts. Rather, it has to do with the limitations under which women in general labor in theater combined with the magnitude of their perceived threat—acute unease is a not uncommon effect of the Brothers' productions.

"The genius of this work is that the Brothers don't use comedy to make a feminist, anti-homophobic point go down easy," wrote Solomon, "the comedy *is* the point—and so is the anxiety and terror."[46] One source of this anxiety is the unnerving way the Brothers fully inhabit white womanhood and perform it with a vengeance. As self-described lesbian brothers, they posit themselves as the epitome of "bad" womanhood while explicitly playing out all the historical and contemporary baggage of proper womanhood. Dibbell has articulated this one-two punch: "We're rebel girls in a nasty way."[47] All WOW girls are rebels, but with the Brothers it is a double whammy.

Like Troyano's *Memorias* in the mid-1980s, the Brothers' first production in 1990, *Voyage to Lesbos,* represents a turning point in WOW's representational history. *Lesbos* was markedly different from other WOW shows, including its own precursors—*Paradykes Alley* (1987) and *Paradykes Lost* (1988)—in which four of the yet to be Brothers performed. In coming together as the Five Lesbian Brothers in 1989, Angelos, Davy, Dibbell, Healey, and Kron adopted an in-your-face style akin to that of Queer Nation, the activist group formed, in part, in response to the AIDS pandemic. Queer Nation abandoned assimilation in favor of direct action in the fight for gay rights, proclaiming, "We're here! We're queer! Get used to it!" In a similar spirit the Brothers unabashedly staged explicit scenarios and images of boy-on-girl sexuality that had been assiduously sidestepped in WOW work.

Voyage to Lesbos is set in a pre-Stonewall midwestern town and focuses on preparations and events leading up to a wedding, the ultimate rite of passage into a future of domestic bliss. The bride is Bonnie, a character who at one time or another has had sex with all four of the other women in the play. Throughout the piece she repeatedly and graphically describes sexual acts with her soon to be husband, Brad, raving about the joys of heterosexual sex. In one of her celebratory rants, Bonnie offers the following advice to her neurotic cousin: "Connie. I always told you. You don't need a PhD. A dick. That's what you need. Find the biggest one you can. Sweetie, if he rams it in you as hard as he can you'll be swell. You won't be feeling nothing but big dick."[48] And to her one lesbian friend, Bonnie says, "You see, Evelyn . . . Brad's peter is about fourteen inches long. And when it's up inside me, I swear, I just see stars. A woman could never give you that. I feel sorry for you. . . . When I'm on top of him, it's like I've got an oak tree growing up inside of me. I can feel the branches branching out, and all the leaves."[49]

At a time when sex-positive lesbians were productively recuperating the dildo—strapping it on and laying claim to it on their own terms, separating it from its connection solely with male bodies—the Brothers focused a spotlight on the literal male organ, demystifying it and undermining its connection with the phallus as a privileged symbol. Healey, who played Bonnie, explained it this way: "The phallus represents society and heterosexual culture. In that sense, it's a very important part of our show."[50] Some spectators found *Voyage to Lesbos* fascinating, others distressing. Those who found it upsetting were used to the respite WOW had provided from a presumptive, imperative heterosexual world and were taken aback by the play's obsessive focus on heterosexuality, not to mention its ending, in which the groom is killed on the eve of his nuptials by a deranged lesbian, portrayed as a cold, vengeful man hater. Although Brad is not a character in the play, Healey shrewdly remarked of her character's phantom beau, "Interestingly, with five lesbians on stage and Brad nowhere to be seen, merely a name on our lips, he somehow managed to get into the reviews."[51]

The play fiercely skewed the demands of normative heterosexuality and also launched the beginnings of a critique of whiteness by exposing white womanhood as more than the property of individuals, setting it up as a kind of institution and eviscerating it from the inside out. To intervene in the good-girl construct by parodying the mainstream forms in which it lives—as in romance novels, television sitcoms, and films, as in *Memorias* or popular songs, as in *Queer Justice*—risks reaffirming the veracity of its original propositions. In the process of defying the norm, the norm itself is re-presented, reassuring audiences that it prevails. As a form of embodied representation, performance unavoidably enacts race, class, gender, and sexuality. Even when these identity categories are culturally unmarked—like whiteness—they are nonetheless presumptively read and produce meanings.

Although the good girl is the foundation on which much popular culture has been built, there is nothing inherently liberatory in the act of inserting lesbian characters into parodies of mainstream representational forms. There is nothing necessarily disruptive and subversive about white women rejecting the privileges whiteness bestows. As the scholar Peggy Phelan has described it, "In abandoning the dream of being a spoiled white girl, I paradoxically confirm the fact that I am spoiled enough and white enough to be able to afford to abandon it."[52] But the "bad girl" plays out in more complex and productive ways at WOW than simply turning one's back on privilege or performing an alternative sexuality as a means of disrupting the good-girl syndrome. Work like that of the Five Lesbian Brothers takes on the entire institutionalized conglomerate "white womanhood," which is more than merely a component of whiteness. Ideologically and symbolically, white womanhood carries the meanings of whiteness itself as a racial category.

Many WOW artists addressed the good-girl construct, but the Brothers did so more pointedly and conspicuously, as if they consciously returned to the origins of true womanhood in the nineteenth century to expose the continuing saliency of its foundational precepts. If such an analysis seems far-fetched, consider this: the musical *Seven Brides for Seven Brothers* was the original concept behind the Brothers's third play, *The Secretaries*. The initial idea was to parody the piece by playing the seven lumberjack brothers as five lumberjack lesbians. When the troupe sat down to watch the film version of the musical, however, they were horrified by the overt sexism driving the narrative. They decided to play the brides, instead of the brothers, as five secretaries working for a lumber mill but with no familial relationship to the lumberjacks. "Sick and disgusting scenes of the ravages of internalized sexism came pouring forth," recalled Dibbell of the collaborative writing process for *The Secretaries*.[53] That the resulting text uncannily parallels nineteenth-century concepts of true womanhood is attributable to the enduring legacy of this ideology, which is archived in cultural memory and ghosted in the bodies of white women.

The cult of true womanhood has been described as premised on and emerging from four overarching qualities: piety, purity, submissiveness, and domesticity.[54] Together these attributes produced an ideal against which all women were measured. The ideal was not monolithic and certainly does not represent the histories of all nineteenth-century women or the diverse ways both white women and women of color actually lived. Still, it strongly informed contemporary notions of legitimate womanhood in the realm of the symbolic. In turn, the ideal's codified, prescriptive nature had its effects on women's lives in the realm of the social—producing the contradictions that inspired abolitionist Sojourner Truth's famous question at Seneca Falls in 1851. When she asked "Ain't I a woman?" the answer was a qualified yes. By definition, true womanhood posits an untrue or incorrect womanhood, which is not exclusively a consequence of aberrant behavior but of racial and class positioning. Respectable, white, bourgeois women were the sole occupants of the category. Truth and others like her were women, of course, but not *truly* so. Working-class and poor white women, too, had been essentially written out of the category of "woman."

A single scene from *Voyage to Lesbos* provides an example of the ways in which true womanhood's major themes are played out textually and performatively in the Brothers' work. With one exception the play's characters are portrayed not as lesbians but as straight, white, stay-at-home, middle-class women attempting to suppress their homosexual leanings; they each represent a variation on the same white-bread model or vacuous type with little emotional depth. When Bonnie and her cousin seek help in exorcising their aberrant desires, Bonnie visits a priest's confessional, and Connie visits a psychiatrist's office. The scene takes place in near darkness, with the priest positioned on one side of the stage and the psychiatrist on the other, both played as male characters, both seated in profile "hidden" behind a scrim and lit from behind. Also in profile, the women each face the silhouetted figure of the authority they have come to consult. As the scene unfolds, the women's lines overlap, revealing little substantive difference as Bonnie confesses her sins against God and Connie confesses her sins against man. The intimate, private spaces a confessional and therapist's office suggest become increasingly sexually charged as the men's overlapping dialogue elicits ever more graphic details of the women's sexual fantasies.[55]

Although scenes such as this throughout the Brothers' repertoire are played with a kind of eerie darkness—as opposed to camped up—humor invariably bubbles up periodically from beneath the surface. Bonnie's sins are absolved through penance when the priest places her hand on his crotch. "Why, Father!" she exclaims, "You have a hard-on the size of a truck!" The stage direction reads, "Bonnie complies good-naturedly with a lackluster hand job." Therapy is the cure for Connie's illness. The psychiatrist concludes, "I feel it is important for you to become physically close to a real man. . . . Now I'm going to ask you to come over here and sit on my lap. . . . That's it. . . . Do you feel a real man's penis inside you?" Connie replies, "I think I'm getting better, Doctor."

Because the characters are played one-dimensionally throughout the piece, and because the action is staged behind a scrim, making it suggestive rather than realistic, the scene is more about the horrors of subjects trapped within ideologies that mask their own contradictions than about the horrors of individuals victimized by sexual abuse. To be absolved and cured, and thereby returned to a state of grace and health, requires submission to institutions that, whether religious or secular, serve their own agendas, institutions that the Brothers draw here as patriarchal. Echoing early feminism, the dialogue makes use of the personal to reveal the political writ large. The scene is paradigmatic in that it works to unmask and expose the contradictions inherent in all ideologies and their institutions, contradictions that sow the seeds of their own demise, creating the possibility for change.

Although the Brothers did not deliberately mine the historical construct "true womanhood" in creating their work, a kind of echo or residue clearly informed their collective imagination. Indeed, the first act of their second play, *Brave Smiles . . . Another Lesbian Tragedy* (1992), quite literally plays out the themes of piety, purity, submissiveness, and domesticity—demonstrating the insidious, enduring nature of cultural memory. The act is set in the Tilue-Pussenheimer Academy, a girls' boarding school "somewhere in Europe, 1920." In this factory for the production of proper women, five prepubescent girls are rigorously subjected to various forms of training deemed necessary to transform them into reverent, chaste, compliant ladies. The act parodies the 1931 Weimar film *Mädchen in Uniform,* and, as in the film, the tension of repressed lesbian desire is palpable. The girls suppress their yearnings for their teachers, and the teachers suppress their desire for each other and the girls.[56]

There are more than fifteen characters in the play, and, as in all their productions, the Brothers play all the roles with lightning-quick character and costume changes. The second act follows each girl to her inevitable tragic end in adulthood, starting with a brilliantly conceived vignette designed to presage their fates from the top of the act. As one of the now grown-up girls tosses her wedding bouquet to her friends from the academy, each woman nonchalantly steps back and lets the bouquet hit the floor. Punishment is exacted as the act unfolds. For failure to resist their deviant desires, the fallen angels of Tilue-Pussenheimer are hit by trucks, electrocuted, blown up in airplanes, and felled by alcoholism and brain tumors. The production both parodies and embraces works like *The Killing of Sister George* (1964), *The Well of Loneliness* (1928), *The Children's Hour* (1961), *Julia* (1977), *I Want to Live* (1958), and Ann Bannon's lesbian pulp novels (1957–62). The Brothers played out the moral that bad girls inevitably come to a bad end while simultaneously presenting five triumphant lesbians in a critically acclaimed tour de force. "The five actresses make a wonderfully comic ensemble," wrote the critic for the *New York Times* of the Brothers' performance. He described the play as "a smart, satirical farce that uses laughter and touches of raunchy humor to debunk the myth of the doomed lesbian."[57] The distance and resulting tension between who they declared themselves to be in life—a performing troupe of lesbian brothers—and the characters they represented onstage is Brechtian in its effect.

Privileging the Bad Good Girl: The Secretaries

Brave Smiles mapped the education and production of ladies, setting up the Brothers' next play, *The Secretaries* (1993), in which women willingly take on the care and maintenance of proper womanhood in sinister ways with murderous results, circumventing punishment entirely. The production turned out to be especially controversial, not only because it depicted straight, white, middle-class women killing off innocent straight, white men. It also engendered anxiety because of its representation of white womanhood run amok—bourgeois white women unmoored and dangerously adrift. *Voyage to Lesbos* foreshadowed *The Secretaries* in that it launched a compelling critique of whiteness, accomplishing intermittently what *The Secretaries* fully achieved. Another *New York Times* critic described *The Secretaries* as a "protracted . . . sometimes very funny, exercise in subverting American images of womanhood." The review goes on to say that the production "plays on anxious male fantasies of what women do when they're alone together . . . and the warping cultural expectations of femininity."[58]

White women's bodies occupy a duplicitous representational space, which the Brothers exploit in their work. White women signify both a pure, chaste, asexual, before-the-fall womanhood (a respectable "next to man and godliness" womanhood) and an uncontrolled and uncontrollable after-the-fall sexuality. This fallen woman status is embodied by some white women (prostitutes, white trash, and lesbians, for example) and all women of color. What is so extraordinary about *The Secretaries* is that the Brothers portray white women engaged in treacherous acts who somehow maintain their before-the-fall status. The characters adhere so fanatically to the rules of proper womanhood that even serial killing is not enough to tip them neatly and dismissively into the category of fallen woman. This enormously productive sleight of hand is readable as such only because the performers are white.

In contrast to the sexual appropriateness "true womanhood" bestowed on bourgeois white women, black women have historically been configured as the epitome of sexual promiscuity and voraciousness. The African American studies scholar Hazel Carby has described one egregious effect of this fabricated configuration. The way black womanhood was constructed allowed the white male to be "represented as being merely prey to the rampant sexuality of his female slaves."[59] History's lingering effects are visible in the way black women are still associated with overt sexuality and taboo sexual practices. As the legal scholar Kimberlé Crenshaw has suggested, "Given their race, black women have . . . always been within the fallen-woman category."[60] Sexual purity is the birthright of white women, while history has consigned women of color in general—albeit in differing ways—to an ostensibly natural and therefore presumed state of sexual deviance. Absent presumptive goodness, women of color are already among the fallen from grace.

White women, however, have access to a historically constituted system of meanings embedded in the phenomenon of white womanhood, and, as Gomez and Troyano have suggested, these meanings are deeply connected with class. At the intersection of gender, sexuality, and race with "middle-classness," white women embody and perform an institutionalized variety of whiteness. *Voyage to Lesbos* worries around the edges of this intersection and articulates it at one point. As Bonnie bestows yet more wisdom on her hapless cousin, who is trying hard not to be a lesbian, she explicitly links sexuality with a stay-at-home class privilege enjoyed overwhelmingly by white women: "Why don't you try settling down with a man? You've no idea the good being with Bradley has done for me. Look at me. Look at us. Two girls leading a life of luxury, drinking highballs at two in the afternoon. A dick. That's what you need. A big, hard, throbbing, veiny dick shoved all the way inside your pussy. Filling you up so much all you feel is dick. We'll get Brad to come and fuck you, Connie."[61] Here heterosexual *practice* signals entre into a specifically bourgeois way of life, acknowledging white women as the social subjects most advantageously positioned to live it. As performed here, middle-class status is conjoined with whiteness and heterosexuality to suggest a paradigm-making alliance with the gender category of "woman."

The critical significance of the nineteenth-century formulation of "true womanhood" is twofold: it was inextricably linked to the period's attributes of middle-class respectability, and it was reserved solely for white women. The descriptor *middle-class* carries far more symbolic weight than merely that of economic standing. Historically, *middle-class* has also denoted a kind of hard-earned respectability (as opposed to birthright) in the form of civility, encompassing a plethora of values and mores that underpinned moral rectitude and determined sexual propriety. The cult of true womanhood brought together gender, class, sexuality, and race dynamically and definitively. In the process the tenets of middle-class propriety became nearly synonymous with those of the racial category "whiteness." When identity categories intersect, they produce something different, if not greater, than the sum of their parts. When the gender-marked category of "woman" intersects with "whiteness" and "middle-classness," with its implicit heterosexuality, white womanhood is the by-product.

In *Voyage to Lesbos* the Brothers render this intersection perceptible by concentrating its salient features in a dry, ironic image—one of their trademark devices. Connie waxes poetically and earnestly on how the four women left behind by Bonnie's marriage might reconfigure themselves to participate in the romance of domesticity and reap its rewards: "We can adopt Evelyn and Janet and get a little house in the country and a rotisserie and a power lawn mower and pretty soon *House & Garden* will do a feature on us: 'The Queer Family at Home.'"[62]

This line drew big laughs from WOW audiences. In the days before gay marriage appeared on the radar of mainstream culture, the idea that normalcy could be accomplished even by queers when dusted off, cleaned up, and dropped into respectable "house and garden" variety family life was hilarious. The point still holds today. The whiteness and middle-classness of

House & Garden magazine in the 1960s was absolute, linked here to the "normal" and normalizing confines of the nuclear family. Historically, the nuclear family was the site where all that constituted prosperity and propriety was understood to reside. In their attempts to convince themselves of heterosexuality as the correct life path, the characters in *Voyage to Lesbos* proselytize, selling the nuclear family as a package deal with extras—appliances, barbeques, lawn mowers—the trappings of middle-class status and single-family life. Incorporating queer into the mix throws Bonnie (with her Bradley) into relief as the true woman.

Many WOW productions eschew any portrayal of middle-class propriety; that the Brothers emphasized it in their work suggests its importance to their overall project. Although they are not the same things, the meanings that adhere in the term *middle class* are virtually laminated with the array of meanings that constitute whiteness. For instance, the respectability inherent in middle-classness requires conformity; to conform requires behaving within set limits, which in turn requires setting boundaries and practicing self-control. These qualities resonate with the sense of "boundariness" the film scholar Richard Dyer has asserted as a basic characteristic of whiteness.[63] The characters in *Voyage to Lesbos* spend their days attempting to maintain appropriate boundaries while their desires insistently work to undermine them. In one scene Bonnie and Connie manage to keep their hands off each other by masturbating—one against a chair, the other against an upright vacuum cleaner. The stage direction reads, "Connie has a repressed yet apoplectic orgasm during which she inadvertently turns on the vacuum cleaner."[64] One reviewer described the scene as "deliriously wicked and funny," but as played in performance it also elicited a sense of abject emptiness.[65] The funny, wretched little act of implosion that characterizes this scene's orgasmic finish is a signature feature of the Brothers' work. Dramatic action revolves around fierce struggles to resist crossing over to the dark side.

In *The Secretaries* vigilant border control becomes the modus operandi of characters so tightly wrapped and highly strung that a series of small implosions drive the action relentlessly toward one big bang. The world of *The Secretaries* is compact, claustrophobic, and complete unto itself. The play focuses on five secretaries who work for the Cooney Lumber Mill in the town of Big Bone, Oregon—a state and an industry overwhelmingly populated by white people. None of the secretaries is married or has a social life that does not revolve around the other women from work. They exist in a spiraling set of boundaries within boundaries. The story unfolds by way of a newcomer to the secretarial pool, Patty. She is the epitome of the good girl, the young woman who has done everything right. "I come from a good family," she says. "I have an excellent education most girls would envy, attending one of the finest institutions in the nation with an advanced degree in secretarial sciences, with an emphasis on foreign study and international keyboards."[66]

When she arrives on the scene, Patty is welcomed by the other secretaries—the sycophant Ashley; the sweet, clueless Peaches; and the office lesbian, Dawn—with the kind of perky, obsequious niceness of bratty, white high school girls. They fawn over her in ways that make them appealing enough for Patty to want to become one of them. The play centers on Patty's dawning awareness of the group and gradual initiation into it. She notices that every morning the other secretaries arrive at the office wearing lumber jackets and hats they hang high on coat hooks, prominently displayed side by side. Eventually she realizes that each jacket is a trophy earned by killing a lumberjack.

Like *Voyage to Lesbos, The Secretaries* ends with the murder of a man, but there are some striking differences. Whereas the text of *Lesbos* as a whole is inchoate, the narrative in *The Secretaries* is fleshed out and keenly focused. It is the skill of the Five Lesbian Brothers *as performers* that makes this production a paradigm-altering piece of theater. Its subversive dimension depends on the characters being understood as the "real thing"—good girls. Simultaneously these good girls must be read as women who murder but *do not fall*. Just as whiteness is so reined in as to be virtually nonperformative, "acting out" is the antithesis of uptight, middle-class respectability. Herein lies the critical balancing act required of the Brothers' performances in *The Secretaries*—representing the ultimate in female dissembling without forfeiting good-girl status, acting out while retaining the semblance of white, middle-class boundaries. Unlike the iconic film characters Thelma and Louise, who were utterly cornered by the authorities and chose to end their own lives rather than "go back," the Brothers' secretaries do not face punishment. Instead, they get a pass for their unwavering allegiance and adherence to the principles of institutionalized white womanhood. All five are standing in the end and will live on to murder another day. This, then, is where terror and anxiety are concentrated. To make the paradox work fully and subversively depends on the Brothers' performances.

Four of the characters are played as heterosexual, and all five women are described as having "a hairdo that would stop a truck."[67] Imagine lesbians in skirts, heels, and big hair playing straight women from Big Bone, Oregon, without invoking images of men in drag. The *New York Daily News* critic Howard Kissel made the point that there is "something deeply unsettling about *The Secretaries*. For me, it was the realization that the roles of the women . . . were actually being played by women! My first fear was that this tokened a hitherto unnoticed shortage of drag queens."[68] Given the troupe's name, it is possible Kissel was surprised simply because he expected to find drag queens in the roles of "lesbian brothers," but this does not explain his choice of words—"deeply unsettling"—when he realizes he is watching women perform. Making a similar point, a college student familiar with the Brothers' work reported on a college production of *Brave Smiles* at New York University. "The performers were great," he said, "but they played the whole thing camped up, like a drag show. What I like about the Brothers is that it's funny but creepy."[69] This dimension of creepiness informs a sentiment like "deeply unsettling."

The Secretaries is so unnerving because the Brothers manage to hold antithetical positions together in single performances. This is achieved through a text and acting style that conjures and sustains all that constitutes true womanhood while simultaneously in the throes of diabolical behavior. An institutionalized form of whiteness begins to appear and become readable. Institutionalized whiteness is the kind used to rationalize white dominion, control, and privilege; it is the kind of whiteness against which white trash, for example, is measured and from which it is distanced. Institutionalized whiteness feeds privilege to all whites, so to speak, without letting all white people sit at the table. Those people of color who occupy a seat at all are bequeathed a status that is honorary and contingent. As Hazel Carby has put it, "[B]lack entry into the so-called mainstream has been on the grounds of middle-class acceptability and not the end of segregation."[70] Whiteness in general is fully mobilized and powerfully deployed through the construction of white womanhood in particular. Whiteness is lodged, for signifying purposes, in the Western ideological phantasm "white womanhood"—a phantasm only in the sense that the full force of its effects exceeds an embodiment of it, which is not to deny or ameliorate the complicity of white women in the ongoing project of leveraging its privileges.

The Secretaries uncannily traces contemporary corollaries to the precepts of true womanhood, perhaps because the traditional construct gained renewed saliency with a resurgence of the conservative Right in the decades immediately preceding and spanning the Brothers' work. Patty's first line is delivered to the audience: "I guess the question I have to ask myself is, 'How

did a decent girl like me get involved with a cult of murderous secretaries?'"[71] Echoing true womanhood's (and the Far Right's) requirement for
religious piety, the Brothers imagine their secretaries as a cult, transforming
the public sphere of the office—where secretaries exist to serve—into the private sphere of a cult, where many of the same dynamics of submission and
obedience are played out.

Those nineteenth-century women most constrained by true womanhood
were often those who most embraced it, manipulating the ideal as a means of
expanding their own influence. This is the role the character Susan Curtis as-
sumes in *The Secretaries*. The kind of female power garnered through compliance with true womanhood's dictates was ostensibly power over the natural promiscuity and unruliness of men. In reality, however, it was power
exercised among and over other women, especially the power of white bourgeois women over those written out of true womanhood—immigrants,
slaves, and laborers, secretaries and factory workers. As office manager, head
secretary, and cult leader, Susan's influence extends far beyond the office. She
is admired and feared by the other secretaries, who follow her lead in all
things. Susan represents perfection, the ideal the other women strive to
achieve. The behaviors that define her as a model evolve into a set of rules
that comes to define the women's lives. She reigns over the women, demanding compliance with the rules, and the women in turn demand it of each
other. As Susan polices the borders of proper conduct, the others fall in step
as her foot soldiers.

One particularly illustrative example is a scene longtime theater critic
John Simon put at the top of his review, describing the play as a "takeoff on
all those nine-to-five working-stiff movies, with the figures reshuffled to from
5 to 69—what with two actresses performing (in simulation, never fear!)
what may be the first all-female oral sex in Off Broadway history."[72] Echoing true womanhood's requisite purity, Susan demands absolute celibacy.
When Dawn, the office lesbian, seduces the newcomer, she is punished *not*
for the nature of the sexual act but for having sex at all. Susan entraps Dawn
by coming on to her. They kiss and Dawn begins to go down on Susan, when
Susan pulls her to her feet, kneels, hikes up Dawn's skirt and buries her face
between Dawn's legs.

Dawn begins to moan ecstatically, then screams out in pain, "You bit
me!" Susan turns to the audience, her mouth covered in blood. "Oh Dawn,"
she says, "I just remembered the celibacy rule. Meaning celibacy. No sex.
None. Nada. . . . That means no checking into the Hollyhock Hotel with the

new recruit. . . . You don't make a move I don't know about. You don't have a thought I don't already know. . . . Don't fuck with my rules. DON'T FUCK, PERIOD. End of discussion."[73] The action suggests an especially virulent hysteria, but Susan is played unrushed, calmly, liquidly in every scene. In performance, Susan's whiteness is manifest in acts of extreme calm and control. As Dawn hobbles out of the room, Susan says, "I hope you know how much I love you. I make these rules for a reason." Dawn thanks her as Susan licks blood off her fingers. Interesting that Simon celebrates *this* as the first example of all-female oral sex on the off-Broadway stage.

From the excruciatingly brutal to the sublimely ridiculous, the play's echoing of true womanhood's mores extends right down to the homemade artsy-craftsy pin Patty wears on her lapel. Those who subscribed to the most genteel form of nineteenth-century womanhood believed women were best suited for such leisure activities as needlework and other handicrafts. Susan makes a big show of admiring Patty's lapel pin and commensurate homemaking ability, not only to point out what it takes to reach this summit of womanly accomplishment but also to engender backstabbing envy among her minions. Competing notions of white womanhood have always existed historically, and the play incorporates nearly all of them. For instance an alternative view advocating health, intelligence, assertiveness, and economic self-reliance emerged from the ranks of working-class women. Susan demands that these qualities be honored as well as those of genteel womanhood, exploiting the crazy-making tension that is created by competing, contradictory expectations.[74] Critics, especially male ones, paid a great deal of attention to the production's final act of violence—the killing of a lumberjack. They ignored the fact that the play predominantly and graphically depicted the cruelty and violence women inflict on each other. These are characters who have so thoroughly internalized middle-class propriety that they function as instruments of their own oppression.

Varying degrees of white women's privilege might be understood in terms of mobility across a continuum representing the mind-body dichotomy of Western thought. Rather than a static binary opposition, it is fluid, with qualities of the mind, culture, and civilization at one extreme and those associated with the body, nature, and savagery at the other. White, straight, bourgeois women—by virtue of these privileged markers—have the ability to travel away from the end of the continuum typically reserved for those subjects considered most embodied, in other words, those who are most encumbered by nature and therefore perceived as the least civilized or most degenerate.

White women can move ever closer to the pinnacle of civilized culture as represented by middle-class, heterosexual, white masculinity.

The Five Lesbian Brothers are not the only WOW troupe to have exploited the dynamics of this continuum. The title alone of Split Britches' third play, *Upwardly Mobile Home,* ingeniously captures this idea. With extraordinary imagination and humor, the piece unsentimentally explores and exposes the promise of mobility. Mired in the conditions of white trailer trash, the play's characters enact their dreams of inhabiting a different kind of home in both the social and symbolic registers. What they lack, however, is the redemptive power of middle-classness necessary to jump-start and fuel the journey.[75] White womanhood informs the material reality of white women as social subjects differently. At the same time, it transcends that reality, legitimizing white domination and control.

No white woman ever reaches the most privileged end of the continuum, though, for "to embody" is still *femininity*'s definition and woman's destiny. In her book *Unmarked,* Peggy Phelan has suggested that the myths of American identity are those "which center on white men's struggle to invent and reinvent their identities in the moment." She adds parenthetically, "The parallel myth for women involves the endless reinvention of their image because how she looks is (still) who she is."[76] The Brothers are explicit about this notion, what they call the "tyranny of the image," and their secretaries slug down the weight-loss drink Slim-Fast all day. "It's healthier than food," they all agree. Consuming solid food is forbidden. In a wonderful bit of shtick, Peaches—at her desk, out of eyeshot of the others—fondles a bagel slowly, preciously, stuffing her mouth until her cheeks puff out and she cannot squeeze in another bite. Just then her phone rings. What happens next is hilariously "Lucyesque" as Peaches picks up the phone and attempts to speak.

In *The Secretaries* it is lesbians who are in drag, playing out the gender-marked categories of "woman" and "secretary." Each scene depicts conflict and psychosis as a product of material conditions rather than personal failure. The obsessive, workaholic, and perfectionist Ashley's adoration of Susan is a consequence of Ashley's severely limited horizons rather than some deep personal trauma. The problems of over-ideal-weight Peaches are primarily the result of nutritional and sexual privation rather than emotional neediness. All five performances have a compelling, disturbing edge to them that derives from each performer's idiosyncratic style, a style in which the culturally ghosted lesbian incessantly lurks and occasionally bleeds through. The Brothers' secretaries are at once enormously reined in and wildly imaginative, both slapstick funny and deadly serious.

Buzz is the only character without an edge, so to speak—a lumberjack done in by his own saw. He is described as a nineties kind of guy, the graduate of a sexual harassment workshop; cute, clean-cut, affable, sensitive, an understanding listener, he is an all-around good guy. When Buzz is targeted for the next ritual murder, Patty pleads with Susan to spare him. In response, Susan delivers the play's infamous summary line: "We don't kill them because they're bad. We kill them because *we're* bad." What the production marks as vicious is not only, or even primarily, the murderous act; rather, it is the ideology and power relations that determine the paradoxical space of true womanhood and its legacies. The Brothers are bad girls in the way all WOW girls are bad—not in reaction or relation to the category of "man" but indifferent to it.

Across the back of the Brothers' T-shirt is a caricature drawing of four historical figures in a row: Groucho, Harpo, Chico, and Sappho. The classically rendered Greek poet of Lesbos glances back over her shoulder at the familiar vaudevillian team. In the work of the Five Lesbian Brothers, agon, hubris, and deus ex machina meet shtick, with a touch of the lesbian poet. The Brothers go far beyond the playful parody their T-shirts suggest. They take parody into the realm of satire and perform it with a lethal edge. "We do a lot of dangerous material," Maureen Angelos has said. "Sometimes it feels like juggling blazing chainsaws."[77] The Brothers are escapees from white womanhood who drag the entire apparatus along with them, throwing it into relief and provoking the acute anxiety engendered by the threat of white womanhood unmoored from the strictures of middle-class propriety.

In assuming the label of lesbian up front, the Brothers celebrate lesbian identity in the sense of gay pride. Like Troyano, they "disidentify," adopting and simultaneously re-forming the egregious historical, psychological, and social baggage the term conjures. The Brothers' work returns "lesbian" to the status of pervert and mines that terrain. Their name also lays claim to masculinity. The neologism "lesbian brother" epitomizes "female masculinity"—not merely impersonating maleness but assuming it as their own. It could be argued that *lesbian brother* privileges the noun *brother* and appends *lesbian* as merely an adjective. But the Brothers' work demonstrates that in their creative world *lesbian* wields the power of all adjectives, the power to change. Their name invokes no less than the brotherhood of man, altering its character, refiguring the fraternity of Groucho, Harpo, and Chico.

Like other groundbreaking work that emerged from WOW, *Memorias de la Revolución* and *The Secretaries* are unimaginable creations apart from WOW. Both plays demonstrate that white women are uniquely positioned to intervene in the symbolic structures of whiteness, as well as its quotidian dimensions, and the seeds of this intervention are inextricably linked to the conditions under which WOW operates. If whiteness is constituted in a kind of rational sense of "boundariness," characterized by order and stability, then the messiness and precariousness of WOW's anarchical organization in itself stands in opposition to its tenets. From the beginning, WOW women created a space designed to continuously teeter on the edge of organizational chaos. If the racialization that produces whiteness is deployed through the construct of white womanhood, then the aggressively oppositional stance WOW women take as self-proclaimed bad girls flies in the face of that process. As Gomez and Troyano have broadly suggested, there is something "not quite white" about WOW. Something different is going on, a difference that contributes to the project of unmasking the dynamics of identity at the intersection of race, gender, class, and sexuality in performance.

Flyer for second Women's One World Festival, October 1981. Artwork by Peggy Shaw.

The Schlockettes, Women's One World Festival, 1980. *Left to right,* Jordy Mark, unidentified dancer, Cathy Gollner, Maggie Hicks, Pamela Camhe, Peggy Shaw, Barbara Baumuller, and Lois Weaver. (Photo by Mariette Pathy-Allen.)

Diane Torr, *Diana Toranado and Her Dicey Dames from Passaic,* Women's One World Festival, 1981. (Photo by Mariette Pathy-Allen.)

Jordy Mark and Pamela Camhe in "A Little Vaudeville" segment, slide show of Camhe's photographs, Women's One World Festival, 1980. (Photo by Pamela Camhe.)

Split Britches, 1981. The Split Britches Company, *from left to right*, Lois Weaver seated, Peggy Shaw standing, and Deb Margolin. (Photo by Pamela Camhe.)

Sex and Drag and Rock 'n' Roles, Women's One World Festival, 1980. *Left to right,* Jordy Mark and Pamela Camhe. (Photo by Mariette Pathy-Allen.)

Paradykes Lost, 1988. *Left to right,* Carolyn Patierno, Peg Healey (holding the arm of Imogen Pipp), Maureen Angelos, and Kate Stafford. (Photo by Dona Ann McAdams.)

Sharon Jane Smith as Garnet McClit, Lady Dick, in Holly Hughes's *The Lady Dick,* 1986. (Photo by Eva Weiss.)

Uzi Parnes as the Virgin (in background video) appears to Carmelita Tropicana as she flees Cuba by boat in *Memorias de la Revolución*, 1986. *Left to right,* Jeep Reis, Alina Troyano/Carmelita Tropicana, and Peg Healey. (Photo by Dona Ann McAdams,)

Alina Troyana/Carmelita Tropicana as Pingalito in *Memorias de la Revolución*, 1986. (Photo by Dona Ann McAdams.)

Kill night scene, *The Secretaries,* 1993.The Five Lesbian Brothers, *from left to right*, Lisa Kron, Maureen Angelos, Dominique Dibbell (collapsed in the arms of Peg Healey), and Babs Davy. (Photo by Joan Marcus.)

Groucho   Harpo   Chico   Sappho

Illustration on the Five Lesbian Brothers's T-shirt. Artist: Donna Evans.

The Five Lesbian Brothers photographed for *The New Yorker*, August 2005. *Left to right,* Lisa Kron, Maureen Angelos, Dominique Dibbell, Peg Healey, and Babs Davy. (Photo by Max Vadukul.)

Epilogue: "Learning to Walk on Our Hands"

If lesbians ever catch up with the limited inroads gay men have made into main-stream culture, they'll do it with work like the stuff at WOW.

—C. CARR, 1985

In the decades since C. Carr made the statement quoted in the epigraph, white gay men *have* made significant inroads into mainstream culture. And, as the scholar David Savran has suggested in his formulation of the "new American queer theater," women theater artists—whether straight or lesbian, white or of color—have not.[1] Although Lisa Kron's play *Well* was an enormous critical success, the production closed on Broadway after a few weeks because, as Kron described it, "[T]here was no shorthand way to say what the play was about in a way people could understand enough to buy a ticket."[2] Rather than bemoaning the limitations of mainstream discourse to succinctly capture a piece like *Well*, I follow Jill Dolan's lead and look instead for hope in the theater.[3] Those of us who wrote about feminist performance a generation ago claimed the power of work like that which was coming out of WOW to engender social change in concert with other forces at work in the larger social landscape. Change is realized only when it can be imagined, and the playground for such imaginings is representation.

In *Well*—an example of representation at the apex of mainstream, commercial theater production—I detect change and find reason to hope in the critical response to a seemingly dumpy midwestern housewife. Scads of reviews of the off-Broadway and Broadway productions of *Well*, written by dozens of different critics, offer an opportunity for patterns of reception to emerge, patterns that not only point to how Kron's aesthetic strategies engender less predictable responses but signal a shift in the larger sociosymbolic landscape. In the absence of a cohesive whole, stable characters, and resolution, what emerges from *Well* is dynamic, a potent blossoming of agency where it is least expected. For every "truth" *Well* asserts, countertruths abound and persuasive evidence is presented for the "truthiness" (as the satirical TV news show host Stephen Colbert would say) of them all.

This is especially apparent in the way the play deals with illness. The character Ann believes allergies are a highly underrated, sinister, life-destroying force kept secret by the evil medical establishment controlled by the American Medical Association. Lisa is angry with Ann over the willfulness of what she believes is Ann's psychosomatic state, yet simultaneously she argues for the "realness" of Ann's condition. She tells about the time her mother almost died and "we didn't notice." Lisa asks, "What is the difference between that body and mine?" Then she answers, "I moved to New York . . . I studied theater . . . I [learned] how to inhabit my body—that there is an alternative to dragging your body around like a stone and wishing it would disappear."[4] This moment in the play captures the split between women and their bodies, between women and discourse, and the transformative potential of art. Lisa and Ann are engaged in the same struggle, but it takes different forms. Allergies are a reaction against something, or someone, a feeling of antipathy, which implies a logical basis for the desire to avoid or reject. Ann describes allergies in terms of fatigue—"the irresistible voice calling you all day to just close your eyes. Just give in and close your eyes." In her struggle against the debilitating seduction of allergies, or a culture that would pull her under if she lived according to form, Ann fully inhabits her body. She is unapologetically and good-humoredly both sick and well.

The many reviews of the production invariably start out describing Ann with phrases like "maternally adorable" and "blissfully endearing," but what characterizes the majority of reviews in the end is a startling lack of condescension. Kron, as playwright, gives the audience every opportunity to dismiss Ann; Lisa, as a character, invites it. However, Kron also infuses the character with an autonomy that supersedes stereotype. Just as she takes charge of her neighborhood within the play's narrative, Ann takes charge of the play onstage. Some critics did respond to Ann condescendingly, but they were few. Ann is described as "unexpectedly engaging," and several reviewers wrote about how they, and by extension at least some other spectators, "fell in love" with her. This reading is not unprecedented since the cast's white actress tells Lisa, "I'm in love with your mother." With a gesture that includes the audience, the black actress says, "I think that's how we all feel." All are "in love" with Ann, suggesting the heart-thumping, erotic dynamics of "falling in love."

This apparent desire strikes me as a consequence, and evidence, of agency played out on a body traditionally denied it. Agency is sexy. Ann quietly, unassumingly, but nonetheless effectively seizes the action, takes center stage, and turns the production on its head. In some reviews, descriptions of Ann shift from the general "dumpy lady" to a "heroic woman" and a "modest kind of hero."[5] Agency is not only sexy, it is the stuff of heroism, helping to explain the apparent change of attitude and heart toward the character. Because of WOW and the strategies developed there, it is possible to transform a disheveled "lumpy, lethargic housewife mother" plopped in a La-Z-Boy in the middle of her living room into an autonomous, desirable, heroic woman on the Broadway stage.[6] *Well* opens wide a space in representation. Hope arises from evidence that spectators may now be in a position to rise to the occasion.

Dolan posits what she calls the "utopian performative," or "the ways in which performance lets audiences see *as if for the first time* or *see anew,* through an alienation effect that's emotionally resonant, how to create moments of a future that might feel like utopia in the present of performance."[7] The transformation of the character of Ann Kron, the "falling-in-love moment," strikes me as an example of the utopian performative. The stirrings of change occur within individuals before they are manifest in the street, hence the avant-garde's emphasis on the aim of art to alter consciousness itself. As Dolan puts it, "[T]he experience of performance, the pleasure of a utopian performative, even if it doesn't change the world, certainly changes the people who feel it."[8] Hope is embedded in the contributions of entities like WOW to the project of social change and political justice regardless of their distance from mainstream culture and in the absence of any guarantee of their ultimate effectiveness.

From 1980 on, the WOW Café Theatre has been a player in providing its participants with a variety of contexts from which to imagine and therefore create alternative futures. In this regard, nothing captures WOW as an entity more accurately, perhaps, than the political and queer theorist Shane Phelan's compelling notion of "(be)coming out." She has used this concept to describe all identities as works in progress, as constituted in processes rather than ontologies.[9] WOW's endless process of becoming, its status as an ongoing work in progress, is at once its great promise and its most frustrating characteristic. Kron's hit play illustrates some of the ways in which an aesthetic associated with WOW works, but WOW's quotidian dynamics and struggles are as important to its past and future as are its aesthetic achievements.

During the summer of 2002, for example, the collective was engaged in what the choreographer and performance artist Jen Abrams has described as an "intense discussion around race," both at meetings and electronically. "We have no societal models for the discourse we are trying to have—not only the specific discourse on race, but the overarching mode of discourse we are trying to invent in an anarchistic, all-women's space," she reflected. "You can't go to Office Max and buy a packaged version of this social contract. We write and rewrite it from scratch, without even a complete awareness of the social contract we're responding against. It's so subtle, what we're trying to re-pattern. It's so integrated into the bedrock of our interactions. No wonder we bang into each other all the time. We're learning to walk on our hands."[10] This intense discussion on race was replaced by an equally intense debate around issues of gender definition. There is reason to find hope in the collective's ongoing willingness to engage in battles over issues that by their very nature are irresolvable in a culture that professes to be beyond racism, sexism, and heterosexism and simultaneously props up the institutions that depend on systems of privilege and discrimination.

There is also hope in the changing composition of the collective's membership. The conceptual foundation of WOW as being more of a city than a community may explain why increasing numbers of women of color have found that they can be productive there. Writer and performance artist Susana Cook came to WOW in 1994 from Argentina. "Some think the first ten years of WOW were the golden years," she said. "I think we're still in the golden years."[11] Cook's production of *Hamletango: Prince of Butches* in WOW's 2001–2 season is a case in point. Billed as "the most feminist, erotic, exotic, hysterical and Argentinean party of classic ghosts and tragic orgasms," *Hamletango* is a smart, witty, complex treatment of Hamlet as a working-class, butch prince. The piece works on several levels, engaging classical tropes to comment on multiple dimensions of culture, colonialism, and the nature of narrative itself. The cast included three white women and fourteen women of color, a number of whom represented transgender communities. It played to sold-out houses of audiences as diverse as the cast over its four-week run. Although the number of women of color in the collective has ebbed and flowed with WOW's ever-changing membership, in 2007 women of color comprised more than half of the collective's active membership.

WOW work, when looked at historically, represents an ongoing trajectory that makes of itself a representational economy greater than the sum of its parts—a robust economy in which the unimaginable is re-presented on its own terms, signaling vital lesbian sexualities and subjectivities in particular and autonomous female-gendered subjectivities in general. As Savran has suggested, the new queer theater phenomenon did little to alter the conditions of visibility and material status for women of any stripe. Although exceptions such as Kron's *Well* exist, they mainly serve to illustrate the durability of the dilemma and continuing salience of WOW's achievement, helping to explain the WOW Café Theatre's continuing existence as both a lesbian and a women's theater. The operative words here, of course, are "WOW's continuing existence."

In the fall of 2000 the collective was faced with an ultimatum. It could either move WOW to a different location or join other tenants in the building in an effort to buy it. The city of New York owned the building and dozens of others in the area and had been renting out space at far below market value. It was forced to sell as a consequence of the lobbying efforts of activists, artists, and other low-income residents who had revitalized the neighborhood over the preceding decades and wanted a stake in its future. The purchase price was one dollar plus the cost of bringing the entire building up to code—a huge sum by any standard, but especially by WOW's, given the utter shoestring nature of the theater's budget.

A meeting was held in the city's Lesbian, Gay, Bisexual and Transgender Community Center to accommodate a large group of current and past members of the collective.[12] Those attending ranged in age from their twenties to their sixties and seventies and included a significant percentage of women of color. The conversation was focused, productive, and dotted with periodic gales of howling laughter. Near the end of the meeting, however, the frustrations of the matter at hand turned the discussion in a predictable direction. Some women argued, "We've got to get a board of directors, apply for grants, and become a serious theater." To which one woman replied, "But then WOW wouldn't be WOW . . . it's always been about anarchy." This bit of cultural memory survived because the group had quite literally been engaged in the same debate for twenty years. It would take many more meetings before the collective ultimately decided to participate in the effort to purchase the building and many more years to raise the money this accomplishment required. The indomitable spirit of WOW prevailed, however, and by 2005 it had secured a permanent space for its future.[13]

Thus WOW lives on to produce another day. Surely this is reason to celebrate. Maureen Angelos, a WOW girl since 1980 and one of the Five Lesbian

Brothers, captured the overall celebratory spirit of WOW in a message she posted on WOW's e-mail discussion list before the 2002 annual summer retreat: "Good luck on the retreat and be sure to have a good time. WOW was founded on the pleasure principle and though everything cannot be fun, most things should be and all should strive to be."

Party on WOW!

Appendix: WOW Production History

Production	*Artist and/or Producer*
Women's One World Festival, 1980	
Oh What a Life	Muriel Miguel New York City (NYC), Eva Bouman (Amsterdam)
The Adventures of Orange Paint	Magic Window (bilingual puppet show/Spanish and English)
An Evening of Disgusting Songs and Pukey Images	Spiderwoman Theater
A Taste	Copenhagen's Women's Theatre (Denmark)
Minni Kabini's Hygiene	Michelle Frankel (London)
My Redheaded Aunt from Redbank	Blondell Cummings
Rice and Beans	Jan Cohen, Amy Trompetter
Split Britches	Naja Beye, Cathy Gollner, Peggy Shaw (Lois Weaver, director)
Tlatilco	Gloria Miguel, Vera Colorado, Hortensia Colorado
WOW Cabaret	The Schlockettes, Lunatune (choreographed by Cheryl Gates McFadden)
Slide and Seek	Pamela Camhe ("slide movie" show)
Women I Have Known	M. Tullis Sessions
The Pause That Refreshes	Lisa Mayo
A Piece of the World	Edwina Lee Tyler
Sex and Drag and Rock 'n' Roles	Jordy Mark, Annie Toone
Sirens	Women's Collage Theatre
Electra Speaks, Part I	Women's Experimental Theatre
First Lover and *The Witch Papers*	Cambridge Lesbian Theatre

Why Don't You Find a Rich Guy and Marry Him?	Word of Mouth Productions (Boston)
Snow White	Snow White Street Theatre (Netherlands/Switzerland)
	Beryl and the Perils (London)
	Robin Tyler (stand-up comedy, Los Angeles)
	Three Clowns Company (Boston)
	Wallflower Order (Oregon)
	OVA (London)
	New Cycle Theatre
	Mischief Mime Company (Ithaca)
	Radical Lesbian Feminist Terrorist Comedy Group
	Suni Paz (Latin American singer, songwriter, guitarist)
	Cheap Perfume (women's rock band)
	New York Women's Chamber Orchestra
	New York Women's String Band (square dancing)

Women's One World Festival, 1981

Twilight in Concordia	Sally Rodwell, Deborah Hunt (New Zealand)
Interact	Jimini Moonlight
Wolf Story	Saara Salminen (Sweden)
Vitale Funeral Home	Teatteri Porquettas (Finland)
Interact	Keiko Kawade (Japan)
A Piece of the World	Edwina Lee Tyler
Shoeshow	Teatro Viola (Rome)
Contraception	Barbara Jo Flemming
Family Album	Katherine Sanderson
Mountain Moving Day	Justine Lewis
Split Britches	Deb Margolin, Peggy Shaw, Lois Weaver
Women I Have Known	Tulis McCall, Nancy Elizabeth Cammer
No False Moves	Sustained Release Organization
Boundaries	Chrysalis Theater Electric Company (Northampton, Mass.)

Cosser y Cantar	Elizabeth Peña, Maria Norman
Food Talk	Women's Experimental Theatre,
	Roberta Sklar, Sondra Segal
Sex and Drag and Rock 'n' Roles	Jordy Mark
Slide and Seek	Pamela Camhe ("slide movie" show)
Incidents	Babazou
Junk Love	Robin Epstein, Dorothy Cantwell
An I for a You	Pro Femina (Washington, D.C.)
Reverberations	The Flamboyant Ladies Theater
	Company (Brooklyn)
Everything You Always Wanted to Know about Nukes	Barbara George
The Exorcism of Cheryl	More Fire! Productions
	Diana Tornado and Her Dicey
	Dames from Passaic (N.J.)
	Radical Lesbian Feminist Terrorist
	Comedy Group
	Mischief Mime Company (Ithaca, N.Y.)
	End and Means Committee (Boston)
	Gay Divorcees (Boston)
	She's Moved (London)
	The "B" Girls (women's rock band, Canada)
	IBIS (women's jazz/funk fusion band)
	Sharon Isbin (classical guitarist)
	The Bloods (girl punk band)
	Lunatune (a cappella theater)
	String Fever (women's all-string big band)
Film Program	*Thriller,* Sally Potter
	Diary of an African Nun, Julie Dash
	Gently Down the Stream, Su Friedrich
	Another Great Day, Jo Bonney, Ruth Peyser
Midnight Cabaret	Judy Remly (performance art)
	Kate Clinton (stand-up comedy)
	Jane Anderson (stand-up comedy)
	Emily Long Trio (jazz)

1982–84*

Beauty and the Beast	Split Britches (scripted by Deb Margolin, additional text by Peggy Shaw, Lois Weaver)
Punch for Boys	P. D. Littlefield
The Snow Queen (adapted by Peggy Shaw and Lois Weaver from the story by Hans Christian Andersen)	Working Girls' Repertory Company
Rosemary and Juliet	Alice Forrester
Carmelita Tropicana Chats/ Chicken Sushi	Alina Troyano
Her Funniest Parts	Lisa Kron
Heart of the Scorpion	Alice Forrester
Shrimp in a Basket	Holly Hughes
The Well of Horniness	Holly Hughes
Snow White, Unadorned	Cheryl Moch
The Weirds	David Cale
The God Show	Deb Margolin
Gorilla Kisses	C. R. Polcovar, Dorothy Friedman
White Gloves	Jean Allen
Tantrums and Fantasies	Dana Rosenfeld
Upwardly Mobile Home	Split Britches
A Tennessee Waltz (based on Tennessee Williams's characters)	The Cast (Lois Weaver, director)
Who's Afraid of Ronald Reagan, Ronald Reagan	Mary Vasiliades
The Rip-It-Up Hate Aggregate Rape Tapes	James Larson
Lesbian Winter Mini Spectacular	Radical Lesbian Feminist Terrorist Comedy Group
"When We Were Young: A Walking Tour through Radical Jewish Women's History on the Lower Eastside, 1879–1919"	Sarah Schulman, Susan Young
Reno: Laff Riot	Reno

*All subsequent dates represent two-year periods, not single seasons.

1985–86

The Swashbuckler (based on a story by Lee Lynch)	Sarah Schulman, Susan Young
Saint Joan of Avenue C	The Cast, with Deb Margolin, Peggy Shaw, Lois Weaver
Cinderella: The Real True Story	Cheryl Moch
Hootenanny Night	Sarah Schulman
The Lady Dick	Holly Hughes
Eclipse (Listen): An Experiment in 3 Movements	Kathryn Wetzel
Erotica	Joan Nestle
Useless Femmes (Band)	Lynn Hayes, Kathy Thomas, Debra Miller
Incest: It's All Relative	Karen Spitfire
Asian Lesbianism Past and Present	Asian Lesbians of the East Coast
Mundane Devastations	Alice Forrester
SEXTRAVAGANZA (Jeep Thrills)	Diane Jeep Ries
Fear of Laughing in the Lower East Side	Alice Forrester
Shari and the Shy-type (Band)	Sharon Jane Smith, Kathryn Wetzel, Laura Lonfranco
Mood Ring	Heidi Griffiths
Long Island Lesbian Thesbians Present a Play	Long Island Lesbian Thesbians
The Pause That Refreshes	Spiderwoman Theater
Hiroshima Beach Party	Val Penn, Hedy Abel
The True Story of the Elephant in the Living Room	Maureen Brady
A Couple of Weirdos	Deb Margolin, Reno
Lipowitz & Fry	Heidi Griffith, Serena Heslop
Immediate Family	Terry Baum
Pickaxe	Ana Maria Simo
Memorias de la Revolución/Memories of the Revolution	Alina Troyano, Uzi Parnes
Patience and Sarah (in collaboration with author Isabel Miller)	Peggy Shaw, Lois Weaver
A Happening	Alina Troyano, Ela Troyano, Uzi Parnes, with Jack Smith
Waaay Beyond the Valley of the Dolls	Alison Rooney
Healers-Original Whirling Lesbian/ Women of Color	Katherine Ekau Amoy Hall, Bina Sharif, Sheila Hallet

More Funny Things and Some Songs with Lisa Kron (and Her All Boy Orchestra)	Lisa Kron

1987–88

School for Scandal (based on the play by Sheridan)	Heidi Griffiths, Alice Forrester
Heidegger/Schmeidegger	M. G. Ward
LEZZYVISION	Maz Troppe
Killing Game (by Eugene Ionesco)	Heidi Griffiths, Alice Forrester
Tart City	Kate Strafford, Karen Crumley
Threads from the Tailor's Granddaughters	Sharon Jane Smith
Little Women (based on the book by Louisa May Alcott)	Split Britches (scripted by Deb Margolin, additional text by Peggy Shaw, Lois Weaver)
Fan Mail	Madeleine Olnek, Nancy Swartz
Star Struck	Lynn Hayes
Case Studies	Dominique Dibbell, with Madeleine Olnek, Nancy Swartz
From Stolen Kisses to Stolen Cars	Nancy Swartz
Paradykes Alley	Lisa Kron, with the cast
Paradykes Lost	Lisa Kron, with the cast
Carmelita Tropicana's Clamcracker Suite	Alina Troyano, Ela Troyano, Uzi Parnes
Sake Sisters Play Mahjong	Asian Lesbians of the East Coast
Lessons out of Time	Terry Dame, Mary Patierno
Rabbit Plantation	Alison Rooney
Tit Bits	Cheryl Moch
Guitar Boy	Lynn Hayes
Dress Suits to Hire	Holly Hughes, with Peggy Shaw, Lois Weaver
Into Temptation	Holly Hughes, with Kate Stafford
LEZZYVISION II: The Sequel	Maz Troppe
Glossed Horizon	Diane Jeep Ries
Carmelita Bears All	Alina Troyano
The Doughs	Lisa Kotin
Is It Love or Just Palmolive	Nancy Swartz
How to Say Kaddish with Your Mouth Shut	Claire Olivia Moed

1989–90

Pinto Heaven	Sabrina Artel, Lucinda Rhea Zoe
Wake the Jessamy Bride (based on Virginia Woolf's *Orlando*)	Terry Dame
I Wish I Had a Real Gun	Dominique Dibbell
Voyage to Lesbos I & II	The Five Lesbian Brothers
The Sublime Imaginings & Sordid Realities of Miss Emily Soldene or "Confessions of a Music Hall Tart" (adapted from the memoirs of Emile Soldene)	Heidi Griffiths
Playground	Lynn Hayes
World without End	Holly Hughes
What's with Hamlet?	Deb Margolin
Queer Justice	The cast (Lois Weaver, director)
Suicide and Other Lovers	Claire Olivia Moed
Through These Walls	Terry Dame, Gabrielle Hamilton
Of Men and Steamboat Men	Sharon Jane Smith
Good Hair	Maureen Burnley
Love Slapped Me Boom Boom Upside My Head	Claire Olivia Moed
Sex Lives and Rape	Susan Young
Agnes de Castro (by Catharine Trotter)	Peggy Shaw
Beyond the Lezbodome	Quinn
I Sleep with the Lights On	Slats Muldoon
Narcissa and the Monday Mob	Elise Tribble
The Curse of the Medusa's Box	Really Incredibly Broke Repertory Company
Parlor Games	Bayla Travis
The Last Repossession	Ann Elizabeth Miller
Two Year Itch	Peg Healey, Maureen Angelos, Lisa Kron
Grand Ole Wowpry	The Traveling Millies
Millie without a Name	The Millies
Kate's Quandary	Terry Diamond
Love's Frantic Yearnings	The cast, with Nancy Swartz

1991–92

Relationship Jones	Theresa Marie Diamond
Go Children Slow	Gabrielle Hamilton
4 Women Snuff 1,000 Points of Light	Susan Young, Amy Meadow

Love Affairs of an Old Maid	Lucinda Rhea Zoe
Double Awareness, Double Awareness	Madeleine Olnek
Catch Her in the Eye	Barbara Bickart, Bridget Hughes
Blaze Craze	Karen Campbell
The Proper Fit	Susan Young, Gail Freund
Millie without a Name	Betsy Crenshaw
Women and Children First: Outstanding Perk or Tool of Oppression?	Babs Davy
A Strong New Cord	Lynn Hayes
Sensuality	Sonia M. Hemphill
What We Saw at the Revolution	Susan Young, with Gail Freund, Dominique Dibbell, Maureen Angelos
Through These Walls	Terry Dame, Gabrielle Hamilton
We Need a Little Love Story	Lynn Hayes
Confessions of a Lesbian Debutante	Terry Dame, Gabrielle Hamilton
Drag Night at the White House	Lynn Hayes
42D/42C (Not a Cup Size)	Terry Dame, with Gabrielle Hamilton
Brave Smiles . . . Another Lesbian Tragedy	The Five Lesbian Brothers
The Re-Wombing	Dana Davis, Cheryl Boyce Taylor, the Mother Spirit Ensemble
The West Wasn't Won on Salad	Sharon Jane Smith
Good Hair	Maureen Burnley
Spooky World	Madeleine Olnek
OH DARN! The World Is a Dangerous Place for Little Buttercups	Dominique Dibbell, Maureen Angelos
Bye Bye Brunhilde	Camille Roy
My Secret Rodeo	Lisa Lerner
Co-Dependent Lesbian Space Alien Seeks Same	Madeleine Olnek
The Jewish Nun	Madeleine Olnek
It's Not the Shoes	Madeleine Olnek, with Alternate Visions Theater Troupe of Youth Enrichment Services at the Lesbian, Gay, Bisexual, Transgender (LGBT) Center
A new play	In collaboration with Heidi Griffiths, Lois Weaver, and the lesbian and gay youth group of the Community Services Center
Salon de la Barky (Art Exhibit)	Donna Evans

1993–94

Cabaret de la Gay (in D Minor)	Sharon Jane Smith
The Second Koan	Kassandra Kaye
Disaster Area Nurse	Madeleine Olnek
Lesbian Bridesmaid	Ellen Wong
The Secretaries	The Five Lesbian Brothers
It's Not Ova Yet	Karen Campbell
Stalling	Sharon Hayes
Lesbian Bathhouse	Helen Eisenbach
Samson and Delilah Brown	Ira Jeffries
The Break	Ira Jeffries
An Evening with Shelly Mars	Shelly Mars
The Personals	Kimberly Gilchrist
Nudes in Repose	Jacqueline Allen
This Girl I Knew	Marcia Wilke
Medusa Project	Lisa Marie Bronson
Susana (and the Elders)	Veronica Mitchell
Hot 'n' Soft	Muriel Miguel
Lesbians Rescue Baby Jessica	Barbara Bickart, Karen Campbell, Betsy Crenshaw, Betsy Farrell, Bridget Hughes
Tami's in Love	Efat Azizi, Betsy Crenshaw
Negotiating Boundaries	Lucinda Rhea Zoe
Destiny of Mimi	Madeleine Olnek
Boxes	Melanie Hope/Deirdre, Boddie-Henderson
The Prisoner	Lexa Rosean
Disfiguration of a Diva	Hattie Gossett
Whose Fault Is It?	Lisa Pitt
Josey's Story	Dorian Beach
Somewhere Along the Way	Lynn Hayes
Sweet Lemon Juice & Broken Glass	Alternate Visions Theater Troupe of Youth Enrichment Services at the LGBT Center and WOW

1995–96

The Truth about Gypsy Byrne	Sharon Jane Smith
I Married a Lesbian Witch	Lexa Rosen
The Lesbian Appetite	Cassie Angely
Time Lines	Carolyn Brown
Upstairs? In the Afternoon?	Nancy Dean
52nd Street	Jess Wilson

Destiny of Mimi	Madeleine Olnek
The Christian and the Jewess & Glory	Ira Jeffries
Suite in 3 Voices	Michelle Colletti
Significant Women	Judith Schray
Once Upon a #%&@*	Piper Macleod
Her Burning Tresses	Vivian Babuts
Tit Tales	Leigh Silverman
Coming to This	Sandra Leon
The Young Skulls	Madeleine Olnek, with Laurie Weeks
To Forgive	Julia Dare
Janis	Carolyn Farhie
The Book of Anger	Jess Wilson
Brides of the Moon	The Five Lesbian Brothers
The Lesbionic Women	Julie Goldman
Museum of the Muse	Deborah Edmeade
Just Pieces	Michelle Coletti
Café Bimbo	Sid Branch
Home: A Boat	Kate Wilson, Susana Cook

1997–98

A Dream Play	S. Ryan Schmidt
Enchanted Laundry: On Rage, Love, and Travel (Astral and Subway)	Laura Marie Thompson
Little Girl Blue	Carolyn Farhie
Book of Anger	J. W. Wilson
Coconut Blood: On Race and Transformation	Laura Marie Thompson
Drag Kings & Subjects	Susana Cook, Diane Torr
Crooked Slough Dyke Road & Other Stories	Sharon Jane Smith
Two Fools	Terry Brown
Xtravagina	Piper Macleod
Delirium	Stanya Kahn
Immoral Threat	Robin Warwick
What Is Said, What Goes Unspoken	Amy Jo Goddard
The Lesbian Afterlife Carnival Extravaganza	Jess Dobkin
Miss Julie	Alison Tartaglia
Hersterical Festival	Piper Macleod
Why She Wears a Suit	Kate Roberts

Felice Brutality	Felice Shays
Quadroon	Danielle Abrams, Moira Cutler
Mickey-O	Sid Branch
Psycho-Semitic	Felice Shays
A Woman in My Life	Carolyn Farhie
Hot Scramble	Leah Kornfeld Friedman
Post-colonial Butches, Post-patriarchal Femmes, and Other Blessings	Susana Cook
The Third Daughter	Beverly Bronson
The Price of a Ticket	Kate Wilson

1999–2000

Diva Construction	Susana Cook
The Skriker (by Caryl Churchill)	Moira Cutler
Breathing Water: On Hitch-Hiking and Love	Laura Marie Thompson
Why We Have a Body	Claire Chafee
Eclectic Little Circus	Alice Gentles
Bloom Festival	Nyonoweh Green, Hanifah Walidah, Dumeha Thompson
Hot Tamale	Susana Cook
Surface Tension	Ladan Nabet
Neurotica	Justine Buchanan
Seven Layers of Skin	Jasmine Presson, Christine White
Blind Visions	Elana Bell
Edge of the World	Jamila Gaskins
Show Me: Shadow Puppet Transformational Journey	Beth Grim
Vulvalution: Her Lips Speak	Amy Jo Goddard, Julia Murphy
Wild Nights with Emily & Gay! Gay! Gay!	Madeleine Olnek
Conga Guerilla Forest	Susana Cook
Eating Cake	Carolin Brown
Lesbian Affairs	Judith Schray
Life, Pain, Triumph	Aleada Minton
The Stories We Buried	Sharon Jane Smith, Beverly Bronson, Lisa Glucken
Daughters from the Stars	Lisa Mayo, Gloria Miguel (Spiderwoman Theater)
The Dating Game and *The Newly Bedded Game*	Aleada Minton

Itch	Jen Abrams
Princess in the Tower	Alison Duncan
Trombone	Leah Kornfeld Friedman
Vulvalution	Amy Jo Goddard

2001–2

She Cuts Herself/She Likes to Write	Gina Young
Learning to Sit	Lisa Glucken
Seven Layers of Skin	Jasmine Presson
Counterfeit Straight	Randi Skaggs
Iolanthe	Alison Duncan
Painted Wings	Elana Bell, Abena Koomsan
Insides/Out	Anne Gadwa
Spic for Export	Susana Cook
Schooled	Carol Thompson
Surfacing	Jen Abrams
Invisible Rocket	Danny McGee, Mika Deutch, Parker Pracjek
Vulvis Presley	Emily Rems
Hamletango: Prince of Butches	Susana Cook
B4T	Imani Henry
A Very Special, One Hour *"Georgie!"*	Lori Bonfitto
Slaughter City (by Naomi Wallace)	Moira Cutler
Mixed Grrrrrill	Lisa Glucken
Saturn Return	Jen Abrams
Spies in the Stacks	Lori Bonfitto, Tom Leger
The Destiny of Mimi (by Madeleine Olnek)	Jasmine Presson, Christie N. G. White
Seven Layers of Skin	Jasmine Presson
The Vagina Dialogues	HAG Theatre
Metameshugenahmorphosis	Moira Cutler, Parker Pracjek, Melissa Shimkovitz, Richard Scudney, Lisa Glucken
How to Write While You Sleep	Madeleine Olnek

2003–4

Burrrrlesque	Erika Bernebei
Monster Babies Project	Anne Gadwa
Wires for Fingers	Alison Duncan
In the Shadow of El's	Karen Campbell
As I Was Saying	Jen Abrams

Slain: Women Going Down	Parker Pracjek
The Carnal Carnival	Felice Shays
Phone Sex Cancer	Gina Young
Some Women Are Like Chocolate	Alice Palau Giovanetti, Ione Lloyd
We Are Petite Neanderthals	Melissa Shimkovitz
Jaded Hokey Love Dance	Anne Gadwa
Son of a Bitch Stew	Moira Cutler
Romeo & Juliet	Kristen Plylar-Moore
Love, Sex, and Dating Deez Dayz	Aleada Minton
Ballin' with my Bois	D'Lo
Stages	Tom Leger, Riley McCleod, Sir Real (aka Amy C. Russell)
Black Folks Guide to Black Folks	Hanifah Walidah
The World May Be Ending but at Least Sex Is Good	Jasmina Sinanovic
God in a Girl	Gina Young
Dykenstein	Susana Cook
Stories and Songs	Sharon Jane Smith
Le Cirque de Bel Canto	Jasmine Presson
(G)riot Festival	Jack Aponte, Jen Abrams, Alison Duncan, Sandra Leon, Erica Weinstein

2005–6

Could You Spare Some Social Change?	Deirdre Boddie-Henderson
Proofs, New Works in Progress	Parker Pracjek
So's Your Uncle	Anne Gadwa
Women Wear Pink	Jaymie Garner
A Black Tale	Ione Lloyd
Oedipus: A Love Story	Raven Koch
A Long Way Home	Shapour Bernard
Galileo (by Bertolt Brecht)	Kristen Plylar-Moore
The Barbarians	Jasmina Sinanovic
Too Late for the Gods . . . Too Early for Being	Chris Ford, Joli Wright
On a Day Which Is Everyday	Nicki Marshall, Helen Styring Tocci
Passing	Nana Dakin
Asunder	Jen Abrams
Moving at the Speed of Sound	Nicki Marshall, Helen Styring Tocci
Ms. Sophie Divine Presents	Andrea Davis
The Idiot King	Susana Cook

Rhamnousia	Joli Wright
Of Love and Bush	Amy Ouzoonian
Faces . . . Voices (by Doreen Perrine)	Miriam Eusebio
The Dawn of Barbarism	Jasmina Sinanovic, Heather Rudzenski, Lissy Kilman, Danni Willis, Ileana Marin
Bloom Fest	Jasmina Sinanovic, Sandra Leon, Hanifah Walidah
An Hour of Fun with Mona	Bina Sharif
Not Alone?	Deirdre Boddie-Henderson
Ecstasy of the Blank Page & *Opening Heart*	Tara Thierry
A Want for Want	Chris Ford

2007–8

Could You Spare Some Social *Change Please?*	Deirdre Boddie-Henderson
Everything Is Hungry	Parker Pracjek
Two: Duets	Nicki Marshall, Helen Styring Tocci
Other People	Joyce Wu
Crosswalk: New Dances	Jen Abrams
Trans/Art	Amy Ouzoonian
On the Verge (by Eric Overmeyer)	Julie Baber
Dancer	Ignacio Rivera
Out of Gas on Lover's Leap (by Mark St Germain)	Keri Seymour
Once in Love with Amy	Amy Dawn Verebay
Mystery School (by Paul Selig)	Julie Baber
La Huella de la Espuma	Rhea Volij
Be Here Now	Seren Divine Brevigleiri
Parallel Lives: The Kathy and Mo Show	Kathy Najimy, Mo Gaffney, Julie Baber
Tic Tic Boom (by Jonathan Larson)	Annie Arthur
Asshole Differential	Moira Cutler
New York City Suite	Jen Abrams

2009–10

Yellow Lens: Asian American *Contemporary One Acts*	KS Stevens
(In)Fidelity—The Musical (by Heather Osterman and Ayhan Sahin)	Heather Osterman

*Butch Mamas! Not Your Butch
    Mama's Comedy*   Kirin Stevens

Waiting for the Show   Theresa Diamond
Rise—Songs for a New Moon   Julia Ostrov
Happy Days (by Samuel Beckett)   Miriam Eusebio
Stop Kiss (by Diana Son)   Keri Seymour
Lesbian Love Octagon (by Will Larche
    and Kimberlea Kresssal)   Seren Divine Brevigleiri
Love in the Time of Terror   Jasmina Sinanovic
Most of This Is True   Jen Abrams
Black Girl Ugly   Ashley Brockington
The Maids (by Jean Genet)   Darya Gerasimenko
*Lynee Breedlove & Silas Howard
    in MIGHTY REAL*   Seren Divine Brevigleiri

MIGHTY LITTLE Works In Progress
    Reading Series   Lucile Scott, Scout Durwood

HERe/nOw: A JOURNEY   Shenelle Eaton Foster
Johnny Blazes' wo(n)man show   Miriam Eusebio

Festivals and Cabarets

High Fiber Comedy (1982–85)   Stand-up comedy, Friday nights,
                                                curated by Reno
Variety Nights (1982–92)   Wednesday nights, multiple curators
WOW Women's Film and Video
    Festival (1988–94)   Mary Patierno, Harriet Hirshorn
Work by Women of Color Festival   Month of December, multiple
    (1991–93)   curators
The Service Economy Vaudeville   Susana Cook, with Piper Macleod
    (1995–96)
All WOW Cabarets (1995–97)   Sharon Jane Smith, Lynn Hayes,
                                                Beverly Bronson, Peggy Shaw
Rivers of Honey (1997–)   Hanifah Walidah, Nyonoweh
                                                Green, many others
Latina Playwrights Festival (1998–99)   Sandra Leon
COCKtail: A Drag King Extravaganza   Amy Jo Goddard
    (1998–99)
Youth Shows   Arturo Schomburg Bronx Satellite
                                                Academy, with Laura Marie
                                                Thompson (1998–2003),
                                                Generation Q with Kristen
                                                Plylar-Moore (2004–7)

Erotica Cabaret (1999–2002)

Christie White, Sugar Finger
Productions

Butch McCloud: Your Friendly
Neighborhood Lesbian Superhero
(2003–4)

Tom Leger, Riley McCleod

The Reality Show (2001–4)

Sir Real (aka Amy C. Russell)

HyperGender Burlesque (2006–)

Jasmina Sinanovic, Agent N

Dates Unknown

The Sin Eaters

Jacki Holborough (Cleanbreak
Theatre Company)

Homegirls on the Prowl

Cyn Cañel Rossi

*Don't Talk about Money: Dykes,
Dough, and Degradation*

Nancy Swartz

Lez Beaux Luv

Honour Molloy

For Life: The Lesbian Bridesmaid

Ellen Wong

Face

Nina Newington

Dream (adaptation of August
Strindberg's *A Dream Play*)

Tammy Rose

Groupies

Lori Bonfitto

Miss Julie (by August Strindberg)

Heather MacDonald

Artists and Producers Unknown

(1989–90) *Love/Suicide*

(1993–94) *Ecdysiast/Yesterday*

(1989–90) *Womb for Rent*

(1993–94) *Merz Werk*

(1993–94) *Tongue in Sheets*

(1995–96) *Open Mouth, Closed Fist*

(1993–94) *Eat Fear*

(1997–98) *Two Fools*

(1993–94) *Springtime for Lysistrata*

(1997–98) *At the End of the Century*

(1993–94) *Lesbians in the Bible*

(1997–98) *Everyday*

Notes

Chapter 1

Epigraphs: Lois Weaver, "Afterword," in *The Routledge Reader in Gender and Performance,* edited by Lizbeth Goodman (London: Routledge, 1998), 304; Lisa Kron, "A Straight Line," in *Cast Out: Queer Lives in Theater,* edited by Robin Bernstein (Ann Arbor: University of Michigan Press, 2006), 53; Jill Dolan, *Utopia in Performance: Finding Hope at the Theater* (Ann Arbor: University of Michigan Press, 2008), 66; Peggy Shaw, Peggy Shaw and Lois Weaver, joint interview with the author, February 12, 2001, New York.

1. Linda Winer, "Mom's in a La-Z-Boy, Daughter's on a Roll," *Newsday,* section B, March 31, 2006; Roma Torre, "Theater Review," *NY1,* March 30, 2006; Michael Kuchwara, "The Hilarious Tribulations of a Mother and Daughter," Associated Press, undated. *Well*'s production publicist, Jackie Green of Boneau, Bryan-Brown, provided publicity blurbs and clippings of twenty-three reviews of the play's Broadway opening. Blurbs are composed of words that appear in a review; they are not necessarily precise quotations, but they represent the reviewer's intent.

2. William Stevenson, "*Well,*" *Broadway.com,* March 31, 2006. This was available online at http://www.broadway.com/gen/ Buzz_Story.aspx?ci=526903 but is no longer accessible. A synopsis of this review can be found at http://www.broad way.com/Did-Critics-Think-Lisa-Krons-Well-Deserves-A-Healthy-Run/broad way_news/526922#.

3. Lisa Kron, as quoted in Torre, "Theater Review."

4. Walter Kirn, "Howler," *New York Times Book Review,* November 19, 2006, 25.

5. Alisa Solomon, "The WOW Café," *Drama Review* 29, no. 1 (spring 1985): 92.

6. WOW Café Theater, "Mission Statement," 2005, WOW archives, New York.

7. David Savran, *A Queer Sort of Materialism: Recontextualizing American Theater* (Ann Arbor: University of Michigan Press, 2003), 79–80.

8. Kron related this anecdote as part of WOW's twentieth anniversary event on December 30, 2000. She elaborated on it in a telephone interview with the author on July 26, 2006. All subsequent quotations in this chapter related to Kron's first encounters with WOW are taken from this interview.

9. Holly Hughes, telephone interview with the author, October 1, 2001.

10. Holly Hughes, *Clit Notes: A Sapphic Sampler* (New York: Grove Press, 1996), 14.

11. Lois Weaver, joint interview.

12. See *Split Britches,* in *Split Britches: Lesbian Practice/Feminist Performance,* edited by Sue-Ellen Case (London: Routledge, 1996), 35–57.

13. Lisa Kron, telephone interview.

14. Claire Moed, interview with the author, August 4, 1992, New York.

15. Lois Weaver, as quoted in Elizabeth C. Stroppel, "Acting from Feminist Approaches: Lois Weaver, Anne Bogart, and Shirlene Holmes," *Theatre Insight 6,* no. 1 (winter 1995): 17.

16. *Paradykes Lost,* press release, 1988, WOW archives, New York.

17. Robert Massa, "Sightlines," *Village Voice,* March 22, 1988, 97.

18. Heidi Griffiths, interview with the author, October 31, 2001, New York.

19. Deb Margolin, "Mining My Own Business: Paths between Text and Self," in *Method Acting Reconsidered: Theory, Practice, Future,* edited by David Krasner (New York: St. Martin's Press, 2000), 130.

20. For a description of the group's history and work, see Susan Stryker, "Queer Nation," available at http://www.glbtq.com/social-sciences/queer_nation.html.

21. Five Lesbian Brothers, *Voyage to Lesbos,* in *The Five Lesbian Brothers: Four Plays* (New York: Theatre Communications Group, 2000), 21.

22. *Queer* became the reified term of the 1990s. As such it signaled everything from a political movement to a cultural aesthetic; the term encompasses an equally wide range of sensibilities, identities, and theories.

23. Jeremy McCarter, "Heal Thyself," *New York,* April 17, 2006, 103.

24. *Well,* unpublished script by Lisa Kron, Broadway production, March 2006. All subsequent quotations from the play are from this source.

25. Torre, "Theater Review."

26. See Teresa de Lauretis, "Eccentric Subjects: Feminist Theory and Historical Consciousness," *Feminist Studies 16,* no. 1 (spring 1990): 115–50.

27. Margolin, "Mining My Own Business," 131.

28. Weaver, "Acting from Feminist Approaches," 17.

29. Ibid.

30. Lisa Merrill, "An Interview with Lois Weaver, Peggy Shaw, and Deb Margolin," *Women in Performance: A Journal of Feminist Theory* 6, no. 1 (1993): 161–63.

31. I am indebted to Lisa Merrill for this suggestion.

32. *Upwardly Mobile Home,* in Case, *Split Britches,* 94–97.

33. The character Lisa claims *not* to have written Lori into the script. At one point the character Lori says, "I don't care if you don't want me in your stupid play. What're you going to do about it? 'Cause I was in your stupid life." This strikes me as a brilliant theatricalization of writer Toni Morrison's argument in *Playing in the Dark: Whiteness and the Literary Imagination* (New York: Vintage Books, 1993).

34. "Best of Manhattan," *New York Press,* September 11–17, 1991, 103.

35. Eileen Myles, telephone interview with the author, June 5, 2001.

36. Joseph Roach, *Cities of the Dead: Circum-Atlantic Performance* (New York: Columbia University Press, 1996), 2.

37. Jane Chambers, "A Decade of Dogma Gives Way to Delight at the Women's One World Festival," *Advocate,* January 22, 1981, 19.

38. Griffiths, interview.

39. In 2000, for example, WOW paid only $545 a month for its space in a city-owned building (plus electricity, insurance, and telephone expenses), while a one-room studio apartment typically rented for $1,200 to $2,000. At $12 a ticket only about a hundred spectators were required to attend WOW productions each month to secure the space financially.

40. See Jo Freeman (pseudonym "Joreen"), "The Tyranny of Structurelessness," in *Radical Feminism,* edited by Anne Koedt, Ellen Levine, and Anita Rapone (New York: Quadrangle Books, 1973), 285–99. I am indebted to scholar Esther Newton for bringing this essay to my attention.

41. Peggy Shaw and Lois Weaver, "MAKE SOMETHING: A Manifesto for Making Performance about Making Change," in *Staging International Feminisms,* edited by Elaine Aston and Sue-Ellen Case (Basingstoke, Hampshire: Palgrave Macmillan, 2007): 180.

42. C. Carr, interview with the author, March 29, 2001, New York.

43. Lisa White, "Partying at the WOW Café with Girls Who Have Fun," *Philadelphia Gay News,* April 18, 1985.

44. Joni Wong, interview with the author, October 29, 2001, New York.

45. Cheryl Moch, *Cinderella: The Real True Story,* in *Lesbian Plays: Two,* edited by Jill Davis (London: Methuen, 1989), 116–17.

46. bell hooks, *Yearning: Race, Gender, and Cultural Politics* (Boston: South End Press, 1990), 171.

47. Hughes, telephone interview.

Chapter 2

Epigraphs: Holly Hughes, *Clit Notes: A Sapphic Sampler* (New York: Grove Press, 1996), 12; Kevin Vance, "The Demented Diva," *Village Voice,* July 1, 1974, 45; Jill Dolan, *Presence and Desire: Essays on Gender, Sexuality, Performance* (Ann Arbor: University of Michigan Press, 1993), 64; Barbara Schwartz and Mara Shelby, "A Survey of Women's/Feminist/Lesbian Theater Groups in New York," *Christopher Street* 2, no. 12, June 1978, 28–32; Sarah Schulman, *Stagestruck: Theater, AIDS, and the Marketing of Gay America* (Durham: Duke University Press, 1998), 65; Clare Whatling, "Reading awry: Joan Nestle and the recontexualization of heterosexuality," in *Sexual Sameness: Textual Differences in Lesbian and Gay Writing,* ed. Joseph Bristow (London: Routledge, 1992), 210; Bette Bourne, Paul Shaw, Peggy Shaw, and Lois Weaver, *Belle Reprieve,* in *Split Britches: Lesbian Practice/Feminist Performance,* ed. Sue-Ellen Case (London/New York: Routledge, 1996), 177; Del Martin and Phyllis Lyon, *Lesbian/Woman* (New York: Bantam Books, 1972), 300; Hughes, *Clit Notes,* 13; Eve Kosofsky Sedgwick, *Epistemology of the Closet* (Berkeley: University of California Press, 1990), 84.

1. Jordy Mark, Pamela Camhe and Jordy Mark, joint interview with the author, March 11, 2001, New York.

2. Jane Chambers, "A Decade of Dogma Gives Way to Delight at the Women's One World Festival," *Advocate,* January 22, 1981, 19.

3. Ibid. Singer-songwriter Chris Williamson and comedian Robin Tyler were key figures in the women's music movement at the time. See Bonnie J. Morris, *Eden Built by Eves: The Culture of Women's Music Festivals* (Los Angeles: Alyson Books, 1999). See also Jane Chambers, *Last Summer at Bluefish Cove* (New York: JH Press, 1982). Chambers's play represents a milestone in lesbian theater history. It was produced by the Glines Theater and ran from December 22, 1980, to March 1, 1981.

4. Eileen Myles, telephone interview with the author, June 5, 2001.

5. Eva Saks, "Hot Peaches," *Christopher Street,* April 1978, 51.

6. Charles Ludlam, interview with the author, October 13, 1974, New York. All subsequent quotations from Ludlam in this chapter are from this source unless otherwise noted.

7. Jimmy Camicia, interview with the author, June 3, 2001, New York. All subsequent quotations from Camicia in this chapter are from this source unless otherwise noted.

8. Francis Levy, "There's a Definite Magic at Work Here," *Village Voice,* August 2, 1973, 60.

9. Camicia, as quoted in Linda Lawrence, "The Watergate Scandals of '73," *Westsider,* August 23, 1973, 8. I saw "Watergate Scandals."

10. Lincoln Perry's filmography spans six decades. See Donald Hogle, *Toms, Coons, Mulattoes, Mammies, and Bucks: An Interpretive History of Blacks in American Films,* 4th ed. (New York: Continuum, 2001), 38–47; and Mel Watkins, *On the Real Side: Laughing, Lying, and Signifying—the Underground Tradition of African-American Humor That Transformed American Culture from Slavery to Richard Pryor* (New York: Simon and Schuster, 1994), 201–2, 226–28, 247–62.

11. Stefan Brecht, *Queer Theatre* (Frankfurt, Germany: Suhrkamp, 1978), 114.

12. Ibid., 123.

13. Camicia, interview.

14. Charles Ludlam, *Ridiculous Theatre: Scourge of Human Folly, the Essays and Opinions of Charles Ludlam,* edited by Steven Samuels (New York: Theatre Communications Groups, 1992), 228–33.

15. Camicia, interview; Michael Feingold, "Prescriptions for Coping," *Village Voice,* June 13, 1974, 83. Peggy Shaw and Lois Weaver, joint interview with the author, February 12, 2001, New York.

16. Steven Watson, "Hot Peaches: Street Theatre with Cream," *Advocate,* September 20, 1978, 34.

17. Camicia, interview.

18. Peggy Shaw, as quoted in Rebecca Lewin, "Peggy Shaw: Master of Her Own Show," *New York Native,* May 20–June 2, 1985, 23.

19. Kate Millet was the author of a best-selling book, *Sexual Politics* (New York: Doubleday, 1970). Camicia, interview. Shaw, joint interview.

20. This monologue was obtained from the private collection of Peggy Shaw and Lois Weaver, New York.

21. Unfortunately, Shaw was unable to recall or locate a copy of this monologue.

22. Camicia, interview.

23. Peggy Shaw, as quoted in Laurie Stone, *Laughing in the Dark: A Decade of Subversive Comedy* (Hopewell, N.J.: Ecco Press, 1997), 172.

24. Stone, *Laughing in the Dark,* 176.

25. Shaw, as quoted in ibid., 173.

26. For biographies of these three sisters, see Kathy A. Perkins and Roberta Uno, eds., *Contemporary Plays by Women of Color: An Anthology* (London: Routledge, 1996), 297–98.

27. Charlotte Canning, *Feminist Theaters in the U.S.A.: Staging Women's Experience* (New York: Routledge, 1996), 33.

28. Mark, joint interview.

29. The emphasis is mine. Both Spedding's and Nicholls's reviews appeared in a publication called *Spare Rib* and were obtained in photocopied form from the private collection of Peggy Shaw and Lois Weaver with no dates or page numbers noted.

30. Ibid.

31. Rebecca Schneider, *The Explicit Body in Performance* (London: Routledge, 1997), 166.

32. Canning, *Feminist Theaters in the U.S.A.*, 123.

33. As quoted by Linda Walsh Jenkins, "Spiderwoman," in *Women in American Theatre*, edited by Helen Krich Chinoy and Linda Walsh Jenkins, rev. ed. (New York: Theatre Communications Group, 1987), 304.

34. Gloria Miguel and Muriel Miguel, as quoted in Barbara Baracks, "Truth Serum," *Village Voice*, May 26, 1981, 39.

35. Canning, *Feminist Theaters in the U.S.A.*, 122.

36. Ana Maria Simo, letter to the author, November 7, 1988. Some of the general information that follows is from this source.

37. Ana Maria Simo, as quoted in Alisa Solomon and Framji Minwalla, eds., *The Queerest Art: Essays on Lesbian and Gay Theater* (New York: New York University Press, 2002), 138–39.

38. The publicity materials and programs for Medusa's Revenge mentioned throughout this chapter were obtained from the Lesbian Herstory Archives, Brooklyn.

39. Peggy Shaw, telephone interview with the author, July 11, 2001.

40. Simo, as quoted in Solomon and Minwalla, *Queerest Art*, 139.

41. Ibid. *Going Slow* and *Bayou* remain unpublished today.

42. Fran Winant, "*Bayou*'s World: Lesbian Bar of the '50s," *Gay Community News*, September 10, 1977, 10.

43. Judith Pasternak, "You Don't Have to Be Lesbian for *Bayou*," *Majority Report*, August 6, 1977, 10.

44. For a cogent discussion of both the politics and theories surrounding butch/femme roles, see Amy Goodloe's online essay "Lesbian Identity and the Politics of Butch-Femme Roles" (1993). Ludlow also provides a comprehensive bibliography. Link at Goodloe's webpage http://www.lesbian.org. Also online see "SAMOIS" by Gayle Rubin in *Leather Times*, spring 2004, http://www.leatherarchives.org/resources/issue21.pdf, 3–7.

45. Peggy Shaw, e-mail message to the author, July 15, 2001.

46. Alan Sinfield, *Out on Stage: Lesbian and Gay Theatre in the Twentieth Century* (New Haven: Yale University Press, 1999), 309.

47. Simo, as quoted in Solomon and Minwalla, *Queerest Art*, 139.

48. Ibid., 140.

49. Holly Hughes, telephone interview with the author, October 1, 2001.

50. See Alice Echols, *Daring to Be Bad: Radical Feminism in America, 1967–1975* (Minneapolis: University of Minnesota Press, 1989), 243–86.

51. See Martha Gever, John Greyson, and Pratibha Parmar, eds., *Queer Looks: Perspectives on Lesbian and Gay Film and Video* (New York: Routledge, 1993);

and B. Ruby Rich, *Chick Flicks: Theories and Memories of the Feminist Film Movement* (Durham: Duke University Press, 1998).

52. Megan Terry, *Willa-Willie-Bill's Dope Garden,* in *Amazon All Stars: Thirteen Lesbian Plays,* edited by Rosemary Keefe Curb (New York: Applause Books, 1996), 423–34.

53. See Andrea Juno and V. Vale, eds., *Angry Women* (San Francisco: Re/Search Publications, 1991), 105–17. See also C. Carr, *On the Edge: Performance at the End of the Twentieth Century* (Hanover, N.H.: Wesleyan University Press, 1993), 141–43.

54. See Sally Banes, *Subversive Expectations: Performance Art and Paratheater in New York, 1976–85* (Ann Arbor: University of Michigan Press, 1998), 71–72.

55. Hughes, *Clit Notes,* 12.

56. Judy Chicago, *The Dinner Party* (New York: Penguin Books, 1996), 6.

57. See Karen Malpede, ed., *Women and Theatre: Compassion and Hope* (New York: Drama Book Publishers, 1983); Krich Chinoy and Walsh Jenkins, *Women in American Theatre;* and Canning, *Feminist Theaters in the U.S.A.*

58. Ntozake Shange, "Author's Note," *for colored girls who have considered suicide/when the rainbow is enuf,* in *Totem Voices: Plays from the Black World Repertory,* edited by Paul Carter Harrison (New York: Grove Press, 1989), 227.

59. Ibid., 261.

60. On the critical reception of *The Dinner Party,* for example, see Whitney Chadwick, *Women, Art, and Society* (London: Thames and Hudson, 1992), 346.

61. For an alternative reading of Saar's work, see Arlene Raven, *Crossing Over: Feminism and Art of Social Concern* (Ann Arbor: UMI Research Press, 1988), 71–82.

62. See Frieda High W. Tesfagiorgis, "In Search of a Discourse and Critique/s That Center the Art of Black Women Artists," in *Theorizing Black Feminisms: The Visionary Pragmatism of Black Women,* edited by Stanlie M. James and Abena P. A. Busia (London: Routledge, 1993), 228–66.

63. See Carrie Rickey, "The Writing on the Wall," *Art in America* 69, no. 5 (May 1981): 54–57; and Kay Mills, "The Great Wall of Los Angeles," *Ms.,* October 1981, 56–58.

64. Lorraine O'Grady, as quoted in Jo Anna Isaak, *Feminism and Contemporary Art: The Revolutionary Power of Women's Laughter* (London: Routledge, 1996), 153.

65. For an alternative reading of body/performance art, see Amelia Jones, *Body Art/Performing the Subject* (Minneapolis: University of Minnesota Press, 1998); and Amelia Jones and Andrew Stephenson, eds., *Performing the Body: Performing the Text* (London: Routledge, 1999).

66. See Moira Roth, ed., *The Amazing Decade: Women and Performance Art in America, 1970–1980* (Los Angeles: Astro Artz, 1983), 14–16.

67. Lois Weaver, interview with the author, August 14, 1993, New York.

68. Lois Weaver, interview with the author, December 29, 2000, London.

69. Ibid.

70. Shaw, joint interview.

71. Amber Hollibaugh, "Desire for the Future: Radical Hope in Passion and Pleasure," in *Pleasure and Danger: Exploring Female Sexuality,* edited by Carol S. Vance (Boston: Routledge and Kegan Paul, 1984), 409.

72. Anne Koedt, "The Myth of the Vaginal Orgasm," reprinted in *Radical Feminism,* edited by Anne Koedt, Ellen Levine, and Anita Rapone (New York: Quadrangle, 1973), 198–207.

73. Pat Robertson, from a fund-raising letter under his name in support of the Iowa Committee to Stop ERA [Equal Rights Amendment], quoted in Pam Keesey, *Vamps: An Illustrated History of the Femme Fatale* (San Francisco: Cleis Press, 1997), 45.

74. The idea of the "desire to be desired" was formulated by the film scholar Mary Ann Doane as a theoretical construct for getting at the operations of spectatorial desire in cinema; it also described what many women recognized as their own desire in the practice of their sexuality. See Mary Ann Doane, *The Desire to Desire: The Woman's Film of the 1940s* (Bloomington: Indiana University Press, 1987).

75. From a talk delivered in 1975 at a meeting of the Eulenspiegel Society, New York, entitled "Why I'm against S/M Liberation" by Ti-Grace Atkinson, originally published in 1977, reprinted in 1982 in *Against Sadomasochism: A Radical Feminist Analysis,* edited by Robin Ruth Linden, Darlene R. Pagano, Diana E. H. Russell, and Susan Leigh Star (San Francisco: Frog in the Well, 1982), 91.

76. For works that recuperate and reflect on the butch/femme experience, see Joan Nestle, ed., *The Persistent Desire: A Femme-Butch Reader* (Boston: Alyson Publications, 1992); and Sally R. Munt, ed., *butch/femme: Inside Lesbian Gender* (London: Cassell, 1998).

77. Catharine MacKinnon, *Only Words* (Cambridge: Harvard University Press, 1993), 17.

78. Gayle Rubin, "The Leather Menace: Comments on Politics and S/M," in *Coming to Power: Writings and Graphics on Lesbian S/M,* edited by SAMOIS, rev. and updated ed. (Boston: Alyson Publications, 1982), 213. See also Rubin, "SAMOIS," 3–7. SAMOIS was a lesbian feminist S/M group that believed in consensual, mutual, and safe S/M sex. The group was active in San Francisco from 1978 to 1983. Samois is the name of an estate in the novel *Story of O* (1965) where the female dominant in the narrative lives and where S/M scenes are enacted among women.

79. Vance, *Pleasure and Danger,* 434.
80. Martin and Lyon, *Lesbian/Woman,* 301.
81. Weaver, interview, 1993.

Chapter 3

Epigraphs: Lois Weaver, quoted in Sue Feinberg and Judd Hollander, "Split Britches: Together or Apart, Still Going Strong," *Off-Off Broadway Review* 6, no. 17, December 23, 1999, available online at http://www.oobr.com/top/volSix/seventeen/britches.html; Women's One World Festival, press release, 1980, from the private collection of Peggy Shaw and Lois Weaver, New York; Howard Smith, in Howard Smith and Lin Harris, "WOW Bows," *Village Voice,* July 15, 1980, 18; Jane Chambers, "A Decade of Dogma Gives Way to Delight at the Women's One World Festival," *Advocate,* January 22, 1981, 19; ibid., 21; Jordy Mark, Pamela Camhe and Jordy Mark, joint interview with the author, March 11, 2001, New York; Barbara Baracks, "Witches, Nuns, and Bearded Ladies," *Soho Weekly News,* October 29, 1980, 23; Audrey Roth, "The Life of W.O.W.," *Womanews,* November 1980, 7. Sherry Rosso, interview with the author, June 25, 2001, New York.

1. Alisa Solomon, "The Wings of Desire: WOW Café Celebrates Twenty Years of Lesbian Performance," *Village Voice,* January 9, 2001, 61.

2. See Helen Krich Chinoy and Linda Walsh Jenkins, eds., *Women in American Theatre* (New York: Crown Publishers, 1981), 343–45.

3. Information was garnered from the First Gay American Festival's program, which was obtained from the Lesbian Herstory Archives, Brooklyn. Jane Chambers's play *Last Summer at Bluefish Cove* was presented, the comic Robin Tyler was featured, and the poet and author Audre Lorde participated in an evening of readings devoted to women poets.

4. C. Carr, interview with the author, March 29, 2001, New York.

5. C. Carr, e-mail message to the author, May 1, 2007.

6. Susan Thames, "WOW Fest in East Village," *Womanews,* October 1981, 14; Catherine Bergart, "W.O.W.: A Place for Something New," *Villager,* October 1, 1981, 11.

7. A grant application to the National Endowment for the Arts, obtained from the private collection of Shaw and Weaver, projected the cost of the second festival at $56,950 (including labor, artists' fees, workshop instructor stipends, and theater rental) and requested $15,000. The application listed expenses for the first festival at $15,937 (which used a free venue and volunteer labor) and revenues at $18,770. If the proposal was submitted, the request was not granted.

8. Percentages were reached by reviewing each event in the two festivals' pro-

grams with the producers. The percentage of lesbian work represents work identifiable as lesbian to anyone, not just to insiders.

9. See Brenda Dixon-Stowell, "Blondell Cummings: *The Ladies and Me*," *Drama Review* 24, no. 4 (December 1980): 37–44; and a review of the piece in *Dancemagazine* 54, no. 9 (September 1980): 106–9.

10. See Julie Malnig and Judy C. Rosenthal, "The Women's Experimental Theatre: Transforming Family Stories into Feminist Questions," in *Acting Out: Feminist Performances,* edited by Lynda Hart and Peggy Phelan (Ann Arbor: University of Michigan Press, 1993), 201–14; and Charlotte Canning, *Feminist Theatres in the U.S.A.: Staging Women's Experience* (London: Routledge, 1996), 88–93.

11. The Schlockettes' musical numbers were choreographed by Cheryl Gates McFadden.

12. Susan Thames, "W.O.W. Wows," *Womanews,* September 1980.

13. Thames, "WOW Fest in East Village," 14.

14. Lois Weaver, as quoted in Leah D. Frank, "Women's One World Festival," *Other Stages,* October 8, 1981.

15. Peggy Shaw, Peggy Shaw and Lois Weaver, joint interview with the author, February 12, 2001, New York. All subsequent quotations from Shaw and Weaver in this chapter are from this source unless otherwise noted.

16. Jordy Mark, Pamela Camhe and Jordy Mark, joint interview with the author, March 11, 2001, New York.

17. Erika Munk, "Outrage Department," *Village Voice,* October 7, 1980, 114.

18. Roth, "Life of W.O.W.," 7.

19. Pamela Camhe, as quoted in Smith and Harris, "WOW Bows," 19.

20. Munk, "Outrage Department," 114.

21. Pamela Camhe, as quoted in Barbara Baracks, "Living on Truth Serum: Gay and Lesbian Performance Artists Look at Themselves," *Village Voice,* May 26, 1981, 39.

22. Pamela Camhe, Pamela Camhe and Jordy Mark, joint interview with the author, New York, June 29, 2001.

23. Deborah Proos, "Theatre . . . as a Cabaret, Old Chum," *Womanews,* November 1980, 9.

24. Prudence Sowers, "Is There Life after WOW?" *Advocate,* December 24, 1981, 48.

25. Donna Allegra, "NYCNews Goes to the WOW Festival," *New York City News,* November 3, 1981, 1.

26. See, as examples, Barbara Findlen, *Listen Up: Voices from the Next Generation* (Seattle: Seal Press, 1995); Rebecca Walker, *To Be Real: Telling the Truth and Changing the Face of Feminism* (New York: Anchor Books, 1995); and Leslie Heywood and Jennifer Drake, *Third Wave Agenda: Being Feminist, Doing Feminism* (Minneapolis: University of Minnesota Press, 1997).

27. Sowers, "Is There Life after WOW?" 40.

28. Baracks, "Witches, Nuns, and Bearded Ladies," 23.

29. Mark, joint interview, June 29.

30. Baracks, "Living on Truth Serum," 39.

31. Camhe and Mark, joint interview, March 11.

32. Sue-Ellen Case, *Feminism and Theatre* (New York: Methuen, 1988), 50.

33. Ibid., 53.

34. Mark, joint interview, June 29.

35. Case, *Feminism and Theatre,* 50.

36. Sowers, "Is There Life after WOW?" 40.

37. Jessica Abbe, "Views from the Women's One World Festival," *Villager,* October 8, 1981, 11.

38. Sarah Schulman, "Riding the Go-Go Bus Home: Interview with Dancer Diane Torr," *Womanews,* November 1982, 11.

39. Jennifer Baumgardner and Amy Richards, *Manifesta: Young Women, Feminism, and the Future* (New York: Farrar, Straus and Giroux, 2000), 137.

40. Ibid., 135.

41. Diane Torr, interview with the author, June 29, 2001, New York.

42. Joan Blair, "Women Are Wowed," *Womanews,* November 1981.

43. Abbe, "Views from the Women's One World Festival," 11.

44. Alexis De Veaux, telephone interview with the author, June 29, 2001.

45. Promotional materials obtained from the Lesbian Herstory Archives, Brooklyn.

46. Shaw, joint interview; De Veaux, telephone interview.

47. Barbara Baracks, "Deja WOW," *Village Voice,* October 20, 1981, 103.

48. Glenda Dickerson, "Wearing Red: When a Rowdy Band of Charismatics Learned to Say 'NO!'" in *Upstaging Big Daddy: Directing Theater as If Gender and Race Matter,* edited by Ellen Donkin and Susan Clement (Ann Arbor: University of Michigan Press, 1993), 160, 158–59.

49. Mel Gussow, "Stage: A Qualified 'No'," *New York Times,* section 1, June 6, 1981.

50. Unnamed reviewer, "'NO' by Alexis De Veaux, Adapted for the Stage and Directed by Glenda Dickerson," *Big Apple Dyke News,* September 1981, 4.

51. Gwendolen Hardwick, interview with the author, June 6, 2001, New York.

52. Dickerson, "Wearing Red," 171, emphasis in original.

53. Alisa Solomon, "The WOW Café," *Drama Review* 29, no.1 (spring 1985): 93.

54. Peg Byron, "Lesbians Too Terrorizing for NYC," *Womanews,* May 1981.

55. Barbara Baracks, "WOW Funky and Feminist," *Village Voice,* October 13, 1981, 93.

56. Mary Anne Bollen, telephone interview with the author, August 3, 2001.

57. Ibid.

58. Chambers, "Decade of Dogma," 19.

59. Mary Anne Bollen, e-mail message to the author, August 5, 2001.

60. Baracks, "Deja WOW," 103.

61. Linda Walsh Jenkins, "Split Britches," in *Women in American Theatre,* edited by Helen Krich Chinoy and Linda Walsh Jenkins, rev. ed. (New York: Theatre Communications Group, 1987), 310.

62. Laurie Stone, "Vixen Fire," *Village Voice,* April 19, 1983, 105.

63. Deb Margolin, interview with the author, June 6, 2001, New York. All subsequent quotations from Margolin in this chapter are from this source.

64. Eileen Myles, telephone interview with the author, June 5, 2001.

65. Vivian M. Patraka, "Split Britches in *Split Britches:* Performing History, Vaudeville, and the Everyday," in Hart and Phelan, *Acting Out,* 216.

66. Chambers, "Decade of Dogma," 20.

67. Patraka, "Split Britches in *Split Britches,*" 217.

68. Shaw, quoted in Laurie Stone, *Laughing in the Dark* (Hopewell, N.J.: Ecco Press, 1997), 173.

69. *Split Britches,* in *Split Britches: Lesbian Practice/Feminist Performance,* edited by Sue-Ellen Case (London: Routledge, 1996), 57.

70. Jo Anna Isaak, *Feminist Contemporary Art: The Revolutionary Power of Women's Laughter* (London: Routledge, 1996), 150.

71. Peggy Shaw, quoted in Rebecca Lewin, "Peggy Shaw: Master of Her Own Show," *New York Native,* May 20–June 2, 1985, 24.

72. Alisa Solomon, *Re-dressing the Canon: Essays on Theater and Gender* (London: Routledge, 1997), 167.

73. Bethany Haye, "Performance," *Soho Weekly News,* October 1, 1980, 71.

74. Baracks, "Witches, Nuns, and Bearded Ladies," 23.

75. Lois Weaver, quoted in Stone, *Laughing in the Dark,* 181.

76. Donna Allegra, "Edwina WOW's 'Em Again," *Womanews,* March 1981, 14.

77. Sowers, "Is There Life after WOW?", 39.

78. Proos, "Theatre . . . as a Cabaret," 8.

79. Sherry Rosso, interview with the author.

80. Shaw, Shaw and Weaver, interview.

81. Weaver, joint interview.

82. Jean Grove, letter to the festival's producers, November 24, 1980, Lesbian Herstory Archives, Brooklyn.

83. Baracks, "Witches, Nuns, and Bearded Ladies," 23.

84. Chambers, "Decade of Dogma," 21, emphasis in original.

85. Proos, "Theatre . . . as a Cabaret," 9; Roth, "Life of W.O.W.," 7.

86. Haye, "Performance," 71.

87. Sowers, "Is There Life after WOW?" 39; Weaver, as quoted in ibid.; and ibid.

88. Solomon, "WOW Café," 94.

89. Case, *Split Britches,* 25.

90. Baracks, "Living on Truth Serum," 39.

91. Carr, interview.

92. Alice Echols, *Daring to Be Bad: Radical Feminism in America, 1967–1975* (Minneapolis: University of Minnesota Press, 1989), 240.

93. Margolin, interview; Myles, telephone interview.

94. Carr, interview.

95. Wendell Ricketts, "Lesbians and Gay Men on Stage: A Necessarily Incomplete History," http://home.earthlink.net/~uur/gla (accessed in 2005). Unfortunately the Web site has been discontinued.

96. Joseph Roach, *Cities of the Dead: Circum-Atlantic Performance* (New York: Columbia University Press, 1996), 2.

97. In the fall of 2000, I attended a talk by the legal scholar Janet Halley on queer theory and the law at New York University. What struck me about the talk and discussion afterward is that "queer" was portrayed as historically contingent while "the feminists" were consistently referred to monolithically, as if all feminists are antipornography and antisex.

98. Esther Newton, *Margaret Mead Made Me Gay: Personal Essays, Public Ideas* (Durham: Duke University Press, 2000), 67.

99. See Esther Newton, *Mother Camp: Female Impersonators in America* (Chicago: University of Chicago Press, 1972).

100. This anecdote has appeared in print at least four times. See Lynda Hart, "Identity and Seduction," in Hart and Phelan, *Acting Out,* 129; Case, *Split Britches,* 4; Stone, *Laughing in the Dark,* 172; and Newton, *Margaret Mead Made Me Gay,* 88.

101. Newton, *Margaret Mead Made Me Gay,* 89, emphasis in original.

102. Camhe, joint interview, June 29; Kathleen M. Conkey, "The East Village as a Way of Life," *Village Voice,* July 2, 1985, 15.

103. See, as examples, Judith Halberstam, *Female Masculinity* (Durham: Duke University Press, 1998); and Del Lagrace Volcano and Judith "Jack" Halberstam, eds., *The Drag King Book* (London: Serpent's Tail, 1999).

104. Baracks, "Deja WOW," 103.

105. Margolin, interview.

106. Jill Dolan, *Presence and Desire: Essays on Gender, Sexuality, Performance* (Ann Arbor: University of Michigan Press, 1993), 47.

Chapter 4

Epigraphs: Carole S. Vance, ed., *Pleasure and Danger: Exploring Female Sexuality* (Boston: Routledge and Kegan Paul, 1984), 437; Lisa Kron, quoted in Steven

Vincent, "The Downtown Alternative: New Theatres on the Lower East Side," *Back Stage,* August 10, 1990, 1, 20; Punk rock vocalist Johnny Rotten of the Sex Pistols, quoted in Dick Hebdige, *Subculture: The Meaning of Style* (London: Routledge, 1988), 109; Reno, interview with the author, October 9, 2001, New York; *She Cuts Herself/She Likes to Write,* press release, 2001, WOW archive, New York.

1. Eileen Myles, telephone interview with the author, June 5, 2001.

2. Donna Allegra, *New York City News,* November 3, 1981, 1.

3. Barbara Barracks, "WOW: Funky and Feminist," *Village Voice,* October 13, 1981, 93.

4. Iris Marion Young, "The Ideal of Community and the Politics of Difference," in *Feminism/Postmodernism,* edited by Linda J. Nicholson (New York: Routledge, 1990), 301.

5. Gloria T. Hull, Patricia Bell Scott, and Barbara Smith, eds., *All the Women Are White, All the Blacks Are Men, but Some of Us Are Brave* (New York: Feminist Press, 1982).

6. Young, "Ideal of Community," 318, 319.

7. Joni Wong, interview with the author, October 29, 2001, New York.

8. C. Carr, interview with the author, March 29, 2001, New York.

9. Heidi Griffiths, interview with the author, October 31, 2001, New York.

10. The sex wars were not the only manifestation of women at odds with each other; women of color were challenging the "feminist subject" as untheorized on the basis of differences other than gender. See, as examples, Hull, Scott, and Smith, *All the Women Are White;* Cherrie Moraga, Gloria Anzaldúa, and Toni Cade Bambara, eds., *This Bridge Called My Back: Writings by Radical Women of Color* (New York: Kitchen Table Women of Color Press, 1983); and Gloria Anzaldúa, *Borderlands/La Frontera: The New Mestiza* (San Francisco: Spinsters/Aunt Lute, 1987).

11. Women's One World Festival, press release, 1980, emphasis added, obtained from the personal collection of Peggy Shaw and Lois Weaver, New York.

12. Throughout the 2000–2001 season, for example, meetings were held to discuss race at WOW, as well as strategies for increasing diversity. In July 2002, WOW's e-mail discussion distribution list included an exchange of views regarding incidents in which some members of color encountered racist attitudes among some white members. When issues of race arise, they are addressed if not resolved.

13. See bell hooks, "Choosing the Margin as a Space of Radical Openness," in *Yearning: Race, Gender, and Cultural Politics* (Boston: South End Press, 1990), 145–53. See also Edward W. Soja, *Thirdspace: Journeys to Los Angeles and Other Real-and-Imagined Places* (Malden, Mass.: Blackwell Publishers, 1996). In theo-

rizing "thirdspace," Soja's text is a kind of exegesis of hook's concept of a "space of radical openness."

14. Gwendolen Hardwick, interview with the author, June 7, 2001, New York.

15. Robert Massa, "SLA Hits Women's Bars," *Village Voice,* September 28, 1982, 11.

16. See Jon Pareles, "Then, Now: New Rock City," *New York Times,* section 2, May 19, 2002. See also Stephen Colegrave and Chris Sullivan, *Punk: The Definitive Record of a Revolution* (New York: Thunder's Mouth Press, 2001).

17. Kathy Rey, telephone interview with the author, May 16, 2002.

18. Tracey Tanenbaum's interview with Patti Smith on National Public Radio (April 12, 2004) can be accessed at http://www.npr.org/templates/story/story/.phb?storyId=1814648.

19. Deborah Glick, telephone interview with the author, August 7, 2001.

20. Ibid.

21. Rey, telephone interview.

22. Myles, telephone interview.

23. Flyer obtained from the Lesbian Herstory Archives, Brooklyn.

24. Holly Hughes, telephone interview with the author, October 1, 2001.

25. Griffiths, interview; Claire Moed, interview with the author, August 4, 1992, New York.

26. Griffiths, interview; Alice Forrester, interview with the author, October 16, 2001, New York.

27. Peggy Shaw, interview with the author, August 3, 1992, New York, subsequently published in *Modern Drama: Plays/Criticism/Theory,* edited by W. B. Worthen (Fort Worth, Tex.: Harcourt Brace, 1995), 1004.

28. Moed, interview.

29. Esther Newton, *Margaret Mead Made Me Gay: Personal Essays, Public Ideas* (Durham: Duke University Press, 2000), 1.

30. Jen Abrams, e-mail message to the author, November 11, 2001.

31. Forrester, interview; Hughes, telephone interview.

32. Ibid.

33. Lois Weaver, interview with the author, February 12, 2001, New York.

34. Madeleine Olnek, e-mail message to the author, October 8, 2009.

35. Madeleine Olnek, interview with the author, May 6, 2002, New York.

36. Susana Cook, interview with the author, April 30, 2002, New York.

37. Dozens of messages on these two issues appeared on WOW's e-mail discussion list between January and April 2002.

38. E-mail exchange on WOW's discussion distribution list, spring 2002.

39. Molly Kleinman, Anne Gadwa, Jen Abrams, Emily Rems, Sandra Leon, Christie White, and Justine Buchanan, group interview with the author, Novem-

ber 13, 2001, New York. All subsequent quotations from these people in this chapter are from this source. Individual speakers are not identified; rather, any quoted comments are those with which the entire group agreed.

40. In recent years the "Rivers of Honey" cabaret moved to 8:00 p.m. on the first Friday of the month.

41. Kleinman et al., group interview.

42. Ibid.

43. On rare occasions, more informal social enforcement of the "rules" can involve passive-aggressive nonaction in the form of refusing to work on the show of a member whom other collective members feel has crossed a line.

44. Joreen [Jo Freeman], "The Tyranny of Structurelessness," in *Radical Feminism,* edited by Anne Koedt, Ellen Levine, and Anita Rapone (New York: Quadrangle Books, 1973), 285–99.

45. Klienman et al., group interview.

46. Hughes, telephone interview.

47. Betsy Crenshaw, interview with the author, August 7, 1992, New York.

48. Wong, interview.

49. Lois Weaver, interview with the author, August 4, 1993, New York, subsequently published in Worthen, *Modern Drama,* 1006.

50. Wong, interview; Forrester, interview; Babs Davy, interview with the author, August 16, 1992, recorded while driving through Virginia. Davy is my sister, so I also learned about her experience with WOW informally.

51. Hughes, telephone interview; Griffiths, interview.

52. Sarah Schulman, interview with the author, October 13, 2001, New York.

53. Sarah Schulman, letter to the author, November 5, 1992.

54. Sarah Schulman, letter to the author, December 11, 1991.

55. Schulman, letter to the author, November 5, 1992.

56. E-mail discussion group, July 10, 2002, summarizing the major points raised at a retreat meeting held on July 7, 2002.

57. Griffiths, interview.

58. Terry Diamond, interview with the author, June 6, 2002, New York.

59. Amy Robinson, seminar paper prepared for the American Society for Theater Research conference, New York, November 1999.

60. Alisa Solomon, "Wings of Desire: WOW Café Celebrates Twenty Years of Lesbian Performance," *Village Voice,* January 9, 2001, 61.

61. Holly Hughes, *Clit Notes: A Sapphic Sampler* (New York: Grove Press, 1996), 14.

62. Holly Hughes, "O Solo Homo: Why This Book?" in *O Solo Homo: The New Queer Performance,* edited by Holly Hughes and David Roman (New York: Grove Press, 1998), 477; Forrester, interview.

63. Obtained from an announcement posted on the collective's e-mail discussion distribution list, June 2002.

Chapter 5

Epigraphs: Tony Kushner, "Part One: The Millennium Approaches," in *Angels in America: A Gay Fantasia on National Themes* (New York: Theatre Communications Group, 1993), 32; Alina Troyano, *I, Carmelita Tropicana: Performing between Cultures,* with Ela Troyano and Uzi Parnes, edited by Chon A. Noriega (Boston: Beacon Press, 2000), xiii; Holly Hughes, *Clit Notes: A Sapphic Sampler* (New York: Grove Press, 1996), 17; Charles Ludlam, "Manifesto: Ridiculous Theatre, Scourge of Human Folly," in *The Complete Plays of Charles Ludlam* (New York: Harper and Row: 1989), vii, first published in *Drama Review* 19, no. 4, December 1975, 70, reprinted in *Ridiculous Theatre: Scourge of Human Folly* (New York: Theatre Communications Group, 1992), 157; Virginia Woolf, *A Room of One's Own* (1929; reprint, San Diego: Harcourt Brace Jovanovich, 1957), 45; Lois Weaver, "Afterword," in *The Routledge Reader in Gender and Performance,* edited by Lizbeth Goodman (London: Routledge, 1998), 304.

1. Shaw, as quoted in Alisa Solomon, "Wings of Desire: WOW Café Celebrates Twenty Years of Lesbian Performance," *Village Voice,* January 9, 2001, 61.

2. Simone de Beauvoir, *The Second Sex,* translated and edited by H. M. Parshley (1952; reprint, New York: Alfred A. Knopf, 1993), xxxix–xl.

3. Woolf, *A Room of One's Own,* 35.

4. Robin Bernstein, "Legends in Queer Performance," opening remarks, roundtable discussion, Harvard University, Cambridge, Mass., October 15, 2007.

5. Michael Kirby, "East Village Performance: An Introduction," *Drama Review* 29, no. 1 (spring 1985): 4.

6. Don Shewey, "Gay Theatre Grows Up," *American Theatre* 5, no. 2 (May 1988): 17.

7. Clive Barnes, "Men Fall for 'Secretaries,'" *New York Post,* September 21, 1994, 38.

8. See Uzi Parnes, "Pop Performance in East Village Clubs," *Drama Review* 29, no. 1 (spring 1985): 5–16.

9. Kathleen M. Conkey, "The East Village as a Way of Life," *Village Voice,* July 2, 1985, 15.

10. Peggy Shaw, letter to the editor, *Village Voice,* July 30, 1985, 8.

11. C. Carr, "The Queer Frontier," *Village Voice,* December 10, 1985, 97.

12. Michel Foucault, *Language, Counter-memory, Practice: Selected Essays and Interviews,* edited by Donald F. Bouchard (Ithaca: Cornell University Press, 1977), 147. Michel Foucault (1926–84) was a French historian and philosopher. He has had wide influence in philosophy and also on a wide range of humanistic and social scientific disciplines.

13. Barnes, "Men Fall for 'Secretaries,'" 38.

14. See Jill Dolan, *The Feminist Spectator as Critic* (Ann Arbor: UMI Research Press, 1988).

15. At the time Jill Dolan was a graduate student at New York University, a founding editor of *Women and Performance: A Journal of Feminist Theory*, and managing editor of the *Drama Review (TDR)*. She went on to become a major figure in the field. In the 1970s I had been a graduate student at NYU and an assistant editor and then managing editor of *TDR*; in 1984 I was an associate editor of *TDR* and a faculty member at NYU.

16. Jill Dolan, "*Carmelita Tropicana Chats* at the Club Chandalier," *Drama Review* 29, no. 1 (spring 1985): 26.

17. Ibid., 30.

18. I knew the couple was heterosexual because they performed it openly, passionately kissing, while waiting for the show to start.

19. Dolan, "*Carmelita Tropicana Chats*," 30.

20. Ibid.

21. See Teresa de Lauretis, "Eccentric Subjects: Feminist Theory and Historical Consciousness," *Feminist Studies* 16, no. 1 (spring 1990): 115–50.

22. See Monique Wittig, *The Straight Mind and Other Essays* (Boston: Beacon Press, 1992), 21–32.

23. Clive Barnes, "Stage: An Oddly Touching 'Camille,'" *New York Times*, May 14, 1974, 31.

24. Bertolt Brecht (1898–1956), was a German poet, playwright, and theatrical theorist. He was concerned with encouraging audiences to think rather than becoming too involved in identifying with the characters. He developed alienation effects (A Effekts) in performance, a technique employed to make spectators aware of the actors as actors rather than losing themselves in the illusion of the characters the actors play.

25. Charles Ludlam, interview with the author, October 13, 1974, New York.

26. *Camille*, in *Complete Plays of Charles Ludlam*, 246.

27. Ludlam, interview.

28. John Simon, "Pianistic Genius and Secretarial Skills," *New York*, October 3, 1994, 107.

29. Maureen Angelos, as quoted in Alisa Solomon, "Five Lesbian Brothers: NO WHINING!" *American Theatre* 15, no. 7 (September 1998): 61.

30. Peggy Phelan, "Serrano, Mapplethorpe, the NEA, and You: 'Money Talks,'" *Drama Review* 34, no. 1 (spring 1990): 14.

31. Eve Kosofsky Sedgwick, *Epistemology of the Closet* (Berkeley: University of California Press, 1990), 18.

32. Phelan, "Serrano, Mapplethorpe, the NEA, and You," 14. I would add that the threat from lesbians stems more from heterosexism (fear of women without men) than homophobia (fear of the sexual act).

33. Terry Castle, *The Apparitional Lesbian: Female Homosexuality and Modern Culture* (New York: Columbia University Press, 1993), 4.

34. Holly Hughes, unpublished interview with Diana Halperin and Peggy Phelan, July 1, 1987, New York.

35. Marilyn Frye, *The Politics of Reality: Essays in Feminist Theory* (Freedom, CA: Crossing Press, 1983), 157.

36. Peg Healey, quoted in Laurie Stone, *Laughing in the Dark: A Decade of Subversive Comedy* (Hopewell, N.J.: Ecco Press, 1997), 193.

37. Lisa Kron, telephone interview with the author, July 26, 2006.

38. See Teresa de Lauretis, "Sexual Indifference and Lesbian Representation," in *Performing Feminisms: Feminist Critical Theory and Theatre,* edited by Sue-Ellen Case (Baltimore: Johns Hopkins University Press, 1990), 17–39.

39. Castle, *Apparitional Lesbian,* 4–5.

40. Ludlam, interview; emphasis added.

41. Teresa de Lauretis, *Technologies of Gender: Essays on Theory, Film, and Fiction* (Bloomington: Indiana University Press, 1987), 17.

42. See Sue-Ellen Case, "Toward a Butch-Femme Aesthetic," in *Making a Spectacle: Feminist Essays on Contemporary Women's Theatre,* edited by Lynda Hart (Ann Arbor: University of Michigan Press, 1989), 291.

43. Robert Massa, "Comedy of Womanners," *Village Voice,* January 10, 1989, 97.

44. See Kate Davy, "Fe/male Impersonation: The Discourse of Camp," in *Critical Theory and Performance,* edited by Janelle Reinelt and Joseph Roach (Ann Arbor: University of Michigan Press, 1992), 231–47.

45. Hughes, "Author's Note," *Well of Horniness,* in *Out Front: Contemporary Gay and Lesbian Plays,* edited by Don Shewey (New York: Grove Press, 1988), 222.

46. Hughes, *Well of Horniness,* 225–29. A different, revised version of the play appears in Hughes, *Clit Notes,* 25–78.

47. C. Carr, "The Lady Is a Dick: The Dyke Noir Theater of Holly Hughes," *Village Voice,* May 19, 1987, 34.

48. See *The Lady Dick,* in Hughes, *Clit Notes,* 79–110; and Kate Davy, "From *Lady Dick* to Ladylike: The Work of Holly Hughes," in *Acting Out: Feminist Performances,* edited by Lynda Hart and Peggy Phelan (Ann Arbor: University of Michigan Press, 1993), 55–84, in which I discuss the production at length and point out some of the material that was cut from the text upon publication.

49. E. Ann Kaplan, "Introduction," in *Women in Film Noir,* edited by E. Ann Kaplan (London: British Film Institute, 1978), 3.

50. Fredric Jameson, *The Political Unconscious: Narrative as a Socially Symbolic Act* (Ithaca: Cornell University Press, 1981), 109–10.

51. Arnold Aronson, *American Avant-Garde Theatre: A History* (London: Routledge, 2000), 6.

52. Teresa de Lauretis, *Alice Doesn't: Feminism, Semiotics, Cinema* (Bloomington: Indiana University Press, 1984), 9.

Chapter 6

Epigraphs: C. Carr, "Party Girls," *Village Voice,* January 8, 1985, 9; Lisa Kron, "A Straight Line," in *Cast Out: Queer Lives in Theater,* edited by Robin Bernstein (Ann Arbor: University of Michigan Press, 2006), 55; Madeleine Olnek, interview with the author, May 6, 2002, New York; *The Secretaries,* in *The Five Lesbian Brothers: Four Plays* (New York: Theatre Communications Group, 2000), 180.

1. Jewelle Gomez, interview with the author, August 6, 1992, New York. All subsequent quotations from Gomez in this chapter are from this source.

2. Alina Troyano, interview with the author, August 7, 1992, New York. All subsequent quotations from Troyano in this chapter are from this source unless otherwise noted.

3. Gomez, interview.

4. See bell hooks, *Yearning: Race, Gender, and Cultural Politics* (Boston: South End Press, 1990), 145–53.

5. See Kate Davy, "Outing Whiteness: A Feminist/Lesbian Project," *Theatre Journal* 47, no. 2 (May 1995): 189–206, which expands on the points presented here.

6. Peggy Shaw, letter to the editor, *Village Voice,* July 30, 1985, 8.

7. Kathleen M. Conkey, "The East Village as a Way of Life," *Village Voice,* July 2, 1985, 14.

8. Ibid.

9. Alan Mace, quoted in ibid., 14.

10. Conkey, "East Village as a Way of Life," 15.

11. Peggy Shaw, interview with the author, June 8, 1985, New York, subsequently published in *Modern Drama: Plays/Criticism/Theory,* edited by W. B. Worthen (Fort Worth, Tex.: Harcourt Brace, 1995), 1003.

12. Ibid.

13. Troyano, interview.

14. Peggy Shaw, interview with the author, August 3, 1992, New York, subsequently published in Worthen, *Modern Drama,* 1004–5.

15. Laurie Stone, "Heroic Acts," *Village Voice,* November 12, 1985, 94.

16. Ibid.

17. José Esteban Muñoz, *Disidentifications: Queers of Color and the Performance of Politics* (Minneapolis: University of Minnesota Press, 1999), 185.

18. C. Carr, "The Queer Frontier," *Village Voice,* December 10, 1985, 97.

19. Muñoz, *Disidentifications,* 192–93.

20. *Saint Joan of Avenue C,* unpublished script, author's personal collection.

21. Muñoz, *Disidentifications,* 39.

22. Alina Troyano, *I, Carmelita Tropicana: Performing between Cultures,*

with Ela Troyano and Uzi Parnes, edited by Chon A. Noriega (Boston: Beacon Press, 2000).

23. Troyano, *Memorias de la Revolución/Memories of the Revolution,* in Troyano, *I, Carmelita Tropicana,* 44.

24. Ibid., 44–45.

25. Ibid., 38.

26. Ibid., 10.

27. Shaw, letter to the editor.

28. Troyano, *Memorias de la Revolución,* 38.

29. Laurie Stone, "Cuba Libre," *Village Voice,* November 22, 1987, 106.

30. Troyano, *Memorias de la Revolución,* 21.

31. Troyano, *I, Carmelita Tropicana,* xiv.

32. Ibid., xix.

33. Troyano, *Memorias de la Revolución,* 11–12.

34. Ibid., 12.

35. Stone, "Cuba Libre," 106.

36. Kevin Grubb, "*Memorias de la Revolución,*" *New York Native,* October 5, 1987.

37. Judith Halberstam, *Female Masculinity* (Durham: Duke University Press, 1998), 258.

38. Troyano, *I, Carmelita Tropicana,* xviii.

39. Richard Dyer, "White," *Screen* 29, no. 4 (fall 1988): 59.

40. Stone, "Cuba Libre," 106.

41. Holly Hughes, quoted in C. Carr, "The Dyke Noir Theater of Holly Hughes," *Village Voice,* May 19, 1987, 34.

42. Holly Hughes, interview with the author, September 1, 1992, New York.

43. Margaret Atwood, as quoted in Laurel Graeber, "Margaret Atwood: 'Zenia Is Sort of Like Madonna,'" *New York Times Book Review,* October 31, 1993, 22.

44. Alisa Solomon, "*Queer Justice,*" *Theatre Journal* 42, no. 3 (October 1990): 366.

45. Jill Dolan was the first scholar to flesh out a feminist critique of the dynamics of desire in performance. See Dolan, *The Feminist Spectator as Critic* (Ann Arbor: University of Michigan Press, 1988), 59–81.

46. Alisa Solomon, "Five Lesbian Brothers: NO WHINING!" *American Theatre* 15, no. 7 (September 1998): 62.

47. Dominique Dibbell, quoted in Dennis Harvey, "Troupe Pools Satiric Talents in 'Secretaries,'" *San Francisco Chronicle,* January 9, 1994, 28.

48. *Voyage to Lesbos,* in *The Five Lesbian Brothers: Four Plays,* 17.

49. Ibid., 26.

50. Peg Healey, quoted in Neil Smith, "'Voyage to Lesbos' Will Embark Tonight," *Daily Pennsylvanian*, February 27, 1991.

51. Peg Healey, "On *Voyage to Lesbos*," in *The Five Lesbian Brothers: Four Plays*, 3.

52. Peggy Phelan, *Unmarked: The Politics of Performance* (New York: Routledge, 1993), 109.

53. Dominique Dibbell, "On *The Secretaries*," in *The Five Lesbian Brothers: Four Plays*, 118.

54. For the original formulation of this construct, see Barbara Welter, "The Cult of True Womanhood, 1820–1860," *American Quarterly* 18 (summer 1966): 151–74; and Carroll Smith-Rosenberg, "The Female World of Love and Ritual: Relations between Women in Nineteenth-Century America," *Signs* 1 (fall 1975): 1–29.

55. *Voyage to Lesbos*, in *The Five Lesbian Brothers: Four Plays*, 31.

56. See *Brave Smiles . . . Another Lesbian Tragedy*, in *The Five Lesbian Brothers: Four Plays*, 43–116.

57. Stephen Holden, "Brave Smiles: Another Lesbian Tragedy," *New York Times*, Arts section, June 19, 1993, 16.

58. Ben Brantley, "A Secretarial Pool Out for Blood," *New York Times*, section C, September 22, 1994, 20.

59. Hazel V. Carby, *Reconstructing Womanhood: The Emergence of the Afro-American Woman Novelist* (New York: Oxford University Press, 1987), 27.

60. Kimberlé Crenshaw, "Whose Story Is It Anyway? Feminist and Antiracist Appropriations of Anita Hill," in *Race-ing Justice, En-gendering Power: Essays on Anita Hill, Clarence Thomas, and the Construction of Social Reality*, edited by Toni Morrison (New York: Pantheon, 1992), 414.

61. *Voyage to Lesbos*, in *The Five Lesbian Brothers: Four Plays*, 18.

62. Ibid., 33.

63. See Dyer, "White," 44–64.

64. *Voyage to Lesbos*, in *The Five Lesbian Brothers: Four Plays*, 28.

65. Maria Maggenti, "The Voyage Out," *Out Week*, June 13, 1990, 67.

66. *The Secretaries*, in *The Five Lesbian Brothers: Four Plays*, 129.

67. Ibid., 128.

68. Howard Kissel, "'Secretaries' on Cutting Edge," *New York Daily News*, September 23, 1994, 41.

69. Isaac-Davy Aronson was in college at Columbia University when he attended this production at NYU with a friend. As the nephew of one of the Five Lesbian Brothers, Babs Davy, and my son, he had attended all of the Brothers' productions.

70. Hazel Carby, "The Multicultural Wars," in *Black Popular Culture*, edited by Gina Dent (Seattle: Bay Press, 1992), 197.

71. *The Secretaries,* in *The Five Lesbian Brothers: Four Plays,* 129.

72. John Simon, "Pianistic Genius and Secretarial Skills," *New York,* October 3, 1994, 107.

73. *The Secretaries,* in *The Five Lesbian Brothers: Four Plays,* 169–70.

74. See Frances B. Cogan, *All-American Girl: The Ideal of Real Womanhood in Mid-nineteenth-century America* (Athens: University of Georgia Press, 1989).

75. See *Upwardly Mobile Home,* in *Split Britches: Lesbian Practice/Feminist Performance,* edited by Sue-Ellen Case (London: Routledge, 1996), 87–118.

76. Phelan, *Unmarked,* 106.

77. Maureen Angelos, quoted in Kris Kovick, "Tits Outta Control: Outrageous Dyke Humor from NY's Five Lesbian Brothers and Seattle's Dos Fallopia," copy obtained from the private collection of the Five Lesbian Brothers, no publication data cited.

Epilogue

Epigraph: C. Carr, "Party Girls," *Village Voice,* January 8, 1985, 9.

1. David Savran, *A Queer Sort of Materialism: Recontextualizing American Theater* (Ann Arbor: University of Michigan Press, 2003), 79–80.

2. Lisa Kron, telephone interview with the author, July 26, 2006.

3. See Jill Dolan, *Utopia in Performance: Finding Hope at the Theater* (Ann Arbor: University of Michigan Press, 2005).

4. Lisa Kron, *Well,* unpublished script, Broadway production, March 2006. All subsequent quotations from the play are from this source.

5. Blurbs quoted, respectively, from Michael Sommers, "'Well' Written, 'Well' Staged, 'Well' Acted," *Star-Ledger* (Newark, N.J.), March 31, 2006; Robert Feldberg, "Tired of Mom's Exhaustion," *Record* (Bergen County, N.J.), March 31, 2006; and Jeremy McCarter, "Heal Thyself," *New York,* April 17, 2006, 103.

6. Kenneth Jones, *Playbill,* March 10, 2006.

7. Dolan, *Utopia in Performance,* 33; emphasis in the original.

8. Ibid., 19.

9. See Shane Phelan, *Getting Specific: Postmodern Lesbian Politics* (Minneapolis: University of Minnesota Press, 1994), 41–56.

10. Jen Abrams, e-mail correspondence with the author, July 24, 2002.

11. Susana Cook, interview with the author, June 5, 2001, New York.

12. I attended this meeting, as well as WOW's first "board of directors" meeting, at an outdoor café, where Peggy Shaw and Lois Weaver were in attendance along with a few current WOW members. (Establishing a board was a requirement for purchasing the building.) A young woman brand new to WOW, having attended her first meeting the week before, was also at this board meeting. I remember thinking, "This is so WOW."

13. Before WOW received an ultimatum in 2000 to either relocate or purchase

its space, the collective had managed for twenty years to avoid the time and labor a fund-raising campaign requires in order to focus its energy and resources on making theater. Until funds were secured and the future of the space was ensured, there were occasional brief periods when no show was presented and an annual festival was not produced. This is precisely why the collective had eschewed fund-raising during WOW's first two decades; it bled away the time and energy needed to make theater.

Index